Jakob Nielsen
Hoa Loranger

Prioritizing
Web Usability

New Riders

New Riders, An Imprint of Peachpit, Berkeley, California USA

Prioritizing Web Usability

Jakob Nielsen and Hoa Loranger

New Riders
1249 Eighth Street
Berkeley, CA 94710
510/524-2178
800/283-9444
510/524-2221 (fax)

Find us on the Web at: www.newriders.com
To report errors, please send a note to errata@peachpit.com

New Riders is an imprint of Peachpit, a division of Pearson Education

Editor: Camille Peri
Production Editors: Lupe Edgar
Compositor: WolfsonDesign
Indexer: Emily Glossbrenner
Cover design: James Tung, Eric Baker Design Associates, NY
Interior design: Elizabeth Keyes

ISBN 0-321-35031-6

9 8 7 6 5 4 3 2 1

Printed and bound in the United States of America

For Hannah,

—Jakob

For Derek,
with appreciation,

—Hoa

Acknowledgments

This book draws upon a myriad of user studies and client projects conducted by current and past members of Nielsen Norman Group, and our insights have been honed by many discussions with this group of supremely talented professionals, including Kara Pernice Coyne, Susan Farrell, Shuli Gilutz, Garrett Goldfield, Chris Nodder, Donald A. Norman, Amy Schade, Suzy Sharpe, Michael Summers, Marie Tahir, Bruce "Tog" Tognazzini, and Jenny Wu. We thank our business staff for making our projects happen: We would have no data if it weren't for Brenda Brozinick, Luice Hwang, and Susan Pernice. They make the company run. We also thank our research assistant, David Philp, who reviewed hundreds of hours of test videos to collect some of the statistics presented in this book. Finally, we thank Marjorie Baer, Davina Baum, Derek Loranger, and John Morkes for contributing additional insights. And a special thanks to Camille Peri for help with the manuscript and providing the encouragement that allowed us to complete this book.

—Jakob Nielsen and Hoa Loranger

About the Authors

Jakob Nielsen

Jakob Nielsen, Ph.D., is a principal of Nielsen Norman Group. He is the founder of the "discount usability engineering" movement, which emphasizes fast and efficient methods for improving the quality of user interfaces. Nielsen, noted as "the world's leading expert on Web usability" by *U.S. News and World Report* and "the next best thing to a true time machine" by *USA Today*, is the author of the best-selling book *Designing Web Usability: The Practice of Simplicity* (New Riders Publishing, 2000), which has sold more than a quarter of a million copies in 22 languages. His other books include *Usability Engineering* (Morgan Kaufmann, 1993); with Robert L. Mack, *Usability Inspection Methods* (Wiley, 1994); *Multimedia and Hypertext: The Internet and Beyond* (Morgan Kaufmann, 1995); *International User Interfaces* (Wiley, 1996); and with Marie Tahir, *Homepage Usability: 50 Websites Deconstructed* (New Riders Publishing, 2001). Nielsen's Alertbox column on Web usability has been published on the Internet since 1995 and currently has about 200,000 readers at www.useit.com.

From 1994 to 1998, Nielsen was a Sun Microsystems Distinguished Engineer. His previous affiliations include Bell Communications Research, the Technical University of Denmark, and the IBM User Interface Institute. He has been awarded 79 United States patents, mainly on ways of making the Internet easier to use. Nielsen holds a Ph.D. in human-computer interaction from the Technical University of Denmark.

Hoa Loranger

Hoa Loranger is a user experience specialist at Nielsen Norman Group and heads the group's San Diego office. She consults with many prominent companies in the entertainment, finance, technology, e-commerce, intranet, and other industries. She has worked with clients to successfully implement user-centered design strategies leading to improved sales and ROI.

Loranger gives keynotes and tutorials on a wide range of topics, including usability principles and guidelines, user-centered design concepts, and applied research methodologies. She produces training videos and authors reports on topics such as: Flash-based applications, teenagers on the Web, "About Us," business-to-business (B2B) Web sites, and paper prototyping techniques. Her extensive usability research has spanned the globe, including Asia, Australia, Europe, and North America.

Before joining Nielsen Norman Group, Loranger served as human factors lead at Intuit, where her group was responsible for the user interaction and visual design for the TurboTax and QuickBooks product line. At TRW (currently Northrop Grumman), she specialized in both hardware and software systems, including navigational and logistical applications, and computer configurations for military vehicles.

Loranger holds a Masters degree in Human Factors and Applied Experimental Psychology from California State University at Northridge, and a B.A. in Psychology from the University of California at Irvine.

Contents

Preface

Ten years ago, the Web was exciting to people. Today it's routine. It's a tool. If it's convenient, they will use it; if not, they won't. With ten times as many sites and probably a hundred times as many pages on the Web, users are getting less tolerant of difficult sites, so every design flaw means lost business. Usability has become more important than ever.

This book has two goals. The most important is implied by its title: to prioritize our extensive knowledge of Web usability into the essentials that all people need to know if they work on a Web project—whether as designers, marketing managers, programmers, or writers. Our second, and related, goal is to update our Web usability guidelines from the 1990s to reflect our findings since 2000.

We began user testing of Web sites in 1994. During the last 20 years, we have identified literally thousands of usability problems and developed as many guidelines for avoiding them. Our company, Nielsen Norman Group, has published almost 5,000 pages of reports from our research into how thousands of users on four continents interact with the Web, with nearly 3,000 screen shots from hundreds of sites. All very good, informative, and valuable research—if we do say so ourselves. But we recognize that you may not have time to read 5,000 pages. So this book distills the most valuable information from our research into a single volume.

Of course, we believe in all our guidelines and we would prefer that all designs complied with everything that's known about how to make sites better for users. But realistically speaking, not every site can do everything. Many projects will have to focus first on the most important usability issues and defer the rest to later. This book will help you do just that.

If anything, Web usability is much more critical now than it was when we began our research because the competitive environment has sharpened. As we discuss further in Chapter 2, the growth of decent search engines means that people use a predominant strategy when they start researching something on the Web (which also happens to be the time when they are susceptible to new brands). They type a few words into a search engine and get a nice list of companies that are competing to solve their problem. All are one click away, and none get the time of day if they impose too many barriers or delays in getting users what they want.

What Is Usability?

Usability is a quality attribute relating to how easy something is to use. More specifically, it refers to how quickly people can learn to use something, how efficient they are while using it, how memorable it is, how error-prone it is, and how much users like using it. If people can't or won't use a feature, it might as well not exist.

If you are considering whether this book contains information that is useful to you, ask yourself: Are users trying to accomplish something when they visit my site? If the answer is "yes," then you should be concerned about usability.

People expect a lot of Web sites today, and they are less and less tolerant of bad design. This book highlights the critical usability mistakes that Web sites make repeatedly—mistakes that lead to customer dissatisfaction and lost business.

The guidelines we offer for better design are based on behavioral research and observation, not on our opinions. Unlike market researchers, we do not simply ask people to speculate how they would use an interface because self-reported data is frequently unreliable and doesn't adequately answer usability questions. Instead, we employ user-testing methods that are based on observational strategies. We give people realistic tasks to perform on the Web and observe them as they interact with various sites. This means that we discover what users actually *do*, not what they *say* they do. Focus groups and surveys are nice at assessing people's general preferences, but they are worthless for discovering whether people can use a site or what specific design elements to use when. Only observational research can get valid answers to these questions.

Don't look for advice on programming language or other implementation details in this book. Our concern is how the user experience feels to the person at the other end of the cable. Ultimately, this book is about your customers and what they need, not about you.

In the early years of the Web, we were the only ones to conduct systematic user testing of sites, so our early findings received substantial attention and were widely cited. That was good back then, but it's a problem now because some people think that our guidelines haven't changed since 1994.

So the second goal of the book is to update our old guidelines from the 1990s in the light of our research findings since 2000. The guidelines that we developed after 2000 have tended to hold up in the studies we have done since then, and we usually end up simply supplementing them with ever-more new ones that reflect new developments on the Web. Not so for the research results from the 1990s. The studies we have done in recent years have sometimes contradicted these findings, so the early guidelines now need to change.

Interestingly, some of our early usability findings do hold true today because the fundamental interactions on the Web haven't changed as much as you might think. People still click on links to navigate through pages. And people's cognitive abilities don't change much from one decade to the next, so usability guidelines, which reflect human capabilities, evolve slowly. The people who use the Web haven't changed that much either; 80 percent of those who will be using your site in ten years are the same people who are using sites now (except they will be older and need bigger font sizes).

Still, designers, users, and technology have all changed, and this book aims to set the record straight on how old usability guidelines have fared in light of these changes. In particular, Chapter 3 contains a detailed analysis of the most important early usability problems and provides advice for how to deal with these issues today.

What has changed is this: Web technology is less brittle, and extremely slow dial-up connections are getting to be rare, so many guidelines that aimed to alleviate early technical constraints are being replaced by equivalent (but different) guidelines that address the corresponding human constraints. For example, in the 1990s most users' connections were too slow to view video over the Internet, and those few who could download video often faced crashes or system incompatibilities. So the main guideline for video was to avoid it. Today, video works from a purely technical perspective, so we can remove this guideline. Instead, we need new ones that address the fact that users watch Web-based video differently than they watch broadcast television.

Because this book includes a fraction of the information that we have accumulated over the years, it is the proverbial tip of the iceberg. In fact, we have boiled down our findings to less than ten percent of our full reports, you could say it's just the tip of the tip. For those interested in reading about our research and documentation in more detail, a box at the end of each chapter provides references to many of our in-depth reports cited within.

Where to Find Detailed User Research

We have conducted immensely more user research than we have room to discuss in this book. These studies are available at www.nngroup.com/reports. If you are not working on the specific type of design project that was the focus of a particular study, the information in that report will most likely be irrelevant. But if you are working on a similar project, it can be very valuable.

Usability Then and Now

Jakob's book *Designing Web Usability: The Practice of Simplicity* (New Riders Publishing, 2000) appeared in print at the cusp of the first Internet bubble and was called a "landmark" because of its role in changing Internet professionals' attitudes toward Web design. Before *DWU*, most companies simply wanted *cool* sites. In fact, the best-selling Web design book at the time, *Creating Killer Websites,* advocated splash screens and other design atrocities. After *DWU* was published, many Internet managers realized that killer sites killed business. They discovered that the best way to do business on the Web was to create sites that their customers could use. The Web is not television. People don't go there to zone out. People go to the Web with a specific purpose in mind. They have their hands on their mouses, ready to interact and be engaged.

Designing Web Usability was a manifesto. It strove to sell readers on the "practice of simplicity" over the cool design and complex user interfaces that dominated the Web at the time, and it did so partly by deconstructing many screen shots of miserable Web sites in the style of the day. In fact, when rereading *DWU* today, the biggest complaint most people have is that the screen shots look outdated. Fortunately, many of the design mistakes we warned against have now gone out of fashion. Unfortunately, new mistakes have arisen to take their place. This book is filled with new screen shots that show what design elements failed current users and caused much misery and lost business.

> *Success rates are up and user failures are not nearly as common as they used to be on the Web. The usability movement has had measurable results in terms of improved user experience.*

Overall, however, the Web has improved. We are now able to include many screen shots of designs that work well. Also, measured usability has increased substantially in terms of how quickly and how well users can get things done on Web sites. The most simple usability measure we collect is the success rate: Can people use the site at all? On average, success rates are up and user failures are not nearly as common as they used to be. In other words, the usability movement has had measurable results in terms of improved user experience.

The Web contained fewer than 10 million sites when *DWU* was published. That was certainly enough to make usability an important issue: If sites were difficult to use, people already had plenty of other places to go. At the time of this writing, the Web has 80 million sites and by the time you read these words, it will probably have crossed the 100 million mark—about ten times as many sites as seven years ago.

More important than the numbers, however, is the change in users' attitudes toward the Web. *DWU* came out at the tail end of the time when the Web was interesting in its own right. It was exciting to be able to reach around the world and have information come to your desktop in an instant—or, more often, 30 seconds. Of course, you couldn't do that much on the Web, and whenever you found what you were looking for, you were grateful.

Today the situation is quite the opposite. People's expectations have expanded with the massive expansion of the Web. People just assume that the Web has what they want. They turn to search engines with all kinds of questions, and usually something comes up that has the answers. They assume that sites work. They assume that they will find whatever they are looking for and can buy almost anything online.

The Web is a tool. Consider the way that people think about that other onetime-dazzling invention, the telephone. They don't wake up in the morning and think, "Today I will experiment with my telephonic apparatus and place a call to somebody so that I can assess the sound quality of the connection." Their use of the telephone is driven by their real-world needs. The same is true for the Web, as far as average users are concerned. You, dear reader, are not the average user, as proven by the fact that you care enough about the Web to buy a book about it. (Just as the people who buy books about how telephones work are telephony engineers, and the way they think about phones is different from the way that most telephone users do.)

> *It's no longer enough to say that you want to design for your customers. If you give usability the priority it deserves on your site, you will be designing for them.*

One of the goals of *Designing Web Usability* was to shake up the world of Web design and make it pay attention to human needs. It succeeded, but only in part. Most Web projects today pay lip service to user experience, and it's rare to find Internet managers who don't list usability as a top goal for their sites. Unfortunately, in practice sites continue to violate many well-documented usability guidelines and as a result do not reach even a fraction of their business potential.

We hope to change that with this book. Our aim is to continue the usability revolution begun with *Designing Web Usability*, and to force Web sites to be successful by following the most important guidelines that have been developed during the last decade. No more excuses. We know what really works on the Web, so it's no longer enough to *say* that you want to design for your customers. If you give usability the priority it deserves on your site, you *will* be designing for them.

Who Should Read This Book?

This book is for people who have business goals for their Web sites. Obviously, this includes e-commerce sites that sell online and corporate sites that promote products that sell through offline channels. But our definition of "business goal" encompasses much more than selling products or services. If yours is a news site, you want people to find, read, and understand your stories, and possibly also sign up for your email newsletter. If you are a nonprofit organization, you want to promote your cause and perhaps attract donations online. And if you are a government agency, you want to support taxpayers by giving them the information they pay you to produce and minimize bureaucracy by allowing them to receive information and even services online.

If you are considering whether this book contains information that is useful to you, the key question to ask yourself is: Are users trying to accomplish something when they visit my site? If the answer is "yes," then you should be concerned about usability.

Of course, there are also Web sites that don't have "business goals." Maybe you have an art site that's a pure expression of creativity. Or maybe you are a Web designer who fields a personal site to show off experimental designs that wouldn't work on client sites. Perhaps you have a site that's only intended for your three best friends. Our guidelines are not geared for these types of sites because they don't aim to attract users who need to be able to get something accomplished. If you have a site that doesn't need to support users' goals, do as you please and you won't lose any business because you are not aiming to get any.

For intranets, on the other hand, there is much applicable information in this book, even though it is geared mainly for Internet sites. There are some differences in the design guidelines for each because of differences in their intended audiences. For example, intranets do not need to compete for users, who go to them primarily for work-directed tasks, whereas Web users' are usually driven by their own needs. Still, intranets use Web technology; they are online information systems, and users navigate their pages using skills, knowledge, and expectations gained from navigating popular Internet sites.

The information and guidelines in this book are for both large and small companies. In fact, we use the word "companies" loosely, to include noncommercial entities such as nonprofits, government agencies, and even personal sites that provide information to outside users. Whether you have hundreds of thousands of employees or just yourself doesn't matter. Users still see one page at a time when they visit your site, and they still click the Back button to leave it if it is too difficult to use.

You may not call the people who use your site "customers," as we tend to do. You may use terms such as "consumers," "members," "volunteers," "readers," "citizens"—something that does not directly imply a business relationship. However, once people visit your site, they become customers of a sort, to the extent that they are in the "market" for something that you may be able to supply. They may or may not pay for this service with money. They surely will pay with their attention and maybe even with their loyalty if you treat them well.

Prioritizing Web Usability

www.myspace.com

Myspace allows young users to create a social environment where they can design their own pages and comment on their friends' pages. If you are designing a page like this, this book is not for you. If you just want to reach a closed clique of your closest friends, usability guidelines are not going to be of much help. Of course, we can say, "Don't use background graphics that obscure the text and make it difficult to read," just as we can advise against having an animated heart that constantly moves around on the left side of the page. And this advice would be correct for a site that has a business goal—including that of selling to teens. In fact, our usability studies with teenage users show that teens don't want business sites or government sites that are made to look as if they were created by teenagers when they were not. But when young people make personal sites to express their personality, traditional usability simply doesn't apply.

In fact, good usability has two benefits: On the one hand, it supports your business goals on the Web and thus helps your company make more money. This is the angle we take throughout this book because we want to motivate you (and your boss) to take usability seriously. On the other hand, usability empowers humans and makes it easier and more pleasant to handle the technology that's infusing every aspect of modern life. We don't want to get all soft-hearted, but making life better and more enjoyable does seem to be a worthy goal. Watching people who feel oppressed by technology is not a happy sight, but it's a common one in user testing.

By improving usability, we can enable people with little education to hold meaningful jobs, we can connect senior citizens with the community, we can give users with disabilities the same information and service as everybody else, and we can allow everyone to spend their time with computers more productively and reduce their feelings of frustration and powerlessness. The happiest thought of all is that these improvements in quality of life don't come at the expense of your profits. On the contrary, usability benefits business *and* it benefits humanity.

—Jakob Nielsen and Hoa Loranger, May 2006

1 Introduction: Nothing to Hide

We'll begin by letting you in on a secret: There are no secrets to doing good usability studies. It's simply a matter of knowing how and where to look, and then documenting your observations.

Usability works because it reveals how the world works. Once you discover how people interact with your design, you can make it better than your competitor's.

This book tells you how people behave on the Internet and what makes Web sites fail or succeed. How do we know this? Because we've spent hundreds of hours looking. If anything, that's our big secret: that we know how to conduct user research. Yet even that is not a secret because we teach a course on how to conduct usability studies correctly.

As much as we try to teach companies to do their own user research and to employ valid methods, however, we keep getting asked for advice on how to make Web sites better. Many people would rather know what works in general than spend time testing their own designs. With so much already known and documented about user behavior on the Web, why not base your design on this general knowledge? Then you can always fine-tune it by conducting research on industry-specific questions that apply to your particular site.

Fair enough. That's why we wrote this book—to bring the best of our extensive knowledge on general usability together in one handy place. The observations here are based on issues that we have seen again and again with many different users as they have tried to use many different Web sites. The guidelines translate our empirical observations into general advice about what usually works on the Web. Although there are exceptions—which is why we advise that you test your own site—these guidelines apply about 90 percent of the time, and the vast majority of Web sites would be better if they complied with them.

Where We Got Our Data

All of our findings and guidelines are based on empirical evidence from two sources. First we rely on our testing of 716 Web sites with 2,163 users around the world. Most of this research was conducted in the United States, but we also ran sessions in Australia, Belgium, Canada, Denmark, Finland, France, Germany, Israel, Italy, Japan, Hong Kong, Korea, Switzerland, and the United Kingdom. Many of these studies were done for our consulting clients, so the details are confidential. But this vast research also provides general insights into user behavior, particularly when we observe the same findings in highly diverse industries.

Other studies were conducted in the process of writing research reports about special issues. Most of the guidelines from these studies are only important if you are working on the exact problem we researched, but we have also abstracted valuable general insights from the thousands of specific observations in these studies. Thus most of what we say here is based on general lessons from a huge number of Web sites and users, whether they were tested for proprietary projects or for our own studies.

Our second source of information was a special study that we conducted for this book. When we talk about "the study" here, we're referring to this smaller set of data.

How We Did the Book Study

We tested 69 users, 57 in the United States and 12 in the United Kingdom, for this book. Slightly less than half (32) were male and slightly more than half (37) were female, in an even distribution of ages from 20 to 60. Each was paid $100 for participating. We didn't test teenagers or senior citizens for this book, though we occasionally offer insights on these special groups, based on the separate studies we have conducted with them.

The users had a broad range of job backgrounds and Web experience. We screened out anybody working in technology, marketing, Web design, or usability because they rarely represent mainstream users. People who work in the biz know too much and have difficulty engaging with a design as regular users. Instead, they tend to criticize the design based on their personal design philosophy, which is invalid as usage data. In fact, whenever you hear a user throw around insider terminology like "information architecture" in testing, you probably have to discard most of what they say.

All the users had at least one year's experience using the Web. We almost never test people who are completely new to the Web because all we would find is that the Web in general and browsers in particular are difficult user interfaces that take some time to learn. We wouldn't learn much that would help us design better Web sites because completely new users wouldn't get very far into the sites.

The experience of brand-new users is generally not that important for Web sites anyway because new users rarely visit one of them on their first Internet expedition. Of course, this is not true if you are Yahoo!, AOL, MSN, or similar Internet service providers that make their sites the default homepage for their customers. However, we are not writing for these few exceptional sites. We are writing for mainstream corporate, e-commerce, news, and government sites, and others that are not among the Web's Top Ten most-visited list. It's actually good news if you're *not* on the Top Ten list because when users visit your site, they already will have learned the basics elsewhere of how to use the Web.

The standard rule for user testing is to employ the equipment that most users are likely to have. For this study, we tested on a Windows machine, running the latest version of Internet Explorer. The monitor had a screen resolution of 1024 by 768 pixels. For Internet connectivity, we used a broadband connection: Depending on the test location, it ranged from 1 to 3 megabits per second (Mbps).

The "Thinking Aloud" Method

In our studies, users are tested one at a time so that they don't bias each other. In each session, the test user sits by a computer while the test facilitator, and sometimes one or two additional observers, sits nearby. If there are many observers, it's better to test in a usability laboratory with two rooms that are separated by a one-way mirror so that the observers can be hidden from view. But with a small number of observers, it works equally well to have them sit behind the user so that they are out of sight and therefore out of mind.

Hearing a user's "thoughts" allows us to understand why they do what they do, and this information is invaluable in testing.

The book study was conducted with the "thinking aloud" method, which is our preferred approach for almost all usability tests. In this method, users are asked to think out loud as they work with the interface. Hearing a user's "thoughts" allows us to understand why they do what they do, and this information is invaluable. It's nice to know that users, say, clicked the wrong button and couldn't check out of an e-commerce site. But if you want to improve the

Large Companies

Nestlé

Cummins (energy company)

United States Postal Service (USPS)

American Honda Motor Co.

Burger King

Medium-Size Companies

BankOne

Dianon Systems (health diagnostics)

Dime Savings Bank of Williamsburgh

Escalade Sports

House of Blues

Pixar Animation Studios

Small Companies

Black Mountain Bicycles

GW Eye Associates

E-commerce

Atlantis, Paradise Island

Bath & Body Works

Kitchen Etc.

Movies.com

The Sharper Image

Whistler Blackcomb Mountains (ski resort)

Government and Nonprofits

American Heart Association

California State Parks

City of San Diego

J. Paul Getty Trust

Her Majesty's Revenue & Customs (United Kingdom customs authority)

United States Social Security Administration (SSA)

checkout process and thus increase sales, you need to know *why* people click the wrong buttons.

We also made two video recordings of each test session: one of the computer monitor and one of the user's face and upper body. These recordings include a sound track with the user's comments. For most usability projects, you don't really need to review the recordings because the main design problems are obvious after the test sessions. For practicality, it is usually best to quickly fix the problems and increase a company's business as soon as possible. But for a research project like ours, it's good to be able to review them and make sure that we have an accurate record of everything the user did.

Site-Specific Testing

For part one of the book study, we systematically tested 25 Web sites that cover a range of genres—from industries like automobiles and financial services to entertainment sites and intellectually oriented medical and cultural sites.

You can see from their homepages that the sites also exhibited a wide variety of design styles, from somewhat primitive to overly glamorous. All in all, our basic goal was to test a good cross-selection of current Web sites.

We didn't pick any site because we wanted to dig into that company's Web strategy. Similarly, our comments on these sites should not be construed as criticism of the companies or teams behind the sites. There are many reasons why a Web site might have a bad design, beginning with a lack of resources. For the purposes of this book, we don't really care why. No matter how understandable the reasons for a mistake, it's still a mistake that our readers should be warned against committing on their Web sites, and that's why we present it here.

Homepages for the 25 sites that were tested systematically in the usability study we conducted for this book. The homepages are shown as they would initially appear in a browser window on a 1024-by-768 monitor.

www.nestle.com

www.cummins.com

www.usps.com

www.honda.com

Prioritizing Web Usability

www.bk.com

www.escaladesports.com

www.bankone.com

www.hob.com

www.dianon.com

www.pixar.com

www.dimewill.com

www.blackmountainbicycles.com

www.drgordonwong.com

www.movies.go.com

www.atlantis.com

www.sharperimage.com

www.bathandbodyworks.com

www.whistlerblackcomb.com

www.kitchenetc.com

www.americanheart.org

www.parks.ca.gov

www.hmrc.gov.uk

www.sandiego.gov

www.ssa.gov

www.getty.edu

It should be noted that the book study was not funded by any of the organizations whose sites we tested. We covered all costs ourselves so that we could be free to speak the truth in reporting on them.

This part of the study was a scavenger hunt of sorts. We gave each user three or four specific tasks to do on each site. While these tasks would not uncover every last usability problem on a site (bigger sites especially offer much more functionality than a few tasks can cover), they were enough for our purposes: to assess how well sites support the most typical goals users have when visiting them.

Some of the tasks we asked users to perform were:

- Go to www.usps.com and find out how much it costs to send a postcard to China.

- Go to www.sandiego.gov and find the name of the city council member for one area.

- You are planning a family reunion at Sugarloaf Ridge, California. Go to www.parks.ca.gov and make a reservation for a campsite that can hold 35 people.

- You are looking for a snack that you can eat during your workout. Go to www.nestle.com and see what products they have for you.

- Go to www.pixar.com and see if you can find out how they came up with the idea for the movie *Monsters, Inc.*

- You want to visit the J. Paul Getty Museum this weekend. Go to www.getty.edu and find out the cost to enter and the time it opens.

- You want to put $1,000 in the bank and keep it there for a long time. Go to www.bankone.com and find the accounts with the best interest rates.

- You read an article about how fuel cell technology may change the world. Go to www.cummins.com and find the top two pros and cons of fuel cell technology.

All of these tasks were eminently feasible to do on the Web sites in question. We almost never ask users to "do the impossible" on a particular site. We observe plenty of difficulties just from watching them try to do the tasks that a site is supposed to support, so that's all we test.

Web-Wide Testing

In the site-specific testing, users were told where to go and were expected to stay there while performing their tasks. This is the way most usability studies are conducted, and is great if you want to find out how elements of a particular site's design works. Of course, that's not the way users work in real life. People have the entire Internet at their fingertips and they'll often jump from one Web site to another to complete a task.

For this reason, in part two of our testing we gave users a range of tasks and told them to go anywhere they pleased. We call these "Web-wide tasks" because users had the entire Web to choose from. These tasks represent a wide range of activities, from highly commercial pursuits to curiosity-based inquiries, and all can realistically be done on the Web today.

The main downside of this approach is that users go to different sites even when working on the same problem, so we didn't get to systematically test those sites with a range of users. The upside is that we get to see how people construct their solutions across multiple sites, as they do when they are not in the lab.

For this section of the testing, we gave each user one of 12 tasks:

- You and your family are interested in going on vacation to Mazatlan, Mexico. Find a travel offer that is both appealing and affordable for your family.

- You have some extra time during the week and want to do something to help the community. Find a community service program that would be a good fit for you.

- Uncle George is interested in getting a personal computer for his home. He's mainly going to use it to surf the Web, e-mail, and print up digital pictures. Find a computer that you would recommend to him.

- Your nephew's birthday is coming up. He's going to be five years old and likes reading. Subscribe to a magazine that he might want.

- You're thinking about investing $10,000 in a retirement plan. Find the best way to invest your money.

- You're planning to purchase a new home and need to finance it. Find a company that will give you the best service and rates.

- There's been a lot of news lately about viruses on the Internet. Find the best way to protect your personal computer from viruses.

- You're doing a report on Marie Curie. Find out who she is and some of her most famous accomplishments.

- What are the three main reasons that Siberian tigers are an endangered species?

- Find out what a "let" is in tennis.

- In August 2003, the United States and Canada experienced an enormous blackout, leaving 50 million people without power. Find out the main cause of the blackout.

- A good friend complains about throbbing pain that usually radiates from one eye to the forehead, temple, and cheek. What might your friend be suffering from?

What if a Site Has Changed?

We include many screen shots in this book because it's much easier to absorb abstract principles when they are illustrated with specific examples. During the year we spent writing the book, however, several of the sites that appear in screen shots here have been redesigned. In some cases, the companies conducted their own usability studies. In others, site representatives attended seminars in which we show video clips of user behavior from recent studies. Thus, even though they didn't know about this book, they still saw previews of our tests of their sites—in effect getting a free usability study!

In either case, this means that if you check out a site after seeing it in this book, it is very likely to look different. Does this make the analysis in this book less relevant to your project? Not at all. The principles and guidelines that a screen shot illustrates are relevant long after a site has changed. In fact, many findings from our user testing in 1994 continue to be seen in studies in 2006 and will probably be found again by unlucky testers in 2020 and beyond.

An example of this is the Web site of the British Broadcasting Corporation (BBC). Jakob and Marie Tahir happened to use bbc.co.uk in *Homepage Usability: 50 Websites Deconstructed* to illustrate the issue of easy access to archives of previously featured homepage stories. The lack of archives was one of the BBC site's usability problems in 2001 and it continued to be a problem in 2005, as the screen shot shows.

The day before this screen shot was taken, the BBC site featured a great recipe for roast goose with sage and onion stuffing and applesauce. How can you find this recipe? An experienced user might be able to conjure up the correct page through a search, but the average user would be at a complete loss.

www.bbc.co.uk

As the second screen shot shows, the BBC was working on an archive in late 2005. If you visit the site now, the homepage may well feature the archive. If so, the BBC will finally have done what we suggested in 2001. Does that change the importance of the comments in *Homepage Usability?* It doesn't, because our guideline to provide an archive of homepage feature stories continues to be relevant for millions of other Web sites. Only 41 percent of corporate homepages follow this guideline, so 59 percent could improve their usability today if they pay attention to the mistake the BBC made in 2001.

Beta release of BBC's service to archive all stories that have run on the homepage so that users can find them later: Let's say that you remember seeing a mouthwatering photo of Rick Stein's Christmas goose when you visited the site yesterday, but you didn't have time to read the recipe. Returning a day later, you discover that the BBC has moved on to a story about Franz Ferdinand's favorite music (see previous screen shot). Even if you like this Scottish rock band, they are not going to help you cook your goose. If you happen to know that the URL for BBC's beta-release archive is www.bbc.co.uk/homearchive, you can easily find the story by scrolling down the list of yesterday's features until you recognize the photo. Hopefully, by the time you read this, the BBC will have promoted the homepage archive from a beta test to a regular feature with a link on the homepage itself.

www.bbc.co.uk

User Testing in Three Days

It's beyond the parameters of this book to explain how to do a usability study, but it's not difficult to learn. So why do so few companies test their sites? Probably out of the misguided belief that doing so will delay their project, although in reality testing can be extremely fast. We teach a course in which we take a team through a simple test of their site in three days.

Some issues are so specific to your site, they aren't covered in any report. That's why you always need to conduct testing with your own users.

Tell Me Again: Why Do I Need to Do User Testing?

By now it's almost a cliché for usability books to exhort readers to conduct their own testing. With all the information out there—including our own book—why are we so emphatic about testing? Isn't it enough for you to benefit from the results of our huge number of tests and simply apply the guidelines to your designs?

The reason is because usability guidelines are based on three levels of research:

- General user behavior across most Web sites

- Specialized findings about specific genres of sites or areas of sites

- Detailed findings about a specific site and its customers

This book encompasses the first type of guidelines. They are related to issues that we see again and again, among all kinds of users on all kinds of sites, so they are relevant to the vast majority of sites. The many reports available on our Web site cover many of the second type of guidelines. The third type of guidelines relates to circumstances that may be specific to your site, and only you can discover what these are.

The Exceptions

It is important to stress that while the guidelines in this book are valid for the vast majority of cases, they are not for all cases. Human behavior is so variable that you may find they don't apply to your site perhaps ten percent of the time. For 1,000 guidelines, that could mean that 100 may not apply—small in the big scheme of things but a sizable number if it is your site. (In fact, we have documented many more than 1,000 usability guidelines, though we are covering only the most important ones in this book.) Thus it's simultaneously true that you should follow the vast majority of guidelines and you should not follow some guidelines.

What should you do about those specialized design questions that are beyond the scope of this book? And how do you know whether they are important enough to warrant deviating from a general guideline? For both questions, you can only discover the answers through your own user testing. Let's look at an example: a site that sells used watches, as shown in this screen shot.

Watches.co.uk should conform to the *general guidelines* for all Web sites, such as minimizing dense text. The site does follow the general guideline to highlight what's inside it by showcasing examples on the homepage. The general guideline cannot state exactly how individual sites should reveal

Users can buy and sell used watches on this site. The long text in the middle of the page violates the general guidelines for writing on the Web. It is preferable for users to see their options in easily scannable menus.

The dense text was probably included for search engine optimization—an attempt to squeeze as many brand names as possible onto the homepage. It would have been better business to design focused topic pages for each brand and aim to have those pages rank highly for users who know what brand they want. If users land directly on a page showing multiple watches from their desired manufacturer, they are more likely to find something that appeals to them. In contrast, somebody who searches for, say, "IWC Mark 10" might find this homepage but would be likely to leave the site without buying because the watch is not visible, nor easy to find.

You might ask, "What's the harm in attracting users even if you don't have the product they want? The worst they can do is leave." But actually, they can do worse than leaving: They can never return. Once users have been disappointed several times after clicking your links in a search engine, they may well decide to ignore your site in the future. Ironically, this would include cases in which you actually do carry the product they want.

www.watches.co.uk

content, but this site's approach of showing photos and prices of some featured watches is good implementation of the guideline.

Since watches.co.uk belongs to the genre of e-commerce sites, its designer should also follow the hundreds of more *specialized guidelines* for e-commerce in our specialized report. For example, we have developed a host of detailed guidelines for site shopping carts, including one to show the cart at the top of all pages, as this site does. Unfortunately, however, the site violates another guideline—to call the cart a "cart"—by calling the cart a "basket." This is an acceptable but slightly less optimal alternative because people scan for the word "cart" first.

Finally, since watches.co.uk sells used watches—as opposed to books, flowers, computers, airline tickets, or any of a thousand other items—its designers should follow *specific guidelines* for selling watches and used items. Some guidelines for selling used items can be gleaned from usability studies of online used-goods vendors, from eBay to antiquarian booksellers. To determine guidelines specific to selling watches, however, the company must do custom research with the site's own users.

The guidelines in this book will help you develop your site, no matter what type of site you are working on. But you should also read additional reports on more specific issues. And some issues are so specific to your site, they aren't covered in any report. There's just no getting around it: To make your site a leader in its genre, you always need to conduct testing with your own users.

In sum, this book condenses thousands of usability findings into a fairly small number of key principles by emphasizing the ones that will have the most impact on your projects. We give you the facts about the top design flaws and strengths on Web sites today and compare them to those of previous years. By the time you have finished reading this book, you will know what works and doesn't work, and how to make your Web site more usable, and thus, more successful.

2 The Web User Experience

You have less than two minutes to communicate the first time a prospective customer visits your Web site. This is the basic fact about the Web experience: As far as users are concerned, every page must justify its claim on their time. If a page doesn't do that immediately and clearly, they go elsewhere. Most don't even bother scrolling to see what's further down the page.

Web users are extremely impatient: In our study, they spent an average of 27 seconds on each Web page. Why the rush? Because there's too much irrelevant junk on the Internet. If people carefully studied everything they came across online, they would never get to log off and have a life.

There's no silver bell that alerts users to a page that is worthy of their attention. You need to convince them. In this chapter we look at users' general behavior on the Web—where they go first, how long they stay, what they do when they get there. We also examine the rise of "information foraging" and changes in the way people use search engines. When designing a site, these are the factors you need to keep in mind if you want people to stay long enough to see all that you have to offer.

How Well Do People Use the Web?

There are more than a billion users on the Internet, so any site that has less than ten million customers (in other words, almost any site) has not tapped into 99 percent of the potential audience.

In the beginning, the question was whether people were even capable of using Web sites. Today the answer is "yes," at least most of the time. When we told people to go to a specific site in the user testing for this book, they completed their tasks successfully 66 percent of the time. Of course, they also failed 34 percent of the time, but on average people did succeed.

Why do people use the Web if they fail a third of the time? Because in reality, they don't fail that often. The failures occur when people use new sites, but most people spend a lot of their time on sites that have proven useful in the past, so their success across a day of Web use is actually higher. Because users choose sites to spend time on based on their prior experience with them, those with high usability have a better chance of being selected. Furthermore, success breeds success: Users get better at using sites that they visit habitually. For example, if you have already bought nine books on Amazon.com, it'll be easier for you to buy the tenth than it was to buy the first.

It may be little comfort to learn that users' overall experience is better than indicated by our statistics, though, because a site's only hope of attracting new customers depends on how easy it is to use during that all-important initial visit. There are more than a billion users on the Internet, so any site that has less than ten million customers (in other words, almost any site) has not tapped into 99 percent of the potential audience.

The 66 percent success rate we measured in our study is actually a great advance over the miserable usability that characterized the Web in the 1990s. At that time usability studies regularly measured success rates at around 40 percent, meaning that more people failed than succeeded at using the Web.

The Measure of Success

We define success rate by the percentage of progress users made in completing their tasks. This is admittedly a coarse measure: It says nothing about why users fail or how well they perform the tasks they complete. Nonetheless, we like success rates because they are easy to collect and are a very telling statistic. After all, user success is the bottom line of usability.

Success rates are easy to measure with one major exception: How do we account for cases of partial success? If users can accomplish part of a task, but fail other parts, how should we score them?

Let's say, for example, that we ask users to order 12 yellow roses to be delivered to their friends on their birthdays. If a test user correctly makes the required arrangements, we can certainly score the task as a success. If the user fails to place any order, we can just as easily determine the task a failure.

But there are other possibilities as well. A user might order 12 yellow tulips or 24 yellow roses, fail to specify a shipping address or give the correct address but the wrong date, or forget to ask that a gift message be enclosed with the shipment. Each of these cases constitutes some degree of failure, so we could score it as such. However, we usually grant partial credit for a partially successful task. To us, it seems unreasonable to give a zero to both users who did nothing and those who successfully completed much of the task. How to score partial success depends on the magnitude of user error.

There is no firm rule for assigning credit for partial success. Partial scores are only estimates, but they still provide a more realistic impression of design quality than an absolute approach to success and failure.

So we have come a long way in just a decade. When will we see success rates of 100 percent? Probably never, because there will always be some sucky sites that almost nobody can use. But if current trends continue and sites invest more in usability, we should approximate 100 percent around 2015. Does this mean that the Web will be perfect by then? Certainly not. Success rates only measure whether it's *possible* for people to use Web sites, not whether it's pleasant or efficient to do so. Furthermore, because the Web is the ultimate competitive environment, once people can use almost all Web sites, they will still tend to use the ones that serve them best.

Web-Wide Success Rates

People succeeded 66 percent of the time when we took them to a homepage and gave them tasks that were possible to do on that site. But when we gave them a blank browser screen and told them to go anywhere they wanted to complete a task, the average success rate dropped to 60 percent. This makes sense because users first have to identify a site that will solve the problem and then use that site to accomplish the task.

If you are collecting usability measures for your own Web site, you should measure your numbers against the success rate we recorded for site-specific tasks, assuming that you too start your test participants on your homepage. This is the most common way to run usability studies because it maximizes the time users spend on the site that you are in charge of redesigning. If your users can perform 70 percent of reasonable and representative tasks on your site, you have above-average usability. Conversely, if their success rate is 50 percent, you have abominable usability and you will need to improve by about a third to bring your usability rates up to the average of 66 percent.

The 60 percent success rate we recorded for the Web-wide tasks is more representative of the overall Web user experience, when users are trying to do something new and they don't already know what site to go to. The lower success rates for Web-wide tasks is a measure of the difficulty of using the Web as a whole and the features that the Web provides to help users identify Web sites (mainly through search engines). So there's still plenty of room for improvement on the Web.

Success by Experience Level

We divided our test users into two groups, based on their amount of Internet experience. All had at least a year's experience using the Web, but there was still a broad range of expertise among them. For the purposes of this analysis, we divided them into "low-experience users" and "high-experience users," according to a variety of issues:

- How many years they had been online

- How many hours per week they used the Web, not counting time spent in email

- How many "advanced" behaviors they exhibited, such as Web chatting, changing the labels on bookmarks, upgrading their browser, and designing their own Web pages

- Whether they fixed problems with their computer equipment themselves

- How much they followed current trends in technology—for example, if they subscribed to computer magazines or were considered by friends to be a source for computer advice

In general people were considered "low experience" if they had been online for no more than three years, used the Web for less than ten hours per week, exhibited less than a third of the advanced behaviors, asked somebody else to fix their computer problems, and weren't consulted for advice on technology. Conversely people were scored as having "high experience" if they had been online for at least four years, used the Web for more than ten hours per week, exhibited more than a third of the advanced behaviors, fixed their own computer problems, and were a source for tech advice for others.

Of course, some people were advanced on some of the rating scales and less advanced on others. In those cases, their final designation as low or high experience depended on their average score.

As this table shows, the gap between the low- and high-experience users was 13 percent for the site-specific tasks and 15 percent for Web-wide tasks. In other words, experience was a stronger advantage when users had to navigate the entire Web instead of being told what site to use. This difference indicates that freedom of movement is more of an advantage for skilled users and more of an impediment for less skilled users. This again vindicates the "walled garden" approach (a closed environment that restricts user access to outside information) that AOL used in the early days when it tried to simplify the online experience for novice users.

Success Rates and Experience

Web Experience	Site-Specific Tasks	Web-Wide Tasks
Low	59%	52%
High	72%	67%

Less experienced Web users have more difficulty than more experienced users accomplishing standard tasks online. Both groups scored lower in completing Web-wide tasks than they did on site-specific tasks.

User Satisfaction with Web Sites

In general, subjective satisfaction ratings are not a very telling usability measure because users tend give generous scores even when they have great difficulty using a design. One reason for this is the general human desire to be polite and fit in. Another reason is that users often don't know how poorly they performed when they tested a site. If they found some information about their problem, they think that the site was helpful—they don't realize that it may have had a great deal more relevant information that it did not make readily available to them.

On a 1-to-7 scale in which 7 is the most satisfactory experience, the average score our users gave the 25 sites we tested was 4.7. In analyzing the usability of a user interface, we rarely analyze these scores except to note if there's something that people particularly like or despise about a site. However, the fact that satisfaction ratings for our study were reasonable indicates that we had picked a representative sample of current Web designs that pretty much matched users' prior expectations as to the current state of usability.

How People Use Sites

Observing how well our test users did with Web-wide tasks tells us how people approach Web sites when they have no predisposition to use a specific site. This is common when users are trying something new, such as researching a purchase of something they haven't bought before, and it is exactly the situation in which a Web site needs to be its most competitive and attractive.

Interior pages accounted for 60 percent of the initial page views. Recognize this and support it. Don't try to force users to enter on the homepage.

On average, our test users spent 1 minute and 49 seconds visiting a Web site before they decided to abandon it and move on. On the final site they visited while working on a task, they spent an average of 3 minutes and 49 seconds.

When doing a task, users visited an average of 3.2 sites in addition to any search engines they might have used to find these sites. More interesting, they revisited sites an average of 0.4 times when performing a task, meaning that basically they didn't. A site has only a 12 percent probability for being revisited, so once you have lost a user, you have almost always lost them for good.

Three Guidelines for Supporting Deep-Link Users

1. Tell users where they have arrived and how they can proceed to other parts of the site by including these three design elements on every page:

   - Company name or logo in upper left corner
   - Direct, one-click link to the homepage
   - Search (preferably in the upper right corner)

2. Orient the user to the rest of the site. If the site has hierarchical information architecture, the best way to do this is usually a "breadcrumb trail"—links that indicate the user's current location in the context of the site's hierarchy and allow users to backtrack or move up the hierarchy. Also include links to other resources that are directly relevant to the current location, but don't flood the user with links to all site areas or to unrelated pages.

3. Don't assume that users have followed a drill-down path to arrive at the current page. They may have taken a different path than what you intended and not have seen information that was contained on higher-level pages.

The users in our testing first went to the homepage of a site 40 percent of the time. Considering that most Web sites have thousands of pages, this means that the homepage gets disproportionately more visits. Furthermore, users often turn to the homepage when they want to get a general idea of what a site does, even if they entered on an interior page. So it's certainly a good idea to pay extra attention to homepage usability.

www.allmusicals.com

Let's say that you were looking for the lyrics to the song Singin' in the Rain and found them on the All Musicals site, maybe from a search engine or through a link from another site. This screen shot shows what you would see above the fold. This site doesn't encourage users to do anything else once they have read the lyrics—which in this case may have been just to check whether it was a "glorious" feeling or a "wonderful" one. The name of the site is at the top of the page, but it is presented in a way that looks like a headline, not a logo. There's no tagline to indicate the purpose of the site. There are a few links, including a money-making link to buying the CD, but these don't look clickable because they are not colored or underlined. Also, taken together, the links don't look like a navigation bar and users will tend to ignore that part of the screen because of its association with the obnoxious banner. Even worse, the title of the musical is not a link, so users have no easy way of clicking through to a list of other songs in the same musical. This site doesn't understand how to exploit deep-link visitors, so it's throwing away a lot of traffic.

Despite the importance of the homepage, however, interior pages accounted for 60 percent of the initial page views. A Web site is like a house with a thousand doors, and visitors can enter anywhere. We strongly encourage you to recognize this and support it. Some Web sites are designed to force users to enter on the homepage, but by doing so they go against a very ingrained element of the Web: the deep link.

Deep links enhance usability because they are more likely to satisfy users' needs. Generic links, such as those to a company's homepage, are less useful than links that take users to a specific article or product. So you want to encourage third-party sites and search engines to link directly to those pages on your site that address specific issues.

News.com offers several follow-ups to users who might arrive at this page via a deep link—for example, from a blog posting about Super Bowl commercials. Below the story are three category links to lists of stories about similar topics. Let's say that you are interested in the concept of showing commercials on cell phones. You can click on "mobile/wireless" to stories about recent developments in mobile technology. Stories that are more specifically about the Super Bowl are listed to the right. Finally, there's a box with unrelated but high-traffic current headlines. (Our main suggestion would be to swap the two sets of headlines so that the list that is the most tightly connected to the current story appears closer to the body text instead of being in the right hand column, where it's more likely to be ignored.) Finally, of course, it's easy to access other features of the site by going to the homepage or using its internal search engine, both of which are represented in the expected location.

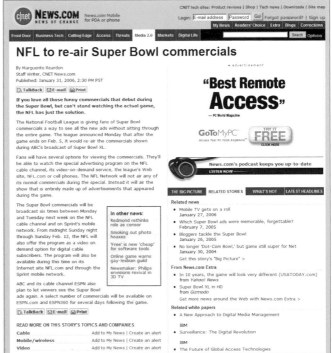

news.com.com

The Homepage: So Much to Say, So Little Time

As this table shows, experienced users who went first to the homepage on a Web site spent an average of ten seconds less time there than did users with less experience. This difference tells us that users get more ruthless in evaluating sites as they gain experience; they become faster at scanning pages and quicker at dismissing things they don't like.

Average Time Spent on the Homepage

Web Experience	Time on Homepage
Low	35 seconds
High	25 seconds

Initial homepage viewings when the homepage is the first page visited on a Web site. Make your point quickly. You have very little time to make a good first impression. For time spent on subsequent visits, see the table on page 32.

Of course, it's always difficult to predict the future, but it's a good bet that this trend will continue. The more years they have been online and the more comfortable they get with judging Web sites, the less time they will spend on the homepage.

With half a minute at your disposal, all messages have to be ultra-lean and to the point. No long-winded paragraphs that users won't read anyway. Most adults can read about 200 to 300 words per minute, depending on their level of education. You might think that this allows you to present a 100-word welcome message on your homepage. Not so. Ten to twenty words are more realistic. Users will spend most of their 25 to 35 seconds figuring out where to go next, not reading word-for-word about what makes you special.

Four Goals in Thirty Seconds

The four most important things a homepage must communicate to new readers in the half-minute they spend on the page:

- What site they have arrived at
- What benefits the organization offers them
- Something about the company and its latest products or new developments
- Their choices and how to get to the most relevant section for them

What does this company do? Even with all the text on this homepage, it doesn't say. A simple tagline or description at the top of the page would help. The strong emphasis on headlines and news overpowers the page, leaving little room to showcase the company's products and services. Also, notice the list of links at the bottom of the page. Cross-linking users to different Web sites without proper context—or warning—is problematic because people aren't expecting it. If you do want to link to other sites, do so by showing their names or a clear description, not their URLs.

www.qg.com

Dial Before You Dig seems to be a simple enough site, with little complexity on the homepage. But what does the company do? Apparently whatever it does has never been easier, but what exactly is that? With only a few seconds to communicate with new users, don't waste it telling people that your new Web service is now available. And the place to tell people how to get their password is on the login page. At any other time they won't be interested.

www.dialbeforeyoudig.com.au

You might be tempted to think that users will read more later in their visit. Unfortunately, this is not so. If people ever return to the homepage, they'll spend even less time admiring your carefully honed slogans. As this table shows, users spend less and less time on the homepage with each subsequent visit. After all, the main goal of a homepage is to guide users somewhere else, and the more people understand the page, the less they will look around on it. They go straight for the navigation and click where they want to go.

Page Views by the Screenful

	Time on Homepage	Users Who Scrolled	Screenfuls Scrolled
1st visit	31 sec	23%	0.8
2nd visit	25 sec	16%	0.8
3rd visit	22 sec	16%	0.8
4th+ visit	19 sec	14%	0.5

Note: A "screenful" is one screen set at 1024 by 768 pixels. One screenful scrolled means seeing the initial screen plus an additional screen length below it. The statistics for scrolling only used those homepages that were so long that they stretched beyond the size of the browser window

Gone in 30 seconds: Users spend very little time on the homepage and scroll minimally, especially on subsequent visits. For simplicity, the numbers in this table are averaged across both high-experience and low-experience users.

Only 23 percent of users scrolled the homepage during their initial visit and even fewer scrolled on subsequent visits. This is because users know—or think they know—where the important areas on the homepage are after one visit. Even those few users who scrolled didn't scroll very much: less than one additional screenful on average.

Interior Page Behavior

Low-experience users who entered a site through a deep link and visited an interior page first spent an average of 60 seconds there. High-experience users spent about 45 seconds on an initial interior page visit.

We see the same phenomenon for interior pages as we do for homepages: With experience, people get faster at scanning their first page view and deciding what they want to do on the site. Users spent about 70 to 80 percent more time reviewing their entry point when they entered on an interior page than they did when they entered on the homepage. This is because the interior pages they visited were more directly related to their tasks.

With 45 to 60 seconds on an interior page, users could theoretically read about 200 words, but they usually spend some of this time assessing the site's navigation system and deciding where to go next. They may read as many as 100 words of initial information, however, which is substantially more than the 10 to 20 words they read when entering on the homepage. One of the major reasons to support deep links is because users read more content on the interior pages of a site.

Homepage vs. Interior Pages

Web Experience	Time Spent on Homepage	Time Spent on Interior Page
Low	35 seconds	60 seconds
High	25 seconds	45 seconds

People spend more time on interior pages than homepages. Again, people with more Web experience fly through screens at a faster pace while novice users tend to scrub the screen more carefully.

Say a user is researching music players and has arrived at the product page for iPods on Apple's Web site. On average, people read about the amount of text we have highlighted with a red box in this figure. In practice, users are not going to read these two paragraphs word-for-word. Instead, they will scan several of the top paragraphs, reading less than half of each of them. Users will spend the remainder of their 45 to 60 seconds looking at the photos and scanning the bulleted feature list and other page elements. In total, this page contains 523 words (including a disclaimer not shown here), which would take the average user two minutes to read—more than twice the time they are likely to spend on the page. The text is written at an eighth-grade reading level, which is our recommendation for adult users, but it will be too difficult for many teenagers, who are an important target audience for this product.

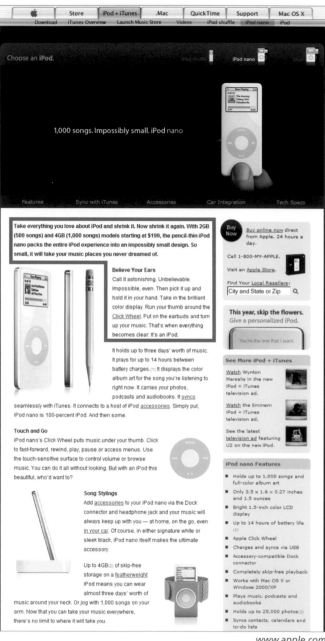

www.apple.com

Tip: Optimizing Interior Page Links

With about half of a minute on interior pages, users spend most of it in the content area, not navigation. Put important links in this area so they are most likely to see them.

When users visited interior pages during their browsing of a site, they spent an average of only 27 seconds on each page. This extremely short time emphasizes the importance of being crystal clear on each page about what users will get out of it. People don't have time to read everything, so they will judge pages in a few seconds.

This pie chart shows where users clicked on the page. It may seem surprising that users spent more time in the content area than in areas that are usually used for navigation, such as the top of the page or the left or right columns. However, we know from eye-tracking studies that users spend the vast majority of their time looking at the content area and only rarely scan navigation areas.

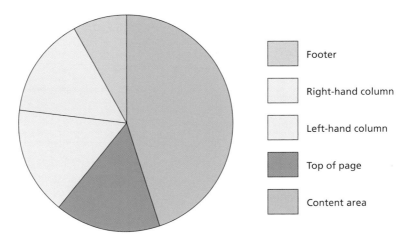

Footer

Right-hand column

Left-hand column

Top of page

Content area

Where users clicked on Web pages to navigate elsewhere on the same site, averaged across 4,719 clicks.

Search Dominance

When we let users loose to go anywhere they wanted on the Web, they went to a search engine 88 percent of the time. Only in 12 percent of cases did they go straight to a Web site that they hoped would help them with their problem. For example, when the task was to research vacation travel to Mexico, only a few users went to a travel site that they already knew and trusted, such as Expedia or Travelocity. The vast majority employed a search engine to help them find sites.

The fact that search engines have become the dominant tool for users looking for solutions is clearly why search advertising has become such a profitable business. Search ads are the main way you get in front of prospective customers at the exact moment they are looking for new vendors.

Increasingly, the Internet user experience is becoming one of dipping a toe into Web sites rather than truly "visiting" them. Using search engines as their Web interface, people often grab query-related nuggets from sites without engaging with the sites themselves.

The search engine has always been an important tool for users. In 1994, when we were trying to understand why people used the Web despite its lousy usability, we asked everyone who came by our lab two questions: What are you doing online? What are your favorite sites? Their answers were strikingly diverse. People's pursuits ranged from golf to knitting to Linux to military history, and their favorite sites varied just as widely. In fact, the only commonality among them was that all users named a search engine among their top sites.

The conclusion was clear: The Web's strength comes from narrowly targeted sites that provide users with highly specialized information that they need or care about passionately. It was also clear that Search was a hugely important general-interest service because even back when the Web had only 30,000 sites, locating specialized ones was nearly impossible without help.

The Rise of "Answer Engines"

The study we conducted for this book confirmed our early conclusion: Users pursue their own idiosyncratic goals and depend on a generic service—Search—for guidance. What has changed: Rather than looking for sites to explore and use in depth, users now hunt for specific answers. Search engines have essentially become "answer engines."

A major change over the years has been a decline in using Search to identify good sites as such. People are looking for answers. The Web as a whole has become one agglomerated resource for people who use search engines to dredge up specific pages related to specific needs, without caring which sites supply them. The job of search engines is no longer resource discovery but to answer questions.

This changing behavior is explained by the theory of "information foraging": The easier it is to track down new resources, the less time users spend at each resource. Thus, improvement in Search quality over time is driving the trend toward answer engines. Always-on connections have a similar effect, because they encourage information snacking and shorter sessions. Finally, Web browsers' despicably weak support for bookmarks/favorites has contributed to the decline in users' interest in building a list of favorite sites.

It's a testament to the Web's growth that users now view it as integrated whole and don't bother with Web sites; they assume that anything they want to know is available somewhere. They just have to ask. "Web sites" weren't really a tangible concept until 1993 anyway. The pre-Mosaic Web in 1991 and 1992 was exactly that: a web of information where the fundamental unit was the article, not the server hosting a particular Web page. So this new user behavior is actually a reversion to the Web's original vision to some extent—though not completely because users still have some favorite sites that they treat as resources.

For search engines, becoming the user interface to the Web's embarrassment of riches is good news. It's also good news for users, who can find answers by visiting a few search hits rather than enduring the obscure design and poor navigation found on many sites. But is this good for Web sites? Unfortunately not. There is very little value in giving answers to users who don't know or care who provides the service.

E-commerce sites are something of an exception, because they often get a sale from users dipping a toe into their catalog. E-commerce sites differ from other Web sites in having confirmation and fulfillment stages that follow up on users' initial visits, and these steps can also grow the site's *mindshare*—the likelihood that the site will come to mind when the user is thinking about the type of products or services it offers. Thus, closing the first sale is one of the most important drivers of subsequent e-commerce sales.

It would be self-defeating for e-commerce sites to refuse shopbots (software that searches the Web for a product's lowest prices), prohibit deep links, or employ other tricks that require users to enter at the homepage and spend time navigating the site. Any barrier between the customer and the product translates into lost sales.

Four Ways to Grab Value from Search Engine Visitors

There are some tactics you can use to gain value for your company from users who dive into your site from a search engine. Unless you use at least one of these four, visitors may only see one or two pages on your site and never know anything about your company.

- Offer flytrap content that attracts users by providing narrowly focused pages with clear answers to common problems. These pages should perform well in Search Engine Optimization (SEO), so remember to write clear headlines.
- Embellish the answer with rich "See Also" links to related content and services. Global navigation won't do the trick because answer-seekers will ignore it. Remember, they are not interested in your site. But contextual links will make the most eager users dig deeper—and the eager people are the ones you'll want to keep as prospects for your for-pay services. "See Also" links can be embedded or placed at the end of the article, where they serve as a follow-up call to action. The latter gives you the opportunity to let people know that you're actually selling something and not just handing out free information.
- Go beyond pure information and provide analysis and insight, preferably from a unique perspective and with a striking personality that supports your positioning. A percentage of users will appreciate your perspective and want more, even after they've found the answer to their immediate question.
- Publish a newsletter with additional tips and useful information. E-mail newsletters set up a relationship with users, offering a more personal experience than page viewing.

Even sites that don't sell must accept the trend toward users' answer-seeking behavior. Walling yourself off from the Web's web-like nature won't solve the problem. Tracking numbers of unique visitors is now irrelevant. Most such visitors are sampling a single page to get an answer, not engaging with your site. Instead of tracking them, count loyal users as a key measure for site success.

How People Use the Search Engine Results Page

The search engine results page is usually referred to as a SERP. It's fitting that this term is rarely used in plural because most users don't see more than one SERP per query. In 93 percent of searches, the users in our study only visited the first SERP, which usually held ten search results plus a number of ads. In only seven percent of cases did users page on to a second SERP, and the number who visited three SERPs for a single query was too small to provide a firm estimate, but it was likely less than one percent.

Not only did most users make do with a single SERP; most of them didn't even bother reviewing the entire page. Only 47 percent of users scrolled the first SERP, which means that 53 percent saw only those search hits that were "above the fold." (Originally a newspaper term, "above the fold" refers to what part of a Web page is visible on a screen without scrolling.) On the most widely used search engine, Google, users can only see four or five results above the fold, if they view the page on the most common screen resolution of 1024-by-768 pixels, like those in our study. In addition to the four or five "organic" search results, there are typically six or seven advertisements above the fold—a total of ten or so items to choose from.

This table shows how often users clicked the search hits at different placements on the SERP list. Since the first SERP only displays ten organic links, users needed to go to the second SERP to click links number 11 or higher. Of the seven percent who actually visited the second page, only five percent clicked there—a discrepancy explained by the fact that a few users who visited the second page returned to the first page. It's no big surprise that the top links get more clicks than bottom links, but it may be surprising to see just how dominant the No. 1 spot is, with more than half of all the clicks.

Where Users Click on the SERP

Position in search results listing	Clicks on links in this position
#1	51%
#2	16%
#3	6%
#4	6%
#5	5%
#6	4%
#7	2%
#8	1%
#9	1%
#10	2%
#11+	5%

Note: Numbers don't add up to 100% due to rounding.

With items 1 through 10 on the first search engine results page, 95 percent of clicks were there. This table only counts clicks on the organic links. Sponsored links follow a similar distribution with disproportionately more clicks on the top ads.

Number One Guideline for Search Engine Optimization

Aim for the top spot in the listings for all the important keywords your users are likely to search for. (Unfortunately, this is an easy guideline to state but a hard one to achieve.) If you don't get the top listing, second or third is certainly good as well. The farther down the list, the less likely your chance of being seen, but if you have a choice between being ninth or tenth, pick the bottom spot on the page, as there is some prominence to being the last element in a list.

If you can't get a decent organic ranking for important query terms, seriously consider running search ads for those terms.

Using Keyword Pricing to Estimate Usability Improvements

It is very expensive and time consuming to conduct broad usability studies like ours of a wide range of Web sites. We can't do it every year, so we can't accurately track usability improvements on a steady basis through direct measurements. Fortunately there is an indirect measurement that's more feasible to acquire and that can be used as a proxy for Web site usability: the prices paid for keyword advertising on major search engines.

On most major search engines, keyword advertising works as follows: First a company must consider how much it is worth paying to try to attract a visitor who has searched for a certain keyword and is presumably interested in a product or service associated with that word. The company then bids for each keyword, and the search engine usually displays the ads from the top eight bidders. (There are many twists to search engine advertising, but the basic principle is an auction in which a limited number of slots are sold to the highest bidders.)

Over time, the price for keyword advertising has shown a distinct upward trend. Future increases in keyword bids will be tightly related to improvements in Web site usability.

For example, our own company, Nielsen Norman Group, usually pays 31 cents per user who searched for "usability training" when that user clicks through from the search engine to the page for our annual usability conference. Similarly, a company that sells vacation packages to Mexico would be willing to pay a substantial amount for users who are searching for "vacation Mexico" or "hotels Yucatan."

Over time, the price for keyword advertising has shown a distinct upward trend. Over the long term, increases in keyword bids will be tightly related to improvements in Web site usability. During the next several years, keyword prices will increase substantially as more companies realize the benefits of search engine advertising. Search ads are the best way to promote a Web site because keyword matching attracts users who are looking for the exact thing you're offering.

Currently most Internet marketing managers are clueless about keyword advertising and spend most of their budgets on advertising techniques that were appropriate in old media but don't work in an interactive medium like the Web. But one of the beauties of the Web is its accountability: You can track the results of advertising expenditures in terms of both click-throughs and the extent to which clickers turn into spenders. Because of this, even clueless managers will gradually reallocate their budgets to the best performing promotions, which will most often be search advertising.

How To Determine the Optimal Bid for a Search Keyword Ad

We say in our discussion of keyword advertising that a company should increase its bids for search keywords as long as it can make more money from the average new visitor than it is paying per click. This is a nice simplification that makes a complicated argument easier to follow, but it's not the best way of actually determining what your bid should be.

In real life, you should maximize your profits, not simply do as much business as possible. For example, let's say that your Web site makes an average profit of $2.00 for each new visitor who arrives after clicking on a certain keyword. (Let's also say that you have a conversion rate of one percent, so the $2.00 profit per visitor was derived from a profit of $200 per buying customer, since only one of every hundred new visitors becomes a customer.)

Your earlier experimentation has established that you will gain the following traffic for each of three possible advertising bids for a keyword that's highly targeted for your product:

- Bidding $1.00 places your ad third from the top and generates 500 visitors per month
- Bidding $1.50 places yours as the second ad from the top and generates 1,500 visitors per month
- Bidding $1.90 places your ad on top and generates 2,000 visitors per month

How much should you bid? Certainly, you could afford to bid $1.90 because you would still make 10 cents per visitor for a profit of $200 a month. On the other hand, bidding $1.00 would gain you a full dollar's profit per user, for a total monthly profit of $500 from the 500 users who were attracted by a third-place ad. Finally, bidding $1.50 will gain you monthly profits of $750. This is obviously the preferred outcome because it has the highest profit margin.

In this example, you are better off doing without the 500 extra users who would be attracted by the top ad but who would not click on a second-position ad. These users are simply not worth the higher cost of the top spot. Users who click on lower-positioned ads are often worth slightly more to companies than users who click on top ads because they tend to be more actively committed to getting a solution to their problem.

Of course, you must gather the detailed data for your customers from your own Web site. In general, though, the main guideline is simple: The higher the worth of a new visitor, the more you should bid to attract them to your site.

As more and more companies discover the high return on investment (ROI) of search advertising, keyword prices will be bid up because of the increased demand for a fixed supply of advertising positions. Of course, a search engine could put more ads on each page but only at the price of diluting the effectiveness of each ad. What search engines are really auctioning off is the attention of motivated users, and as long as motivation stays the same, there's a limit to how much a page can be subdivided and remain profitable.

It's difficult to estimate when all companies will fully understand the benefits of search advertising, but 2010 might be a reasonable guess. When that happens, further growth in keyword pricing will be due to improvements in the target Web sites.

As we've said, each company should bid no higher than what it takes to get a positive ROI. So let's say that a company brings in an average profit of $2.00 for each new customer. It might bid up to $1.99 for a click, for marginal profits of one cent per new visitor. Bidding $2.01 would be too much and would result in losses.

Now let's assume that this company performed enough usability work on its Web site to double the conversion rate for new visitors, which is a likely result. The company now makes an average of $4.00 per new visitor, so it can bid up to $3.99 for each click on the keywords that generate the $4.00 visitors. Improving usability and doubling the conversion rate doubles the bid that the company can afford to pay the search engine.

Of course, our example company would hope that it wouldn't have to increase its search engine bids by quite as much. It would be preferable to pocket some of the increased profits from usability improvements instead of handing them over to a search engine. In the short term, the company would indeed be able to retain some of the profits because its site would be better than its competitors'. Until its competitors also increase the value of their visitors, they could not afford higher search bids. Sooner or later, however, they will conduct their own usability projects and improve their profits, allowing them to increase their bids. As soon as eight competitors have doubled their bids, it will be necessary for our example company to double its bid again. Since even one cent's profit is better than no profit, rational companies will increase their bids accordingly.

In the long term, keyword prices will tend to increase at about the same pace as Web site conversion rates. Since the conversion rate is a key measure of usability, bids for search engine advertising will continue to indicate the extent to which Web sites are improving their designs.

As Web sites improve, search engines will confiscate almost all the increased profits they gain from increased usability. In other words, search engines need do nothing but watch their incomes grow as mainstream Web sites do all the hard work of improving the Web. Is this fair? No. But the reality is that search engines drive much of the new traffic that a site can hope to attract.

Three Reasons to Improve Your Site

Why should a Web site bother with usability if most of the value of improvements accrues to search engines? There are three reasons:

- If you don't improve, your keyword bids will gradually become insufficient to get your ads shown, and your Search-derived traffic will shrivel to nothing.
- If you do improve, there will be a window of opportunity when you're better than the competition and you won't have to increase your keyword bids to the max. During this time, you get to keep the fruits of your labor, so you can hope that your competitors don't read this book and are slow to improve their sites.

- Finally, you do get to keep the increased profits from customers who arrive through other means. Although search ads are a great way of driving traffic, they're not the only way. Links from other sites, word of mouth, offline advertising, and many other techniques can drive traffic as well. Also, most search engines allow so-called "organic results," which are free listings where your site is shown because it naturally scores well for the user's query, even if you are not running any ads.

Scrolling

Users are lazy and ignorant. That's one conclusion we can draw from the fact that they don't even bother using the scroll wheel on their mouse most of the time.

A different, and more appropriate, conclusion is that users are so busy and there's so much information on the Web that it's not worth it to them to dig into a Web page unless the information that's initially viewable clearly communicates that the page has value to them. Sadly, since most pages have little value, users rightly decide to avoid scrolling most of the time. If you are designing Web pages, you must acknowledge this fact and make sure to present enough information above the fold to make them want to see what's below it.

In our study, 35 percent of pages were so short that they didn't require any scrolling. We won't go so far as to recommend such ultra-short pages, however, even though they obviously solve the problem of scrolling aversion. Our test users did not scroll more than half of the other 65 percent of pages that were longer. All the carefully designed information below the fold might as well have not existed as far as most users were concerned.

Tip: Design for Short Scrolling

Most users don't scroll, and when they do, they don't scroll very much. Our users who did scrolled through 1.3 screens worth of information on average—meaning that they saw a total of 2.3 screens, including the initial one above the fold. Any page longer than 2.3 screens risks being overlooked, even by those few users who care enough about the page to scroll it.

In our study for this book, users visited 3,992 pages that were longer than the browser window. This chart shows how many screenfuls of information users viewed on those pages. Obviously all users saw the first screenful (the one above the fold). But viewing frequency dropped off rapidly after that. More than half the users didn't scroll at all, so only 42% of users saw any information on the second screenful (the one immediately below the fold). Only 14 percent of users viewed beyond two screenfuls. Only the most persistent 1 percent of users viewed more than seven screens worth of information. (This doesn't mean that they read all of it, just that it was visible to them because they had scrolled that far down the page.)

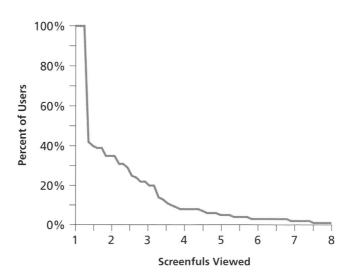

Users with more Web experience scrolled more than those with less experience. Our low-experience users only scrolled 38 percent of long pages, whereas the high-experience users scrolled 46 percent of these pages. There are two possible explanations for this: First, experienced users are more aware that poorly designed Web sites sometimes hide important information below the fold, and second, they are faster at picking out relevant information by scanning Web pages, so they are more willing to take the time to do it.

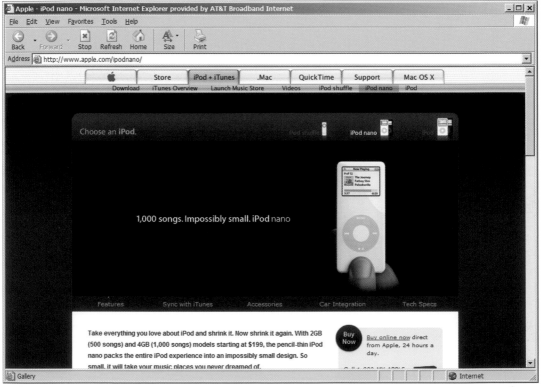

www.apple.com

This is the way the iPod page on page 34 of this chapter appears to a user viewing the page on a 1024-by-768 sized monitor, which was the most common screen size among home users at the time this screen shot was taken. Almost no information is visible without scrolling, but at least the most important facts are above the fold: what the product is and how it looks. Most likely Apple's fans are sufficiently committed to begin scrolling once these two facts have convinced them that they are on the right page. Other sites are strongly advised to be less arrogant.

Scrolling by Page Type

Type of page	Users who scrolled
Homepage, 1st visit	23%
Homepage, 4th & later visits	14%
Interior pages	42%
Search engine results page	47%

The percentage of users who scrolled the different kinds of Web pages in this table was calculated based only on those pages that required scrolling to be seen in their entirety on a monitor with a resolution of 1024-by-768 pixels. SERPs were scrolled the most, while homepages were scrolled the least. Note that even users who scrolled may not have scrolled enough to see the entire page.

Complying with Design Conventions and Usability Guidelines

The entire concept of "Web design" is a misnomer. Individual project teams are not designing the Web any more than individual ants are designing an anthill. Site designers build components of a whole—especially now that users are viewing the Web as a single, integrated resource. Unfortunately, much of the Web is like an anthill built by ants on LSD. Many sites don't fit into the big picture and are too difficult to use because they deviate from expected norms.

Defining Standards and Conventions

- Standard: Eighty percent or more of Web sites use the same design approach. Users strongly expect standard elements to work a certain way when they visit a new site because that's how things almost always work.
- Convention: About 50 to 79 percent of Websites use the same design approach. Users expect conventional elements to work a certain way when they visit a new site because that's how things usually work.
- Confusion: With these elements, no single design approach dominates, and even the most popular approach is used by less than half of Web sites. For such design elements, users don't know what to expect when they visit a new site.

We must eliminate confusing design elements and move as far as possible into the realm of design conventions. Even better, we should establish design standards for every important Web site task. Standards enhance users' sense of mastery over a site, help them get things done, and increase their overall satisfaction with a site.

Even if you don't believe in the theoretical arguments in favor of user interface standards, the empirical evidence strongly favors complying with existing design conventions and usability guidelines. In this chapter, we have seen that the users most often:

1. Go to a search engine and type in two to three words

2. Look at the top few listings on the SERP

3. Visit some of these sites but leave them after less than two minutes if they don't seem sufficiently useful

4. View most site pages for less than half a minute

With this little time to communicate your product benefits to prospective customers, you want everything else out of the way. If a user spends 27 seconds looking at a product page, you don't want them to spend most of it wondering about your navigation design or puzzling over other user interface elements. If your design follows conventions, they can allocate their attention to your content. That's the simple business rationale for complying with standards.

There are certainly cases where it's OK to deviate from the usability guidelines. That's why they are called "guidelines"—because they usually, but not always, hold. Take Victoria's Secret as an example. The very successful e-commerce site of this famous fashion and lingerie company usually scores among the top sellers on the Web. The nature of the company's products and positioning mean that it can do certain things on its site that would be a mistake for almost any other company. For example, the Web site attracts large numbers of visitors every time it streams an hour-long video production. Most Web sites would do better with shorter video clips.

Even those sites that violate some guidelines are only successful if they comply with the vast majority of them. A few sites are so special that they can get away with violating most of the guidelines, but they are truly the exceptions.

Every year Victoria's Secret produces a fashion show that is broadcast on television and available as streamed video off its Web site. This video is usually one of the most downloaded videos on the Internet and clips from it are available on many other sites. A full hour of video much exceeds our recommendation that Web videos be no longer than one or two minutes. Unless yours feature supermodels in lingerie, you are better off sticking to the guideline and producing short videos for your site instead of recycling television productions.

Victoria's Secret may violate the usability guideline on Web videos, but the company's e-commerce pages are pretty much by the book. On this page, however, there ought to be a buy button next to the main product, and it would be better if the model in the photo were wearing the shoes that the site is promoting in the cross-sales area of the page. This disparity emphasizes the need for e-commerce sites to shoot their own photos instead of repurposing images from a print catalog.

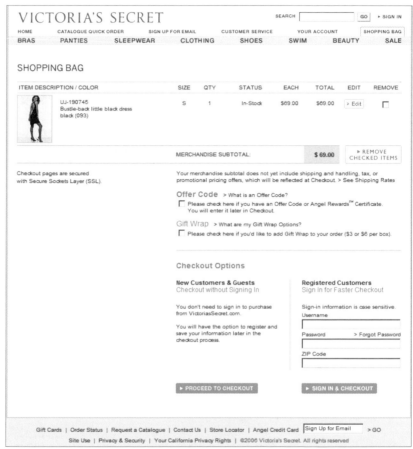

Victoria's Secret continues to comply with usability guidelines in its shopping cart. It follows standard guidelines such as indicating whether a product is in stock (though it should do so on the product page as well), providing an easy link for checking shipping and handling fees, and letting users check out without having to register. Despite the site's emphasis on glamour, this is an easy place to shop, and as a result, it is among the 25 best-selling e-commerce sites in the world.

Information Foraging

Information foraging is the most important concept to emerge from human–computer interaction research since 1993. Developed at the Palo Alto Research Center (previously Xerox PARC) by Stuart Card, Peter Pirolli, and colleagues, information foraging uses the analogy of wild animals gathering food to analyze how humans collect information online.

Web users behaving like beasts in a jungle? There is ample data to support this claim. Animals make decisions on where, when, and how to eat on the basis of highly optimized formulas that have been developed over generations as behaviors that result in starvation are discarded. Humans are under less evolutionary pressure to improve their Web use, but basic laziness is a human characteristic that might be survival-related. ("Don't exert yourself unless you have to.") In any case, people like to get maximum benefit for minimum effort. That's what makes information foraging a useful tool for analyzing online media.

Information Scent: Predicting a Path's Success

Information foraging's most famous concept is "information scent": Figuratively speaking, users estimate their hunt's likely success from the spoor, assessing whether their path exhibits cues related to the desired outcome. Informavores will keep clicking as long as they sense that they're "getting warmer"—the scent must keep getting stronger and stronger or they will give up. Their progress must seem rapid enough to be worth the effort required to reach their goal.

Diet Selection: What Sites to Visit

A fox lives in a forest with big rabbits and small rabbits. Which should it eat? This is a question of diet selection, and the answer is not always the big rabbits. Whether to eat big or small depends on how easy a rabbit is to catch. If big rabbits are very difficult to catch, the fox is better off letting them go and concentrating on the small ones—the probability of a catch is too low to justify the energy consumed by the hunt.

Three Ways to Enhance Information Scent

1. Ensure that links and category descriptions explicitly describe what users will find at the destination. Faced with several navigation options, it's best if users can clearly identify the trail to the prey and see that other trails are devoid of anything edible.
2. Don't use made-up words or your own slogans as navigation options, since they don't have the scent of the sought-after item. (Plain language also works best for search engine visibility.)
3. Remind users that they're still on the path to the food as they drill down the site. In other words, provide feedback about their location and how it relates to their tasks.

The big difference between Web sites and rabbits is that Web sites want to be caught—big ones as well as small ones. So how can you design a site that will attract ravenous beasts? The two main strategies are to make your content look like a nutritious meal and signal that it's an easy catch. These strategies must be used together: Users will leave if the content is good but hard to find or if it's easy to find but not satisfying.

This dual strategy is the reason that Jakob's book with Marie Tahir, *Homepage Usability: 50 Websites Deconstructed* (New Riders Publishing, 2002), recommended showcasing sample content on the homepage (appear nutritious) and prominently display navigation and Search features (be an easy catch). Diet selection also supports our traditional advice against splash screens and vacuous content. These elements convey to users that they're in for a tedious ordeal that serves up only scrawny rodents as rewards.

Patch Abandonment: When to Hunt Elsewhere

Grazing environments often feature several different areas where game congregates. So where should predators hunt? In whatever patch has the most prey, of course. And after predators have eaten some of that game, should they continue to hunt in the same patch or move to another one? The answer depends on how far is it to the next patch.

If getting to the next patch is easy, predators are better off moving on. No need to deplete all the game in the current patch; when it becomes a bit difficult to find their next prey, they can move to richer hunting grounds. On the other hand, if it's difficult to move—say, if they have to cross a river—predators are more likely to hunt each patch more extensively before going to the next.

For informavores, each site is a patch and each site's information is their prey. Moving between sites has always been easy, but for information foraging, it used to be best if users stayed put. The vast majority of sites were horrible and the probability that the next site would be better was extremely low.

We used to advise Web site designers to follow two strategies: Convince users that the site is worthy of their attention (by having good information and making it easy to find), and make it easy for users to find even more good stuff once they arrive so that they don't go elsewhere. An entire movement was devoted to the idea of "sticky sites" and extended visits.

In recent years, highly improved search engines have reversed this equation by emphasizing quality in their sorting of search results. It is now extremely easy for users to find other good sites. Information foraging predicts that the easier it is to find good patches, the quicker users will leave a patch. Thus, the better search engines get at highlighting quality sites, the less time users will spend on any one site. This theoretical prediction was amply confirmed by the empirical data we collected for this book: People left the sites they found useless within less than two minutes.

The growth of always-on broadband connections also encourages this trend toward shorter visits. With dial-up, connecting to the Internet was somewhat difficult, and users mainly did it in big time chunks. In contrast, always-on connections encourage "information snacking": brief online searches for quick answers. The upside of this trend is that users will visit the Web more frequently and therefore find you more often, and will leave other sites faster.

Better intra-site navigation and site maps may tip the balance slightly back in favor of longer stays, but it's safest to assume that users' visits to any individual Web site will become ever shorter. This prediction is supported by our empirical data showing that high-experience users spent less time on pages than the low-experience users.

New Design Strategies for Attracting Information Foragers

- Support short visits; be a snack.
- Encourage users to return; use strategies such as newsletters as a reminder.
- Emphasize search engine visibility and other ways of increasing frequent visits by addressing users' immediate needs.

More Information

For details on our study of usability returns on investment, visit www.nngroup.com/reports, and see "Return on Investment."

Informavore Navigation Behavior

Information foraging presents many interesting metaphors and mathematical models for analyzing user behavior. The most important is that of cost–benefit analysis for navigation. Users make tradeoffs based on two questions:

- What gain can I expect from a specific information nugget (such as a Web page)?

- What is the likely cost to discover and consume that information?

Both questions involve *estimates*, which users make from either experience or design cues. Web site designers can thus influence users' decisions by designing to enhance their expectations of gains and reduce their expectations of costs. Ultimately, of course, what a site actually delivers is most important, but it will never get experienced repeat visitors unless their first encounter is fruitful.

Users optimize cost–benefit relative to personal criteria and within a system that's larger than any single Web site. It's helpful to remember that they are selfish, lazy, and ruthless in applying their cost–benefit analyses.

3 Revisiting Early Web Usability Findings

The Web has changed dramatically since we began identifying usability problems in 1994. How do our early guidelines from the '90s hold up against evolving technology and Web design? Have changes in users' skill levels, Web sophistication, or expectations had an impact?

This chapter revisits 34 of the most significant usability problems to see which have improved, which are irrelevant, and which are as important now as they ever were.

Eight of our original guidelines are as important today as they were when we first identified them. Some bad design practices are actually more of a problem now because continued abuse has made users ever more sensitive to them.

We conducted our first user studies of Web sites and intranets in 1994. Even the first study, which tested only five sites with three users, identified a number of usability problems. For example, it was clear that users didn't want to read very much; detested long pages with dense, unstructured text; and preferred scannable content. In 1997 we conducted more thorough research into how people read online. It confirmed our early findings and resulted in refined analysis of design flaws and more detailed guidelines for avoiding them. This research was confirmed in yet another project in 2004 and led to even more detailed guidelines for specialized Web writing.

In this chapter, we review 34 of the most prevalent usability issues and our guidelines for addressing them, developed during our initial period of user research, from 1994 to 1999. First, we discuss eight issues that continue to be as critical as ever to usable Web design; then we talk about those that have become less important over time. We have assigned each of the 34 problem areas a skull rating, with up to three skulls indicating how important it continues to be. The rating scheme is as follows:

☠ ☠ ☠	Still a high-impact usability problem. It is very important that designers continue to pay attention to this problem and that interface evaluations check meticulously for it.
☠ ☠	Now a medium-impact usability problem. It is still important that designers avoid making this mistake, but it is no longer a top priority.
☠	Now a minor issue. Designers should remember our guidelines and try to avoid this design error, but it will rarely cause Web sites to fail.
0 skulls	No longer a problem and need not be checked systematically in interface evaluations.

There are three reasons why a usability problem may be less of an issue today, and we discuss each of these in turn:

- **Technology has improved.** When you consider the primitive state of the Web in the 1990s, it is understandable that several approaches caused dramatic usability problems even if they were not inherently bad designs. Improved technology has alleviated some of the difficulties users had in the past.

- **Users adapt to Web site designs.** Confusing designs create many usability problems. When people get accustomed to certain design approaches, however, they are no longer confused, and those design flaws are less of a problem.

- **Designers refrain from the worst abuses.** To the extent that designers have shown increased understanding of particular design flaws and restraint in using approaches that increase the potential for problems, we consider that element to be less important, and we don't need to warn against it as strongly anymore.

Under Construction

Unfortunately, we can't revisit many of our minor findings in detail here. For example, in 1994 we found that it was a bad idea to post "under construction" signs on Web sites. Users said, "Either you have it or you don't," and they didn't want to be teased with links to material that was not yet available.

The main guideline for under-construction signs is to avoid them and not advertise features until you have them. If this is not possible, at least provide an estimate of when the information will be available. Even better, if it is an important feature or a product that you will be selling, offer users the option of receiving an email announcement when the page goes live.

Even though "under construction" signs are not nearly as common as they were in the 1990s, we still see them from time to time. For example, in a recent consulting project for a big company's intranet, we followed a link for a useful feature, only to land on a page that read, "coming soon." Our early finding certainly remains true today—users *still* don't like clicking in vain—but we don't emphasize it anymore because under-construction signs have become so rare.

Eight Problems That Haven't Changed

Eight of the original usability problems are as important today as they were when we first identified them. Though some of these bad design practices are less common on the Web now, others are actually more of a problem because continued abuse has made users ever more sensitive to them.

Areas that still cause major problems include:

- Links that don't change color when visited
- Breaking the back button
- Opening new browser windows
- Pop-up windows
- Design elements that look like advertisements
- Violating Web-wide conventions
- Vaporous content and empty hype
- Dense content and unscannable text

Links That Don't Change Color When Visited ☠ ☠ ☠

The oldest usability guideline for any type of navigational design is to help users understand where they've **been**, where they **are**, and where they can **go**—their online past, present, and future. The three are somewhat interrelated: A good grasp of past navigation helps you understand your current location, since it's the culmination of your journey. Knowing your past and present locations in turn makes it easier to decide where to go next.

On the Web, links are a key factor in this navigation process. Users can stop using links that proved fruitless in the past. Conversely, they might revisit links they found helpful in the past. Most important, when users know which pages they've already visited, they are less likely to unintentionally revisit them.

Generally, Web browsers are severely deficient in supporting user navigation, but they do provide one important navigation feature: They allow designers to change the color of a page link when a user has already visited the page. Changing the color of visited links has been part of Web browsing since Mosaic arrived from National Center for Supercomputing Applications (NCSA) in 1993. Currently 74 percent of Web sites use this design approach, making it a convention that people have come to expect.

On sites that violate this convention, however, there can be serious usability problems. Users in our testing unintentionally revisited pages and got lost more easily, misinterpreted or overlooked the difference between similar links if they were unsure which they had already visited, and gave up on the site faster. They felt less mastery over sites that failed to reflect their actions and help them navigate.

Such usability problems are aggravated for users with weak short-term memory, who often can't remember what they've clicked without a visual representation. Of course, all humans suffer from weak short-term memory to some degree, which is why all users are better served by changing link colors. Since this definitely impacts some people more than others, it's particularly important to change link colors if your audience includes, for example, many older users, as our research with senior citizens shows.

Unchanging link colors create navigational confusion because users don't quite understand their different choices or where they are. This is as serious a usability problem as it has ever been, so it continues to deserve three skulls.

Even people who agree with other usability guidelines sometimes question the need for changing link colors. This is probably because they don't pick up on the problems caused by unchanging links when they conduct their own user testing. Unfortunately, the problems can be among the most difficult to detect.

User testing is easy: We offer a course to teach a team valid test methods in three days. Most important usability problems are so glaring they can be identified through a simple test. Once you know the basics of how to write good tasks and facilitate the session without biasing user behavior, you can clearly see users get into trouble when they encounter poorly designed components of your site.

Say, for example, that a user clicks the wrong button. It's obvious to any observer that this signals a design error. Listening to users' comments prior to clicking usually tells you why they misunderstood the design, thus guiding you in fixing it.

Although it is more difficult to detect the problem when users *don't* do something, most usability facilitators can still identify many problems. They might, for example, observe that no one in their test clicked a major feature. Users' "thinking aloud" comments will clarify whether they saw the feature but didn't find it relevant, or never considered the feature because it looked too much like an advertisement.

Some usability problems require more detective work and are often overlooked by people relatively new to user testing. This is particularly true for problems that arise from multiple individual issues, none of which cause difficulties on their own.

The problems that unchanging link colors cause are very difficult to identify in user testing. On any given page, users seem to understand the links just fine. Users almost never complain about link colors, as long as they're distinct from the rest of the text. Life is good, or so it seems. Observe carefully, though, and you'll notice that the users are moving in circles. They'll visit the same page multiple times—not because they want to, but because they don't realize that they've already been there. Or they'll skip links to places they haven't been because they don't realize they haven't been there. Users give up when they've tried most links in a list even if there's a link or two that they haven't tried.

The kinds of problems that unchanging link colors create could also be symptoms of muddled information architecture or poorly written labels, which is why it requires experience to identify the true root cause. The downsides of unchanging link colors may be easily overlooked in user testing, but they're very real and problematic for users.

The Exception: Command-Oriented Functionality

Command-oriented functionality is the exception to this rule. Showing visited areas is unnecessary for applications in which people might want to repeat actions multiple times. When deciding whether to show visited areas, consider if the action takes people to other screens or merely lets them repeat activities on the same screen. If users are going to other areas, especially to get content, they might only need one visit, so showing a visited link is appropriate. However, if people want to repeat an activity on the same screen, showing visited links is unnecessary.

Breaking the Back Button ☠ ☠ ☠

Some things in life can't be undone: For example, once you sell stock from your brokerage account, those shares are gone and you can't take them back if the price goes up. On the Web, however, people should be comfortable knowing that they can undo or alter their actions. Encouraging users to explore a site freely, secure in knowing that they can escape any problems they may encounter, is one of the most fundamental principles of human-computer interaction.

In traditional software applications, the "undo" command serves this purpose. If you are exploring, say, a graphics program, you can color parts of a picture red and see if you like it. If not, Command-Z to the rescue and the red gets zapped. Since the early 1980s it has been a firm design guideline for all software platforms to support "undo" as much as possible in all applications.

Back is the second most used feature of Web browsing. Assuming, of course, that it works as intended.

Backtracking serves the purpose of "undo" in hypertext navigation. You can move around in the information space as much as you like and never truly get lost because you can retrace your path and revert to safe ground. In Web browsers, backtracking is implemented through the Back button. Users just keep clicking this button until they return to the place they want to be. Expert users can also click the pointer over the Back button to pull down a menu of their full backtrack history and revert directly to a previous location.

In statistical studies, the Back button is usually the second most-used feature of Web browsing. (The most-frequently used feature is links to new pages.) In user testing, we often see people click Back repeatedly even when there is a direct link to the place where they want to return. At first, this behavior seems paradoxical because users must click more and spend extra time backtracking. But when we factor in the brain time required for people to use direct links on different sites, we understand why they prefer Back even to a faster way.

Back provides two huge benefits and one smaller benefit:

- The Back button is always available, it's always in the same location, and it always works the same way, retracing one step at a time. This strong user interface consistency means that people don't have to scan the page for a link: They know right where to go. In contrast, Web pages rarely following design standards and users can't rely on finding specific types of links in the same spot on all pages. Worse, some pages may not have the desired link at all, making it a wasted effort to scan the page looking for it.

- As a rule, recognition is better than recall for user interface design because it's easier and faster to recognize something than it is to remember and construct a description of it. In the case of subsequent clicks on the Back button, users must simply glance at each page as it unloads (quickly out of the cache since it was just visited), and if it's not the one they want, click the Back button again. To use a direct navigation link, on the other hand, users must first remember and reconstruct an image of the place they want to return to, then scan the current page to see if any links come close to the image in their head. Quite a lot of thinking, relatively, and substantial likelihood of failure, either because there's no direct link after all or because the user misjudgesd the link and is taken to the wrong destination.

- Finally, because the Back button is a fairly large click target, it's faster to use than the average navigation link. This is a great advantage for users with motor skills impairments, who benefit from having a large target. It is not particularly important to the average user, who probably saves about 0.3 seconds. For them, the time saved in physical movements is dwarfed by that from reduced cognitive overhead.

Back, then, is the user's lifeline. No matter what happens, Back will save you. Assuming, of course, that it works as intended. Unfortunately, Web sites can employ several coding tricks that disable Back buttons and seriously thwart users' movements.

Fitts' Law of Click Times

The speed of clicking onscreen elements is determined by Fitts' Law, which states that the time it takes for a pointing device to reach a target is proportional to the logarithm of the distance to the target divided by the size of the target.

The farther away something is, the more time it will take to click on it. This is obvious, but note that the law holds that the time increases only by the logarithm of the distance, which means it increases fairly slowly. This is because people accelerate their movements when moving their pointers to something that's a long distance away.

Fitts' Law also states that the bigger something is, the less time it takes to click on it. This is because users won't need to point as precisely,

which takes more time. Because it's big, the Back button is fast to click—and easy to click if you're moving to it quickly. The convenience of clicking big targets is one reason we recommend making logos link to the homepage.

Fitts' Law was established in 1954 by Dr. Paul M. Fitts, the first head of the U.S. Air Force Human Engineering Division, as well as a professor at Ohio State University and the University of Michigan. It has proven to hold for many pointing devices—mouses, trackballs, joysticks, foot pedals, touch screens, and even for eye tracking to select objects on the screen. The law is a good example of the longevity of usability findings, which usually depend more on human characteristics and less on specific technologies.

The most insidious way to disable the Back button is to remove it from the browser window through a JavaScript instruction to hide the chrome. Though it has connotations of frivolous decorations like the tail fins on 1960s Cadillacs, the chrome actually includes several of the most useful features of Web browsing, such as Back, Forward, Print, Refresh, and Change Font Size. A browser window without its chrome cripples users. (The exception is certain types of Internet applications that technically are displayed in browser windows but don't involve hypertext navigation or the viewing of documents. These are sometimes presented better without the chrome because they are not browsing tasks, even if a browser's code is used as a rendering platform.)

Clicking a link to open a new browser window also disables the Back button because the new window typically doesn't inherit the history of the original window. Making users open windows that they didn't ask for is a mistake in its own right, as discussed in the following section, so this is just one reason to avoid this design technique.

Finally, the Back button can be broken through the use of redirects that are embedded on a Web page instead of being communicated behind the scenes by server redirects. If a Web page has moved, it is certainly a good idea to leave behind a redirect to avoid broken links. But this redirect should be implemented as an HTTP 301 or 302 response from the Web server because these codes instruct the browser to move to the new URL immediately and forget about the old one. (The difference between the two status codes is that 301 indicates a page that has moved permanently, whereas 302 indicates a page that has moved temporarily.)

Unfortunately, some Web sites implement the redirect by placing a meta-tag refresh instruction on the old page that causes it to be immediately replaced by the new page. When users try to revert to a previous location, their first click on Back will take them to the old page on which the refresh code was embedded. Of course, loading this page activates the forwarding instructions, and the user is immediately bounced to the new location. But that's the page the user was just trying to leave! Every additional click on Back has the same effect, so the user is trapped on this new page.

In user testing, we observe significant confusion whenever the Back button is not available or doesn't work. Expert users may know how to overcome the problems we have just described, but most users simply feel stuck and abandoned. Breaking the Back button continues to cause severe usability problems and still deserves three skulls.

Opening New Browser Windows ☠ ☠ ☠

When users click a link or a button, they usually expect a new Web page to appear in place of the last. To undo their action, they click the Back button, as discussed in the previous section. Violating these expectations intrudes on their experience and free navigation through cyberspace.

Unfortunately, many Web site designers insist on displaying new information in a new browser window instead of reusing the existing window. Sometimes these are small pop-ups, a phenomenon that's annoying enough to warrant its own separate discussion. (See "Pop-Up Windows" in this chapter.) Other times, the new page is displayed in a new, full-sized browser window.

Designers often tell us that they open new windows so they don't lose visitors to their site. But ultimately that's a lost cause. If people really want to leave, they will.

Designers often tell us that they open new windows so they don't lose visitors to their sites. For this reason, new windows are particularly common when linking to material on other Web sites. But ultimately it's a lost cause to trap users on your site. If people really want to leave, they will. And if users follow a link to another site and want to return to your site, they will invariably do so by clicking Back, since that's the most popular way to revisit pages.

Proliferating browser windows present a plethora of usability problems. Most fundamentally, they pollute users' workspaces with more windows than they request, sometimes causing crashes or memory errors. Users are left to clean up these surplus windows, assuming that they can even find them in the system taskbar.

Web browsers include a perfectly fine feature to open a link in a new window: The user can right-click on the link. Admittedly, this is an expert-user feature, but only experienced users should use multiple windows in any case. In testing, we often see experienced users open additional windows to parallel-browse multiple sites or products, or to preserve the old context while exploring a new direction. Bottom line: If users want extra windows, they can ask for them.

Since Back will only take users as far as the first page displayed in a window, expert users may realize that they must close the offending new window in order to get back to the original. But most users don't really understand how to manipulate multiple windows and are focused on working in the front-most window on the screen. If they can't go back, they are trapped.

If the new window doesn't take up the entire screen or completely obscure the original window, people sometimes return to it by clicking in the part of the window that is visible (although this is often by mistake when they are trying to use the scrollbar in the front-most window). Clicking in another window pops it to the front and hides the window that was previously on top. This is a very simple way of multiwindowing for experienced users, but even some of them cannot always keep track of all the windows on their screen.

Commonly, after a user has opened a separate window, he accidentally or deliberately pops the original window back on top, obscuring the new one. Later he might click a link that causes information to appear in the new window, but because it's now obscured, he never sees it. The designer may have intended to make the information more prominent by displaying it in a new window but in reality the user doesn't even know it's there.

The Microsoft Windows operating system lists currently open windows at the bottom of the screen in the taskbar. This bar is small and subtle, however, and placed in an out-of-sight-out-of-mind location. From user testing, we know that people often overlook the taskbar and its reminder that important content is available in an obscured window.

One of the very unfortunate elements of current graphical user interfaces (GUIs) is the way the Maximize button on windows is usually interpreted by designers as "make the window cover the entire monitor." This function should really just make the window its biggest *useful* size.

On small monitors, "biggest useful size" and "entire screen" is nearly the same thing. Seeing more information usually increases usability, but as monitors get bigger and bigger, the difference between screen size and window size becomes more important.

While the Maximize button tempts many users, they are often poorly served by it. For example, a 1024-pixel-wide window will result in overly long lines for text-heavy applications such as Web browsing. The preponderance of

maximized windows also makes it difficult for users to understand the multiwindow nature of modern GUIs. In theory people are supposed to work with overlapping windows, but in practice they can't when windows take up the entire screen. Maximized windows deceive people into thinking of the computer as a full-screen environment rather than one with multiple, simultaneously active areas.

Fortunately, maximized windows will gradually vanish as people get bigger monitors. With a 2048-pixel-wide screen, a maximized window is so grotesquely oversized that most users will resize it and work with two or more windows at a time. Tiled windows may also enjoy a renaissance with huge screens, making it easy to deal with two or four windows simultaneously.

www.latimes.com

New browser windows, such as the one on the LA Times site, causes problems for users who don't understand the concept of multiple windows. When possible, keep your Web site in the same browser window and ensure that the Back button works. Launching new windows on top of the parent window can stop many users from interacting with your site. For example, we've seen people accidentally click outside the parent browser window and bury the new window underneath it, then try to reopen the new window from the parent window and nothing appears to happen. They can't find their way back to the new window and conclude that the site is broken.

As we have seen, opening new browser windows has the following ill effects:

- It disrupts the expected user experience

- It pollutes the user's screen with unwanted objects (sometimes causing crashes or memory errors)

- It hampers the user's ability to return to visited pages

- It obscures the window the user is currently working on

- It can make users believe that links are inactive because they appear to have no effect, when in fact the information is rendered in an obscured window

All these usability problems are as bad as ever, and we see them in test after test. The design mistake of opening new browser windows thus continues to deserve a full compliment of three skulls.

The Exception: PDF and Similar Documents

In user testing, we often observe that when people are finished using Adobe PDF files, Microsoft Word memos and PowerPoint slides, Excel spreadsheets, and similar documents, they click the window's Close box instead of the Back button. This gets them out of the document, all right, but not back to the Web page where they started. Blowing away browser windows is particularly bad on intranets, where users often have to log in or jump through other hoops to access document repositories.

Because people frequently close document windows, the best guidelines for linking to non-Web documents are:

- Open non-Web documents in a new browser window.

- Warn users in advance that a new window will appear.

- Remove the browser chrome (such as the Back button) from the new window.

- Best of all, prevent the browser from opening the document in the first place. Instead, offer users the choice to save the file on their hard disk or to open it in its native application (Adobe Reader for PDF, PowerPoint for slides, and so on). Unfortunately, doing so requires a bit of technical trickery: Designers must add an extra HTTP header to the transmission of the offending file.

The header line to be added is "**Content-disposition: Attachment**." If possible, designers should also add "; filename=somefile.pdf" at the end of this line, to give the browser an explicit filename if the user chooses to save the file.

All these guidelines stem from the same underlying phenomenon: Non-Web documents are native PC formats. These formats have their own applications, each of which gives users a set of commands and navigation options that are different from the ones for browsing Web sites.

How Can You Use Windows if You Don't Understand Windows?

Many readers may believe that we are overstating the difficulty some users have handling multiple windows. How can the most basic concepts of graphical user interfaces be beyond the grasp of many users? How can you use Microsoft Windows if you don't understand windows? How can people be inexperienced using the taskbar when it's staring them in the face every minute they use their computers?

Trust us, the difficulties we are describing are indeed common. We see them year after year in study after study. Most readers of this book are probably very skilled in the use of computers, but many other people are not. Even people who use computers several hours a day often don't have sophisticated understanding of them.

Less-skilled users commonly aren't aware of the difference between concepts such as files, applications, and different kinds of windows—say, operating system windows where icons represent files and application windows where each window represents a file. Often they are also unclear on the difference between Web browsers and other windows, and miss the distinctions between different type-in fields on their screen.

One of the most frequent queries at Yahoo! Is "www.google.com." Why would people *search* for Google if they know its URL? Because they don't fully understand the concept of URLs or the difference between typing something in the browser's address bar and typing something into a field on a page inside the browser. After all, both areas are places where you can type in a Web address and you'll go there.

One of the main reasons we have the field of usability is to address the wide range of user skills. Designers, programmers, Internet marketing managers, and almost everybody else who is a member of a development team will score high in the skills range. That's how they got jobs working professionally with computers. Once you know something, it's difficult to imagine not knowing it. It becomes second nature, for example, to manipulate multiple overlapping windows. But when we test representative end-users, we often find that they know much less and need a drastically simplified user interface.

Why don't people learn the basics of computers if they work with them every day? Because the computer is a tool, not a mission for most people. Once they know enough to get their jobs done, they focus on that, not on ascending the geek scale. Those of us who are interested in technology may find this sad, but it's a fact, and it's better to design for the way the world is than for the way you wish it were.

When users work with, say, a PowerPoint slideshow, their focus is on PowerPoint's slide-manipulation features. Because the experience is so similar to that of working with their own local slides, it's easy to tune out the fact that they downloaded these slides from a Web site. When they're finished with the slides, they do what one always does when finished using PowerPoint: reach for the Close box.

When a PC-native application opens inside a browser window, a second—and equally unfortunate—phenomenon occurs. If users can still see browser commands and buttons, they'll sometimes assume they can use these features to manipulate the document. Unfortunately, features like "Make Text Bigger," "Print," and "Find in Page" don't work while in a native application document. Given this, it's better not to show users familiar (and nonfunctional) browser buttons while they're working with a non-Web document.

Remember that this is an exception, not a guideline. The guideline for Web pages is to keep them within the same window and avoid opening new browser windows.

Pop-Up Windows ☠ ☠ ☠

If anything, pop-up windows are an even worse offense against usability now than they were in the past. Users have become ever more annoyed with pop-ups, and many have gone so far as to install special pop-up blocking software. Since we know that people hate installing new software, the fact that they are doing so is testimony to how far they'll go to rid themselves of pop-up intrusions.

To most users, the popping aspect of pop-ups is reason enough to avoid them. Pop-ups often come as a surprise and deviate from what users expect on the Web, which is to have information rendered in the main browser window. Furthermore, pop-ups have seedy connotations because they most often appear on gambling and porn sites.

Citibank warns its customers against pop-ups because they are often used for "phishing"—tricking people into providing sensitive information by masquerading as a trustworthy business or person. This is just one more example of why pop-ups have a bad name. Obviously, when big, respected companies warn against pop-ups, users are going to be even more reluctant to interact with them on other sites. A bit of this warning is going to keep nagging them and reduce their trust in any site that throws them a pop-up, even if that site is respectable and doesn't intend any harm.

Email Security Zone: Jakob Nielsen
For your account ending in

Dear Jakob Nielsen,

You may have heard the term "phishing" in the news lately.

In case you haven't, it's not just "fishing" misspelled. It actually refers to unsolicited email that looks like it's from a trusted institution — but in reality is an attempt to lure people into providing personal or sensitive account information on phony web sites. The information collected is later used to commit fraud.

Citi Cards holds your security in the highest regard. For that reason, we're working diligently with law enforcement, industry organizations, and governments overseas to shut down these scams permanently.

But there are a few simple things you can do as well to protect yourself:

- **Look for your "personal header" on all emails.** For your protection, effective immediately look for your first name, last name and the last 4 digits of your account number in an "email security zone" at the top of email we send you. Be suspicious of emails claiming to be from us that do not include this information.

- **Never type account information into a pop-up window.** Don't type account information into a pop-up window, even if it looks legitimate. We never request account information through pop-up windows.

- **Don't respond to emails asking you to verify information.** We'll never send you an email asking you to verify information. If we have an issue with your records, we'll contact you another way.

- **Be suspicious of grammatical or spelling errors.** These are usually indications of a fraudulent message.

If you happen to receive a suspicious-looking email claiming to be from Citi Cards, please forward it to spoof@citicorp.com. We have agents on staff around the clock monitoring these reports and acting on them immediately.

If you'd like more information on phishing, please visit our "Security and You" module. Or, you can contact one of our Internet Security Specialists at 1-888-285-9696.

ABOUT THIS MESSAGE

This is a message from Citi Cards. If you'd like to choose the kinds of email messages you receive regarding special offers and promotions, or if you'd prefer not to receive future email updates about the exciting offers and services available to you, please go to: http://email.citicards.com

HAVE QUESTIONS ABOUT YOUR ACCOUNT?
We cannot respond to individual messages through this email address, because we are unable to verify the sender's identity. You can, however, correspond with us electronically through our secure messaging feature. Please sign-on at www.citicards.com and choose Contact Us from the Help/Contact Us menu. Then select the Send New Message link under Write to Customer Care. You can also call the Customer Service phone number on the back of your card.

WE ARE COMMITTED TO YOUR PRIVACY

SECURITY / PROTECTING YOURSELF ONLINE
There are simple steps you can take to protect yourself from fraud while online, such as never sending personal or financial information by email. (We'll never ask for it.) For more information, please review the recommendations of the U.S. Government and others at the following sites:
http://www.nipc.gov/warnings/computertips.htm
http://iisw.cerias.purdue.edu/home_computing/topten.php

www.citicards.com

> *Many users close pop-ups as fast as possible—often even before the content has been rendered. The fact that it is a pop-up is reason enough to want it gone, and fast.*

Users with many different types of disabilities have particular problems managing extra windows. People with motor skills impairments certainly don't relish having to struggle to click unwanted Close boxes. And low-vision users may not even know that a pop-up has appeared if they have zoomed in their screen magnifier to inspect a different part of the screen. Finally, blind users are severely impacted by the additional cognitive load of having to cope with multiple windows and remember what information was read aloud from which pop-up.

Empirically, we see many users close pop-ups as fast as possible—often even before the content has been rendered. The fact that it is a pop-up is reason enough to want it *gone*, and fast.

Pop-ups actually can be used legitimately in interaction design. In the old days, a pop-up was a good solution to display a small amount of supplementary information while keeping most of the user's primary workspace in view. Two classic examples of legitimate use are for help information and glossary definitions. Users like to read help in a small window, so they can refer back to the problem without losing the context.

Sad to say, even good pop-ups are rarely appropriate these days, however, because evil pop-ups have tarnished their reputation. One e-commerce site recently started losing significant sales because it used pop-ups for a critical element of its checkout process. This design had worked reasonably well with customers in the past, but suddenly many users were not seeing the pop-up information, either because they employed pop-up blockers or manually killed them off without reading them.

Pop-ups have always been annoying enough to deserve three skulls and they are now working so poorly that we ought to give them four. But since the rating scale doesn't go that low, we'll have to settle for three.

At Nielsen Norman Group's User Experience 2004 conference, John Boyd, Manager of Platform Research at Yahoo!, and Christian Rohrer, Director of User Research at eBay, presented a large body of research on how users perceive online advertising. This table shows the responses from a 2004 survey of 605 Web users who were asked how various aspects of online ads affected their Web experience.

Design Element	Users Who Answered "Very Negatively" or "Negatively"
Pops-up in front of your window	95%
Loads slowly	94%
Tries to trick you into clicking it	94%
Does not have a Close button	93%
Covers what you are trying to see	93%
Doesn't say what it is for	92%
Moves content around	92%
Occupies most of the page	90%
Blinks on and off	87%
Floats across the screen	79%
Automatically plays sound	79%

As the table shows, pop-ups were the most-hated advertising technique on the Web. Users surveyed today would likely be even more negative.

One user entered the following comment on a major Web site's feedback form: "You people should be ashamed of yourself! I did not ask to have three pop-ups come across my screen when I visited you. I do not visit singles sites, and I don't want to add four inches to my penis. As a matter of fact, I don't use any of the services that pop up on my screen. I think it is disgusting that you money-hungry bastards have infringed on my computer for your own selfish gain. From this moment on, I am boycotting you, and I am advising everyone I know to do the same thing. Down with you and your pop-up ads."

Users transfer their dislike of pop-ups to the advertisers behind the ads and the Web sites that run the ads. In a survey of 18,808 users that Yahoo! conducted in 2004, more than half reported that a pop-up ad influenced their opinion of the advertiser very negatively, and nearly 40 percent reported that it influenced their opinion of the Web site very negatively. When users feel this strongly about a design element, don't use it.

Design Elements That Look Like Advertisements ☠ ☠ ☠

Web users are extremely goal oriented. They look for the information they care about and ignore anything others want to push on them. In fact, users don't just passively ignore unwanted information; they have evolved an active system of self-defense against it. That's because on the Web they are constantly barraged with attempts to capture their attention and divert it from their own goals.

Banner Blindness and Other User Ad Radar

Most famously, users exhibit incredibly powerful "banner blindness." Eye-tracking studies have recorded microseconds-long fixations inside banners but almost never longer gazes or reading. Users dodge even the most obnoxiously flashing banners by training their eyes to avoid this attack on the senses.

"Banner blindness" has expanded beyond the deliberate act of not looking at banners to encompass avoidance of anything that usually signals irrelevant information or advertisements. People also disregard colorful boxes in the margin of the page because they are commonly used in ads. In fact, anything that's overly large or colorful risks being ignored, particularly if it includes animation. We frequently see users try anything except clicking an item that's clearly what they want on a Web page. When questioned after the test, they tell us again and again, "Oh, I saw that, but it looked like an ad, so I ignored it."

> *It is irrelevant whether the design element actually is an ad. Since people don't read it, they won't ever know.*

Users have been conditioned to assume that all useful parts of Web sites appear as plain text, with the exception of fairly small "Add to Cart" buttons next to product photos. We have even observed people not buying products on e-commerce sites because they couldn't find the Buy button—it was too big and colorful, so they subconsciously filtered it out.

Ironically, in these situations, it is irrelevant whether the design element actually *is* an ad. Since people don't read it, they won't ever know. Their reflex reaction to disregard it prevents them from ever considering reading it.

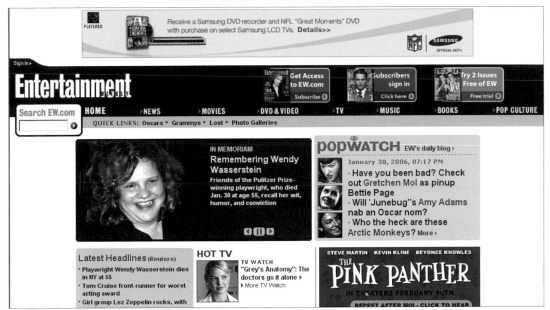

The highly graphical rectangular boxes at the top of this page can easily be confused with external advertising because they look like ads. If you want people to notice something on your site, make sure it doesn't look like advertising; people tend to divert their attention from ad-like items. Simple text links on appropriate areas of the page can attract more attention than highly graphical or dynamic elements because they're contextual and appear more credible. In addition, the Search box is not standard and therefore can easily be missed.

There's also a technical reason to avoid elements that look like ad banners: Some users have advertising-blockers installed to prevent ads from ever appearing on their screens. This software can't read the content—all it knows is to discard any graphic that has the dimensions of an approved advertising banner (say, 728-by-90 pixels).

If anything, users have become more adept at banner blindness and other ad avoidance techniques over time. Including elements that resemble ads is a sure way to inflict usability damages on a Web site, so it still merits all three skulls.

Violating Web-Wide Conventions ☠ ☠ ☠

Let us remind you of Jakob's Law of the Internet User Experience: Users spend most of their time on *other* Web sites. (The law is discussed in more detail in Nielsen and Marie Tahir's *Homepage Usability: 50 Websites Deconstructed*.) Even if users come to your site in droves because it's the biggest and most prominent on the Web, their accumulated visits to other sites will still vastly outnumber their visits to yours.

This means that users gear their expectations for your site by what they have learned to expect elsewhere. If they are accustomed to prevailing design standards and conventions, they'll expect to encounter those on your site as well. With 1 minute and 49 seconds on average to convince potential customers that you are worth doing business with, don't waste it on making them struggle with a deviant user interface.

Avoid Influencing Users During Testing

Many companies employ flawed methodology for their user studies, and this may be one reason why we continue to see so many failed designs on the Web. The design may pass "user testing" with flying colors, so the site manager feels safe launching it. But if the test facilitator biased the study, the results are worthless.

In our three-day courses, it is difficult to cover all the details and nuances of user testing. So it is worth emphasizing here an important point to help facilitators avoid inadvertently diverting users' attention while they are being tested.

If you ask users to comment on each item on a page during a test, they will comment on ads and other elements that look like ads along with the rest. As soon as they have noticed these items, they will certainly also use them if they seem useful. Even worse, if you ask people what they think about a specific design element, you alert them to that item and this colors their actions during the rest of the study. So even a small weakness in the way one asks questions can make it impossible to observe the ad-avoidance that is users' natural behavior.

In the case of design elements that look like advertisements (or anything else the user ignores), the proper protocol is to refrain from making any comments during the test. Once the test is finished and you are in the debriefing segment of the session, you can point to the design element in question and ask about it. That is how we have heard so many people say that they ignored things they thought they were ads.

We continue to see users get confused when sites do things in unexpected ways and to see them pleased when they immediately understand a site because it does things they expect. Therefore, we continue to give three skulls to the problem of violating Web-wide conventions.

www.zincbistroaz.com

This design neglects interaction conventions, making it unnecessarily difficult for people to find what they need. The words Lunch, Dinner, and Navigate provide strong cues for clickablity when they're not selectable. The only selectable items on this homepage are five of the eggs. If you happen to click on the egg holder at the wrong place, you might think that there is no more information than what's shown here. Obscure interface elements degrade the user experience and discourage people from using the site. When information is hidden, people assume it's not there. Interactions that are predictable empower people to navigate without fear of encountering obstacles.

Vaporous Content and Empty Hype ☠ ☠ ☠

One of the biggest problems on the Web is that companies don't want to come clean and say what they are doing in plainspoken language on their sites. This continues to be critical because Web users are extremely impatient and allocate so little time to each page. The more florid the descriptions, the more users tune them out and go elsewhere. It's essential to quickly state what you are offering users and what's in it for them.

The more bad writing you push on your users, the more you train them to disregard your message. Useless content doesn't just annoy people; it's one of the leading causes of lost sales.

Interestingly, one of the oldest guidelines for sales and marketing in any medium is to sell the benefits, not the features, so we shouldn't really have to harp on this here. Sadly, the Web is so smothered in vaporous content and intangible verbiage that users simply skip over it. Of course, the more bad writing you push on your users, the more you train them to disregard your message in general. Useless content doesn't just annoy people; it's a leading cause of lost sales.

www.montblanc.com

The practice of making Web sites more visible by search engines is called Search Engine Optimization (SEO). The more concrete your text, the better your site will rank in search engines. As we saw in Chapter 2, users researching a potential purchase almost always start with a search. This makes SEO the No. 1 marketing technique for Web sites, and using clear, basic words is the No. 1 SEO technique because these are the words that people enter into search engines.

Using fluffy language doesn't just hurt you while users are on your site. It can prevent users from finding your site in the first place because sites that use plain language will outrank you in the search engine results page listings.

Dense Content and Unscannable Text ☠ ☠ ☠

Dense blocks of text are a major turn-off for Web users. The plain look of a page packed with type immediately suggests to users that they will have to work hard to extract the information they want. In information-foraging terms, blocks of text are analogous to the hard shell of a tortoise. Many predators will let the sluggish critter go because it's simply not worth their time and effort to break open the shell to get at the meat. Similarly, Web users often think that digging through dense type takes more time than it's worth.

Government agencies are often the worst offenders in this category. This is probably because civil servants are used to working with long, dense documents that are written for internal audiences and richly salted with specialized bureaucratic terminology. When government agencies tone this down a little, they think they have made the content more accessible to the average Web reader. And they have, but not enough. Bureaucratese must be toned down a lot. This is a classic example of a usability problem caused by designers and authors being too steeped in their internal culture to recognize the huge gap between it and the larger world.

Web text should be short, scannable, and approachable. Typically, you should write half as many words for the Web as you would for print. If targeting a broad consumer audience that includes people with no or little education, it's

(Facing page) Montblanc makes nice pens, but it's impossible to find out anything about them on the company's Web site. This screen is the category page for their collection of classic designs, but users can get an overview of the types of pens that are available (fountain pen, ballpoint, pencil, highlighter) only by clicking through the tiny triangular arrows next to the photos. Also, the site does not provide the type of information users are looking for, such as size, color, or price.

better to aim at 25 percent of the print word count. And in Web writing, it's always best to start with the conclusion, so that people who read only the first line or two on a page still get the main point. Until Web content is written clearly and concisely, this remains a three-skull problem.

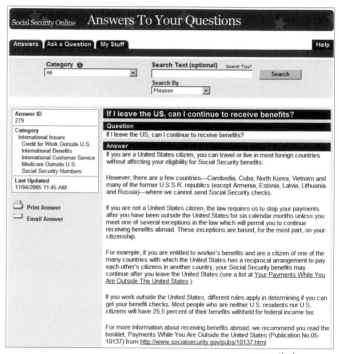

ssa-custhelp.ssa.gov

The U.S. Social Security Administration's information about receiving benefits abroad is written at the reading level of a college senior. Basically, it requires a college degree to easily understand this Web page.

The text here is not horrible compared to that on some federal government sites. For example, this page does start with the conclusion. Still, many sentences cry out for a rewrite. At 61 words, this is the worst offender: "For example, if you are entitled to worker's benefits and are a citizen of one of the many countries with which the United States has a reciprocal arrangement to pay each other's citizens in another country, your Social Security benefits may continue after you leave the United States (see a list at Your Payments While You Are Outside The United States)."

Directgov
www.direct.gov.uk

Straight through to public services

Search this site [   ] **Go** ➡

Home | Directories | Guide to Govt | Do it online | Newsroom

Tuesday, 8 November 2005

◀ Money

Britons living abroad

Pensions

If you are retiring abroad, you can continue to receive your UK state pension.

If you are moving permanently, you will only get yearly increases in your pension if you are in an European Economic Area (EEA) country or one of the other countries that have a special agreement with the UK. You will also need to match the relevant regulations.

You will find a link to a list of countries in the EEA below.

If you are living in the UK and are not planning to live in another EEA country for some time, you will need application form BR19 from your local Jobcentre Plus office or social security office.

If you are moving to another EEA country or anywhere else in the world you will need to inform The UK Pensions Service that you are moving abroad and give them your new address (contact details are below).

Do it online

▸ Be a volunteer (opens new window)
▸ Search for childcare
▸ Find a school
▸ Apply for a driving licence
▸ Find a course
▸ Search for jobs
▸ List of services available online...

Useful contacts

▸ Britons living abroad contacts

direct.gov.uk

The British government provides information about pensions abroad at an 11th grade reading level. This is still too complicated for information targeted at a broad audience of senior citizens, who are less likely than younger people to have completed high school. Aging can also diminish any elderly person's ability to read complicated text.

Our research on low-literacy users indicates that it's best to write for an eighth-grade reading level when targeting a broad consumer audience (and taxpayers are the broadest audience of them all). Still, the British government's site outdid that of the American Social Security Administration. For example, the conclusion it begins with—"If you are retiring abroad, you can continue to receive your UK state pension"—is stated clearly and in larger font than the text that contains the various exceptions to this rule.

Technological Change: Its Impact on Usability

The Web has changed drastically since it started as a collection of physics papers in 1991. The first two years, it was a small type-only hypertext system used by a bunch of researchers, but in 1993 the first major GUI to the Web was introduced with the Mosaic browser. Our research into users' interaction with Web sites and intranets has continued as the Web has evolved through generations of technology—from the gray pages in Mosaic through the colorful pages with table-based layout in Netscape to the multilayered, functionality-rich pages in Microsoft's Internet Explorer (IE), which uses JavaScript and ever-growing Cascading Style Sheets (CSS).

When we began our research in 1994, home users accessed the Internet primarily by dial-up modems with 28.8 kilobits per second (Kbps) throughput, while today most home users in the United States and many other countries have so-called broadband connections running at a few megabits per second (Mbps). (We refer to current cable modems and Digital Subscriber Lines, or DSL, as "so-called broadband" because they are still not as fast as we would ideally like in order to offer an optimal user experience. Fiber-to-the-home service will eventually give us hundreds of Mbps, and that's when we will be able to talk about a truly broadband Internet.)

Seven of the 34 original usability problems have become less important today because of changes in browsers, bandwidth, or other Internet technology.

Haven't these substantial technological advances caused radical changes in usability issues as well? Mainly, the answer is "no." Usability guidelines remain remarkably steady through generations of technology because usability is a matter of human behavior, and people don't change much from one decade to the next. In fact, the great majority of users today are the people who were using the Web ten years ago. Their characteristics are about the same, as are their behaviors. Human short-term memory holds only about seven (plus or minus two) chunks of information, and the last time this design constraint changed was probably at the time of the Neanderthals.

Still, seven of the 34 original usability problems we named have become less important today because of changes in browsers, bandwidth, or other Internet technology. These improvements have somewhat reduced problems with

- Slow download time

- Frames

- Flash

- Low-relevancy search listings

- Multimedia and videos

- Frozen layouts

- Cross-platform incompatibility

In this section we look at those problem areas that lost skulls due to improved technology. Remember that skulls indicate the amount of trouble a usability problem causes. Fewer skulls imply less trouble, and that's indeed a happy side effect of some of the technological advances that have been made since we started developing usability guidelines in 1994.

1986 Air Force Guidelines Stand the Test of Time

From 1984 to 1986, the U.S. Air Force compiled existing usability knowledge into a single, well-organized set of guidelines for its user interface designers called *Guidelines for Designing User Interface Software, ESD-TR-86-278.* Jakob Nielsen was one of several people who advised the undertaking. The project identified 944 guidelines, most of them related to military command and control systems built in the 1970s and early 1980s, which used mainframe technology.

You might think that these old findings would be irrelevant to today's designers. If so, you'd be wrong. As an experiment, we retested 60 of the 1986 guidelines in 2005. Of these, 54 continue to be valid today. Of the total 944 guidelines, we deduced that 10 percent are no longer valid and 20 percent are irrelevant because they relate to rarely used interface technologies. But nearly 70 percent of the original guidelines continue to be both correct and relevant 20 years later.

Slow Download Time ☠

Download times used to be one of the most important issues in Web usability: In every study we ran, users complained about waiting for pages to download. They rarely praised sites for being snappy.

Most of the sites that grew big in the 1990s featured bare-bones designs with few graphics and fast-downloading pages. Graphic designers complained that Yahoo! (1994), Amazon (1995), eBay (1995), and Google (1998) looked primitive—or outright ugly—but users loved these sites and gave them ever-more business because it felt *good* to get the next page immediately after each click.

On a smaller scale, our site www.useit.com grew to become the world's dominating usability site while deliberately sporting an ugly, nondesign look. In the beginning, we felt this was necessary for quick downloading, but today we have retained it as a branding approach because of its strong positive connotations for users. This is an example of how people relate to design on the reflective level outlined in Don Norman's model of emotional design.

> *Most of the sites that grew big in the 1990s featured bare-bones designs with few graphics and fast-downloading pages. Graphic designers complained, but users loved them.*

Don Norman's Three Levels of Emotional Design

In his book *Emotional Design: Why We Love (Or Hate) Everyday Things,* our colleague Donald A. Norman describes three levels at which people relate to design:

The visceral level is the most immediate and is dominated by appearance. Smooth or round objects have cuddly or pleasant connotations; sharp or pointed objects connote feelings of fear or danger. Spiders give you the shakes when you spot them, and babies make you feel protective. Most visceral emotions are hard-wired and triggered immediately because they are based on evolutionary advantages and survival principles. Most graphic design attempts to operate at the visceral level, evoking positive emotions as soon as we look at something.

The behavioral level is based on use of the object. How does it feel to operate it? Is it annoying or pleasant to use? Most usability issues relate to the behavioral level. Response times are a classic example of an issue that affects behavioral emotions: It simply feels bad to sit and wait, and wait, and wait.

The reflective level is based on how we think about, or reflect on, an object. Does it have positive or prestigious connotations? Does it evoke a happy memory? Branding often works at the reflective level by making people think in advance that a certain product or vendor is special.

A Crash Diet for Web Sites?

Today, it's less important for Web pages to slim down to a design that eschews all graphics. When most users have broadband connections, pages with pictures download reasonably fast. At the 3 Mbps that's typical of cable modems, the browser can download about 300 kilobytes (KB) within the one-second limit that's required for pleasant hypertext navigation. In practice, data download can't fill the entire second because there's some latency in communicating requests back and forth across the Internet. But 100 KB is certainly a reasonable page weight for fast downloads.

This means that a Web page can easily combine a fair amount of text with some formatting markup, a style sheet, and even a few small photos or other images. Initial pages still can't include a lot of big graphics. But if users click a thumbnail photo and request a bigger image, they can receive a huge 200 KB enlargement within a good response time.

Still, slow downloads have been reduced to one skull instead of zero for a few reasons. People who live in rural areas, use mobile connections, or are connecting from a hotel room that hasn't been upgraded to broadband are still restricted to dial-up. Second, even broadband users can only download so much within a second, so there's still reason to watch page weights. Finally, response times are determined by server speed just as much as they are by the number of kilobytes being transmitted. There are still too many sites running on overloaded servers that don't send out the next page view immediately.

Frames ☠

Frames were one of the most incompetently designed "advances" in Web technology. They were bolted onto the very clean page model that was the foundation of original Web browsers and broke many interface conventions that users had grown to rely on, such as being able to bookmark a piece of information or email its URL to a friend. In early browsers, printing pages that used frames was extremely difficult, and they interfered with search engines as well.

Worst of all, frames broke the Back button in Netscape, version 2. (As discussed earlier in this chapter, breaking the Back button is a three-skull usability problem to this day, and any technology that does so can only be described as a usability disaster.) It is still best to avoid frames most of the time, but they are not nearly as serious a problem with modern browsers. The Back button works now, and printing pages with them is easier.

Flash ☠ ☠

In the early years, we deemed Macromedia Flash "99 percent bad" because it broke the Back button, didn't work with bookmarks, and caused accessibility problems for users with disabilities.

Flash introduced several serious usability problems in its early versions. First, it encouraged gratuitous animation. ("Since we *can* make things move, why *not* make things move?") Animation clearly has its place in online communication, but that place is limited.

Second, it stopped users from controlling their own destiny. One of the most powerful aspects of the Web is that users can go where they want when they want. This is what makes the Web so usable, despite its many usability problems. Unfortunately, many Flash designers violated this principle by employing television-style presentations rather than interactive media. Regardless of how cool a presentation looks, when users are required to sit through it with nothing to do, they become bored and lose their enthusiastic for the site.

Third, many Flash designers introduced their own non-standard GUI controls. How many scrollbar designs do we need? The world's best interaction designers worked for years testing numerous design alternatives to come up with the current Macintosh and Windows scrollbars. A new scrollbar designed over the weekend is likely to get many details wrong. And even if the new design is workable, it still reduces a site's overall usability because users must figure out how it works. They already know how to operate the standard widget.

None of these usability problems are inherent in Flash. You can design usable multimedia objects that comply with the guidelines and are easy to use. The problem is simply that early Flash design tended to encourage abuse.

After we campaigned incessantly against bad Flash, Macromedia began promoting Flash's ability to add functionality and advanced features to Web sites over the product's glitz. In 2002 a new version was launched that improved Flash accessibility and corrected most of its other usability problems, such as breaking the Back button and using nonstandard GUI controls. Flash seemed well on its way to become a positive contributor to increased Web usability.

www.tiffany.com

Nonstandard scrollbars are almost always a bad idea, but our user testing has revealed a few nonstandard designs that work well. The small gray triangles on the Tiffany site work because the site is so sparse and elegant that these GUI controls stand out despite their size.

> *Flash should not be used to jazz up a page. If your content is boring, rewrite it and hire a professional photographer to shoot better photos. Don't make your pages move.*

Despite such good intentions, however, most of the Flash that we encounter on the Web today is still bad, with no discernible purpose beyond annoying people. The one bright point is that Flash intros are almost extinct. They are held in such low esteem that even the most clueless Web designers won't recommend them, although a few (even more clueless) clients continue to request them.

Flash is a programming environment and should be used to offer users additional power and features that are unavailable on a static page. It should not be used to jazz up a page. If your content is boring, rewrite it and hire a professional photographer to shoot better photos. Don't make your pages move. It doesn't grab users' attention; it drives them away. Using Flash for navigation is not a good idea either. People prefer predictable navigation and static menus.

Flash: The Good, the Bad, and the Usable

In 2002 we conducted user testing of 46 Flash designs and summarized our findings in a report that includes 117 usability guidelines for Flash. Conducting these sessions with Flash applications reminded us of our tests with the first crop of Macintosh applications in the 1980s. Many of the Flash usability issues we identified related to basic GUI concepts such as making controls obvious and easy to grab.

One of our Flash guidelines is a virtual copy of a guideline from the 1980s: You must provide generous click zones around active screen areas or users will think that they clicked something even when the computer's strict definition of clickable pixels says they didn't. We also repeated a finding from early tests of MacDraw and Lotus Freelance Graphics: When you create new objects on a drawing canvas, they should be staggered relative to other objects so that they're all visible.

Other Flash guidelines are new and irrelevant to traditional software. For example, we discovered many usability issues relating to sound and animated objects, both positive—they can indicate change and direction—and negative—they can be distracting, annoying, and difficult for users with disabilities. Some Flash applications have apparently inherited bad habits from Web design.

One particular usability problem is worth emphasizing: In several applications, users missed options because of nonstandard scrollbars. A scrolling control is a standard user interface element in application design, and it should be designed in accordance with users' expectations. We did see a few nonstandard scrollbars that worked—notably on Tiffany's site, which is so simplified that users couldn't miss the scroll controls even though they were fairly small and violated GUI recommendations. (These deviations caused other usability problems, but at least people used the scrollbar.) In general, users often overlooked nonstandard scrolling controls and couldn't scroll the lists to see all their options.

The welcome decline in Flash means it doesn't deserve three skulls any more. Many designers are learning to relegate Flash to when it serves a user purpose and not use it purely for show. In fact, Flash technology itself doesn't even deserve two skulls. However, we still give it two skulls because of the way other Web designers implement it. Some designers continue to ignore usability guidelines for Flash, so some new Flash actually degrades the user experience by creating obstacles that prevent people from obtaining what they need quickly.

Low-Relevancy Search Listings 💀 💀

Next to navigating, Search is the most common way that people find what they're looking for on Web sites. Until recently, most sites had miserable Search capabilities that didn't prioritize page hits intelligently.

Early Search software was ineffective in retrieving useful hits because it sorted listings according to how frequently users' query terms occurred on each Web page, not by their relevance. Who cares how often a term appears on a page? It's much better to place the most relevant pages on top.

For example, when a product name is searched, the core product page for that item should be a top hit, not seemingly arbitrary press releases and papers. The product page acts as the central place to get information about that product and is a springboard from which users can access to other relevant information.

Even today, few Web sites have smooth, efficient Search, and many sites return such irrelevant Search results that *they* ought to get three skulls for bad Search usability. However, Search on many bigger sites is useful enough to be a single-skull issue. On average, across the Web, we now give low-relevancy search listings two skulls.

Multimedia and Long Videos 💀 💀

Three developments have made multimedia and video clips more acceptable on the Web today. First, bandwidth has increased sufficiently to make it much faster to download videos and other media presentations. Second, the technical quality of videos has improved so that viewing them is no longer like watching jerky postage stamp-sized movies. (This is partly due to more bandwidth and partly to better media player software.) Third, Web producers have become better at creating videos and other multimedia presentations *for* the Web instead of using repurposed television programs.

Multimedia usability is still a problem, but much less so than in the days when we had only one guideline for Internet video: Don't do it. We still need to design multimedia that really works well in the online medium, where users tend to be very impatient. And most video clips need to be shorter than a minute, to keep their attention. Until then, this is still a two-skull problem.

Frozen Layouts ☠ ☠

To say that a Web page has a "frozen layout" means that the information displayed on it is fixed in width, no matter what window it's displayed inside. If the window is too narrow, part of the information will be cut off and only visible after horizontal scrolling.

We know from our testing that users hate horizontal scrolling and always disparage when they encounter it. That is surely reason enough to avoid horizontal scrolling, but there are two other reasons to as well. First, users expect

---

Teenagers: Masters of Technology?

Teens are often stereotyped as being much more comfortable and adept with new technology than are adults. While this is sometimes true, it is an oversimplification. Believing those teens are masters of technology can lead to disastrous outcomes for sites aimed at them. Teens are much more apprehensive about technology than it might seem. In fact, we have found that most teens veer away from downloading plug-ins and clicking the unknown because teachers or parents have instructed them to avoid all downloads for fear of viruses.

In addition, when online multimedia doesn't work the way young people expect it to—for example, when a video doesn't play automatically or requires complex user input—they lose patience and blame the Web site. In our tests with teenagers, we found that they will give up rather than try to figure out how to overcome technical difficulties. Young audiences have less success with Web sites than adults do because they have less patience. And while teenagers appreciate some graphics and multimedia, they often don't have the computer setup to support them. Most of the teenagers we visited at home and school had outdated, older computers that ran slowly and lacked current software, plug-ins, and speakers.

vertical scrolling on the Web. As with all standard design elements, it's better to meet user expectations than to deviate from them. Second, when pages feature both vertical and horizontal scrolling, users must move their view port in two dimensions, which makes it difficult to cover the entire space. For people with poor spatial visualization skills, it's especially challenging to plan movements along two axes across an invisible plane. (Typically, users score lower than designers on spatial reasoning and visualization tests.) In contrast, one-dimensional vertical scrolling is a simple way to traverse content without advance planning: You just keep moving down or up.

The risk of inducing horizontal scrolling is an obvious reason not to freeze layouts—or at least not to freeze page widths to a size that's wider than most users' windows. How do you know how big your users' browser windows are? If people maximize their windows, then browser width can be derived from monitor width, and most people currently have screens that are 1024-pixels wide. In the future, bigger monitors will be more common, and many users already have monitors that are 1600-pixels wide or wider. People tend to utilize the space on these big screens to show multiple narrower windows, however, instead of enlarging one window to fill the entire screen. But frozen layouts are undesirable even if the page is narrower than the user's window. The user loses the benefit of having a big monitor because the page doesn't expand even when more space is available.

Frozen layouts cause usability problems, but they have dropped in severity from three to two skulls because of the increased prevalence of big screens. It's very rare for a site to have frozen pages wider than the 1024 pixels of most users' monitors. As an alternative, however, we recommended a "liquid layout"—a Web page that expands and contracts with windows so that it's always exactly as wide as the browser, neither more nor less. Users with sufficiently big monitors who want longer lines of information can have them, and those who prefer reading shorter lines get those.

Cross-Platform Incompatibility ☠ ☠

Worldwide sales of PCs reached 183 million in 2004. Of these, only three million were Macintoshes, leaving the Mac with two percent of the market. Going forward, the Mac will probably continue its decline because most of the growth in Web use will come in countries where Apple has little or no presence. (Apple's market share is 3 percent in the United States, 1.5 percent in Europe, and about 1 percent in the rest of the world—where the growth is.)

Is it worth testing your Web site on the Mac in order to cater to that two percent of the market (three percent if you are a United States-only site)? We would probably still say "yes," at least for bigger Web sites for which a two percent increase in business is worth more than a few tests and easy fixes. Smaller sites, on the other hand, might decide that the financial return is insufficient to bother testing on the Mac. As always, with a limited budget, you must choose your battles.

Cross-platform design is still of some importance, which is why we give it two skulls. We had reduced this guideline to one skull in presentations we gave in 2005, but it's been bounced back up because of the success of the Firefox browser. For Web sites, cross-platform compatibility means the ability to work on different browsers, not just on different computers. After Microsoft wiped out Netscape in the original browser wars of 1997 to 2002, almost all users employed Internet Explorer, version 5, drastically reducing the need for a site to work across browsers. With little competition, Microsoft reduced the pace of new browser releases, so there was also not much need to test across browser versions. As of 2003, only two percent of Internet users were on version 4 browsers, so it was getting to be reasonably safe to ignore them. By 2006 even these last holdouts had abandoned version 4—at least as far as can be measured reasonably. In 2006, Internet Explorer, version 5 had become the minority browser, with five percent of users. Such is the cycle of life.

> *For Web sites, cross-platform compatibility means the ability to work on different browsers, not just on different computers.*

Sad Mac

It saddens us to state that the Mac is approximating insignificance because of its tiny market share. Our company was cofounded by a former vice-president at Apple Computer, Don Norman, and one of our other colleagues, Bruce "Tog" Tognazzini, wrote Apple's first human interface guidelines. We were happy and loyal Macintosh users for 12 years; Nielsen got his first Mac in 1986 and even used a Lisa in earlier years. Still, business is business, and you gotta go with the numbers, not with your memories.

Our general advice is to wait five to six years after the launch of a new browser version before you stop caring about the previous one. For example, IE 5 was launched in 1999, so you could safely ignore version 4 in 2004. IE 6 was launched in 2001, so you can probably start ignoring IE 5 in 2007. IE 7 was introduced in 2006, so you probably will need to support IE 6 until 2012. (The five-to-six years rule is useful for long-term planning; to actually make the decision to stop supporting a browser, check your server logs to see what percentage of your current customers employs that version.)

More recently, new browsers such as Firefox, Apple's Safari, and Opera have gained some market share, and Microsoft has resumed development of Internet Explorer and is launching new versions. This means that at any given time, a Web site will be visited by users on several different versions of IE, as well as by people using third-party browsers, including earlier versions of these browsers.

Given this renewed diversity in the browser space, you might imagine that cross-platform incompatibility would remain a three-skull problem. Not so. Advances in technology came to our rescue and reduced the status of the cross-platform problem. New browsers are more standards-compliant than the browsers in the 1990s, so it's more rare for a Web site to work in one browser and break in another. Breakage still happens, so you should test your site in several browsers and several versions, but the problem is not nearly as bad as it used to be.

Even though we credit technological developments for the reduced skull rating, designer restraint is also partially responsible. Heavy-duty cutting-edge design is rare these days, which is good because such it is more likely to fail in minority browsers.

We used to think that the growing prevalence of mobile devices with Internet access would be a strong argument in favor of cross-platform Web design. After all, cellular phones, Blackberries, PocketPCs, and other handhelds are very different from PCs and won't display sites that are coded too narrowly for a big-screen environment. Our studies of users accessing mobile content and services have convinced us otherwise. Mobile is so different from PC that it really requires a separate Web site with a much simplified user experience.

Cross-platform really only means "across fairly similar platforms." Mac vs. PC vs. Linux? Yes, they are similar enough that one design should work for all three. IE vs. Firefox? Same thing.

Fourteen-inch monitor vs. 28-inch monitor? Again, the same site ought to work when there's only a factor-four difference in available pixels, especially since users with huge monitors tend not to maximize windows and spend all their pixels on just one.

On the other hand, there's a factor-eight difference in screen size between a Treo smartphone and a smallish 1024-by-768 PC monitor, and that's simply too much for the same user interface to scale nicely. A more traditional cell phone display is 31 times smaller than the desktop monitor. This gap is so huge that a single user interface simply can't scale and provide good service to both classes of users.

Adaptation:
How Users Have Influenced Usability

As users have adapted to the online environment and learned more about how to use Web sites, six usability issues have become less of a problem.

Even though we have many of the same users today as we did ten years ago, they have adapted over time to the online environment and learned more about how to use Web sites. As a result, six usability issues have become less of a problem and have lost skulls in our rating.

Over years of Web exposure, audiences are slowing adapting to these problems:

- Uncertain clickability
- Links that aren't blue
- Scrolling
- Registration
- Complex URLs
- Pull-down and cascading menus

Uncertain Clickability ☠

In early studies, we often found that users didn't know where to click on screens. Early Web pages were often highly graphical, and links were hidden in pictures that gave no suggestion of clickability. Of course, if users overlook a link, they will never find whatever information is lurking at the other end of it, so this is a very serious usability problem.

Whenever you find yourself having to give instructions for where users can click, you know you have a usability problem. The Diamond K site needs to say, "click a product for more information" because the product photos don't look clickable. Making the product names into hypertext links would have solved the problem and eliminated superfluous instructions. (It would have been fine to retain the product photos as supplementary links, but it's better not to rely on users clicking things that don't look like links or buttons.)

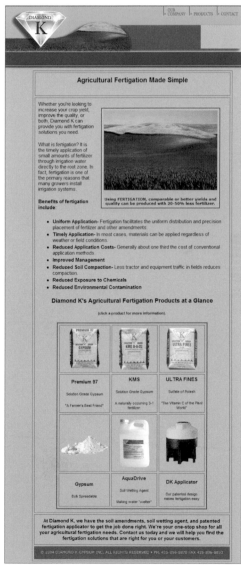

www.diamondkgypsum.com

Today users are very accustomed to the conventions for clickability on the Web. They know that text can be clicked if it's colored and underlined. And they know that graphics can be clicked if they have a raised, 3D appearance that makes them look somewhat like buttons. As long as you stick to these two design conventions, your users should have no problem knowing where they can click. (Knowing *why* they should click on a link is another matter, of course.)

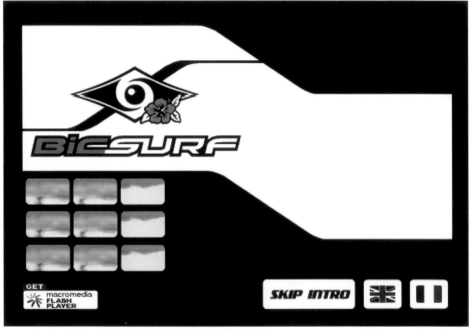

www.bicsportsurfboards.com

What would you select to bypass the intro page? How about "skip intro"? On this page, "skip intro" does nothing. Contrary to user expectations, the way to bypass the intro page is to select the British or American flag. One might argue that this saves people time by combining two steps into one—selecting a country and skipping the intro. However, contradicting users' interaction models causes more harm than good. Any timesaving is overshadowed by the potential for errors and frustration. Besides, intro pages are a waste of time.

(Facing page, bottom)   The bold blue underlined headings on this page indicate clickability when in fact they're not clickable. Blue text provides strong cues of clickability, especially when underlined or used for menu items. The misuse of visual cues causes confusion because the interface doesn't respond according to people's expectations. Violating Web conventions reduces user confidence and discourages people from using a site.

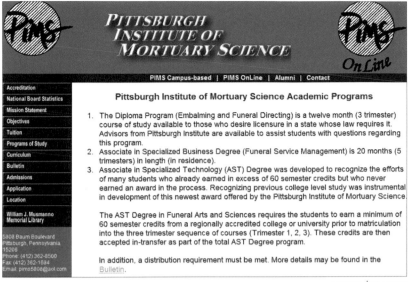

Links no longer *have* to be blue. Here it's obvious that Bulletin and "Cooperative Bachelors Degrees" are the links in the body text because they are colored and underlined. It's also reasonably obvious that the user has already visited Bulletin because this link is a less-luminous version of the primary link color.

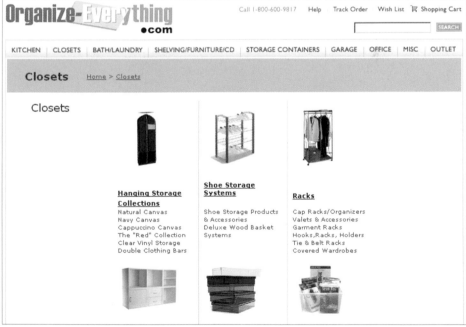

This problem now merits only one skull because it's so relatively rare. Yet sometimes we come across Web sites with headlines that are clickable even if they don't look it, and we have found a good deal of clickability problems with young children. So this issue is not down to zero skulls yet.

Links That Aren't Blue

In earlier years, we recommended that links be blue because that was the color people associated with clickability. But today's users have seen links in many other colors. Other colors work just as well as long as they stand out clearly from the body text and change to a different color after the page they link to is visited.

If you don't have a particular reason to prefer another color, we still recommend blue as the safest choice. But going with another color has such tiny potential for causing trouble these days that it is no longer worth even one skull.

Scrolling 💀 💀

As discussed in Chapter 2, some users still don't scroll Web pages when they navigate a site to determine where to go (or whether to leave). This is not nearly as serious a problem as it was in the early days of the Web, when we saw many users rarely or never scroll. Now people have gotten used to long Web pages and have learned that they sometimes have to scroll. If users decide to dig into a page, they usually know how to scroll.

Yet reluctance to scroll persists. This issue is not endemic to the Internet. Newspaper people put their top stories above the fold on the front page to make sure they're seen on newsstands and doorsteps even before readers unfold their papers to read them. On the Web, it's still fairly common to see users give up on a page too quickly because it doesn't seem relevant to them when in reality the information they needed was "below the fold" and just not visible during first scan.

Reluctance to scroll persists. It's still fairly common to see users give up on a page too quickly because it doesn't seem relevant to them.

(Facing page, top) The graphical design and layout of the Atlantis homepage provides inadequate cues to let people know that there's more information below the viewable browser window. The image of the resort fits perfectly within the window and the "Begin Your Adventure" heading at the bottom looks like it marks the end of the page.

Make sure that design elements don't look like end-page markers. Even experienced Web users need cues to indicate that there is relevant information below the viewable area. Unfortunately, on this site there are many more interesting areas at the bottom of this page that people won't know about.

www.atlantis.com

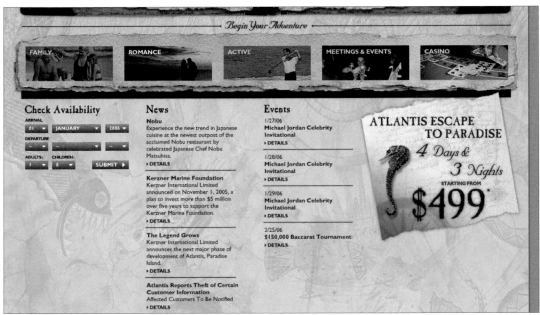

www.atlantis.com

The Atlantis homepage, scrolled down: Look at all the interesting information people can miss. All key information should be visible on the initial screen. Customers often decide whether to do business based on what they see without scrolling. Remember to check your pages on different screen resolutions to make sure that there are sufficient visual cues in the viewable area to pique people's interest and let them know there's more below.

We still give scrolling two skulls as a usability issue because it continues to hurt sites more than it should. This is probably because of differences in how designers and users judge relevancy. People who work on Web sites know when a given page is the solution to a given problem, and they may assume that users will scroll down to look for the link to that solution. And readers would if they knew that it was waiting for them. But of course, users don't know any such thing. During the initial few seconds when they judge a page, they may make their decision based on what's visible. If this doesn't seem promising enough, some will leave without investing the extra time to scroll.

Registration ☠

In the early days of the Web, registration was a huge barrier, and people didn't know whether to trust sites with their personal information. Now people are more used to entering this information as long as they trust the site and want the service or products it offers. Today users know how to register on a site if they have decided to do business there.

Also, many e-commerce sites have designed alternate checkout paths where users can complete their purchases without officially having to register. Of course, users must enter most of the same personal information, including their credit card numbers, but to many people that's less intrusive when it's part of a checkout process.

The United States Postal Service requires customers to register before purchasing products from its site. Allowing people to buy without registering is a better approach for sales because there are fewer opportunities for drop off. For example, it's common for people try to register by creating a new user name and password in the wrong area, even if it's labeled "Existing Users." People are simply drawn to text boxes and immediately fill in information and then are confused when the system returns error messages. Making registration optional at the end of a purchase is less offensive to customers because it doesn't interrupt shopping and gives them a choice.

Sign In

It's easy to use the United States Postal Service® online services.

Existing Users

Please fill in the following information:
(* Required fields)

* Username [   ] (minimum 6 characters)

* Password [   ] (minimum 8 characters)

I forgot my password

☐ Edit/View my profile

(Sign In >)

New Users

Register now for USPS® online services, and create an account that allows you to:

- Print Shipping Labels
- Request a Carrier pickup
- Buy Stamps & Shop
- Mail Letters & Postcards
- Send Greeting Cards
- Mail Glossy Postcards
- Send Business Greetings

(Sign Up >)

www.usps.com

Still, users don't like to register on Web sites, and sites lose a lot of business if they force users to register prematurely or if they ask too many nosy, privacy-invading questions. All in all, registration is still a cause of lost business, but not nearly as much as it was in the past. One skull.

Complex URLs ☠ ☠

URLs are as bad as ever, even though complex URLs hurt both usability and search engine optimization. There is no reason for URLs that are several hundred characters long, since that's more than necessary to provide a unique address for every atom in the known universe. Most Web sites have less than a million pages and should work fine with URLs of 20 to 50 characters.

There is no reason for URLs that are several hundred characters long, since that's more than necessary to provide a unique address for every atom in the known universe.

We have downgraded complex URLs to a two-skull usability problem because users no longer rely on them very much when interpreting a Web page or navigating a site. Expert users will still "hack" a URL from time to time, but this is now relatively rare, so URLs that are difficult to manipulate are not as harmful as they used to be. There are also services like TinyURL to help expert users create a shorter URL if they want to email a reference to friends or colleagues.

Pull-Down and Cascading Menus ☠

In the past, any dynamic element on the Web commonly confused users, but now people are used to dynamic elements such as pull-down menus and even hierarchical menus that cascade a few levels. The more complex the menu, the more difficult it is to manipulate, so we still give one skull to cascading menus, which present usability problems when they are overly elaborate or long. Think twice any time you are tempted to use anything beyond a simple menu, but you can do it if it truly helps the site. Do watch out for accessibility problems, though, and remember that people with physical disabilities have more difficulty controlling the pointer.

Restraint: How Designers Have Alleviated Usability Problems

Thirteen early usability issues are less problematic now because most designers have learned how to design for the Web.

We've seen gradual improvement in 13 usability problems as a result of Web designers gaining experience and showing restraint. These issues are still *potential* problems because inexperienced designers who have not had to watch their early sites fail might be tempted to resurrect them. But seasoned designers now know when and how to use technology to create a good user experience.

The problem areas where we have seen improvements are

- Plug-ins and bleeding-edge technology
- 3D user interface
- Bloated design
- Splash pages
- Moving graphics and scrolling text
- Custom GUI widgets
- Not disclosing who's behind information
- Made-up words
- Outdated content
- Inconsistency within a Web site
- Premature requests for personal information
- Multiple sites
- Orphan pages

As mentioned earlier, we are not able to discuss in detail here many small and focused usability guidelines that may still cause problems for users. In fact, most Web sites still violate a number of specialized guidelines.

For example, our research has identified 207 usability guidelines for designing e-commerce sites. It has long been a guideline for those offering a product in multiple colors to label color swatches. But we still find e-commerce sites that violate this obvious guideline. (Of course, usability guidelines are not really "obvious" until they have been pointed out after the fact. That's why we compile them in checklists —to minimize the risk that something is overlooked.)

Because Hurricane Pass Traders doesn't label color swatches, users don't know what each option in the color drop-down menu refers to. It is conceivable that the swatches and the menu options are sorted in the same order (black certainly seems to be at the bottom in both cases), but users would feel much more confident in their choice of color if the swatches were labeled, especially since some of the color names are rather ambiguous. (What is "asparagus," for example? The asparagus we buy in our supermarkets is a vivid green that doesn't match any of the swatches in the screen shot.)

The site violates another guideline for the use of color on product pages: There is no option to see the shorts in any of the alternative colors, so you are left guessing how they might look in, say, "almond." It's not particularly helpful to refer shoppers to telephone number for color information. Colors, of course, are better seen than described over the phone.

www.store.nordstrom.com

By labeling color swatches, Nordstrom makes it easy to understand the color names, even when they are slightly odd, such as "pink martini." Unfortunately, Nordstrom's site does not enable users to see the product in their preferred colors. The link to "view colors/patterns" sounds promising but results in a lame pop-up showing slightly staggered sweaters in four of the five available colors. While better than nothing, it's weird that one color is missing and it's difficult to visualize the "dreamy blue" sweater when you can only see a corner of it.

www.cadillac.com

Cadillac provides labeled swatches and also changes the photos of the vehicle's exterior and interior as the user experiments with different colors. Here the user has chosen a "crimson pearl" exterior and "shale" interior. Such real-time feedback is particularly important when a customer is coordinating two color choices.

Plug-Ins and Bleeding-Edge Technology ☠

Bleeding-edge technology was a curse of the early Web, and sites lost many potential customers who refused to download yet another plug-in or software upgrade to use them.

Two things have happened since then. First, designers have come to their senses and recognized that they can't force new technology on users. When people encounter a download dialog, they simply select Cancel. People fear getting viruses, and they don't want to wait for a download and maybe even a reboot to see a Web page. Today most designers rely on proven technology that's a few years old to avoid this issue.

Design restraint is the main reason for this change. But improvements in technology have also had an impact. Refinements in bleeding-edge technologies and plug-ins have made it smoother to upgrade and use them. The Firefox browser in particular has a nifty interface for keeping plug-ins up to date.

Both of these improvements have helped reduce plug-ins and bleeding-edge technology to a one-skull problem. We still recommend that you stick to technologies that are at least two years old and don't force users to upgrade anything in order to visit your site. Problems still occur, so it's not a zero-skull problem.

3D User Interface 💀

Three-dimensional user interfaces on the Web are almost always overly difficult to use and rarely worth the effort. The basic problem is that 3D images are displayed on a two-dimensional surface, the screen, and are controlled through a two-dimensional input device, the mouse. Add in zooming and multiple camera angles, and the potential for trouble multiplies. Users find it very difficult to get 3D interfaces to show products at good angles. They spend most of their time struggling with the interface instead of viewing the product.

It's better to optimize the user interface for the reality of the flat screen than to overwhelm users with fancy 3D mannequins that are difficult to manipulate.

Three-dimensional interfaces have a role in software programs such as medical applications, where it can be critical to visualize tumors, surgical incisions and patients in three dimensions. Similarly, architectural applications are a natural for 3D because real-life structures are built in three dimensions. But most Web applications do not innately require 3D. When shopping for products on e-commerce sites, for example, users seem to have no trouble selecting 3D objects based on 2D pictures. It's better to optimize the user interface for the reality of the flat screen than to overwhelm users with fancy 3D mannequins that are difficult to manipulate.

For the most part, 3D interfaces are history. Most early 3D technologies didn't work, so designers stopped torturing their users with them. Every so often, however, a new 3D technology vendor pops up and talks some poor, unsuspecting e-commerce manager into gussying up his site with 3D, so we still give it a one-skull warning.

PREV <u>1</u> | 2 | 3 | 4 | NEXT

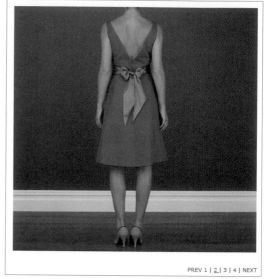

PREV 1 | <u>2</u> | 3 | 4 | NEXT

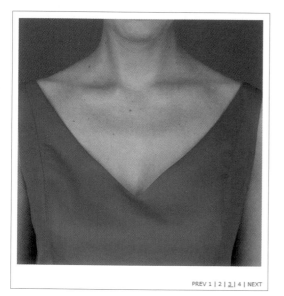

PREV 1 | 2 | <u>3</u> | 4 | NEXT

PREV 1 | 2 | 3 | <u>4</u> | NEXT

www.jcrew.com

Instead of an all-spinning, all-zooming 3D model, J. Crew provides four professional photos of this dress, close up and at well-chosen angles. The site also allows users to view the dress in each of the available colors. Two small quibbles with this design: The current view should be indicated with a boldfaced number instead of underlining because underlined text indicates clickability, and there should be no "next" link when users are on the last image in the series (nor a "prev" link when users are on the first image).

Bloated Design ☠

Pages that overwhelm users with a profusion of moving elements, blinking lights, and poorly structured links were a curse in the early years of the Web. Designers seemed to believe that the more you threw at users, the better the chance that something would attract their attention. Of course, what really happened was that users gave up on those sites and spent their time on scaled-back ones.

Today some sites still have more features than they need, and others have too many big, irrelevant graphics, but overblown design is not nearly as common, so we have downgraded it to one skull. Web sites focus much more on getting straight to business, and that's what customers want to do too.

Splash Pages ☠

Splash pages were an early sin of abusive Web design because they hindered people from getting to what they came for. We were very close to awarding zero skulls to splash screens because we almost never see them anymore. But there are still a few sites that insist on slowing down users with this abomination of a design technique, so we retain a one-skull warning against them. New small-business sites seem particularly susceptible to the lure of splash pages—possibly because their owners insist on fancy designs at the expense of catering to customers and their needs.

Splash screens must die. They give users the first impression that a site cares more about its image than about solving their problems. It is true that a homepage must immediately communicate what the site is about and what a user will get out of visiting it, but it also must communicate respect for the visitor's time or people will simply leave.

One of the original, and flawed, arguments for the splash screen was that it functions like a magazine cover, setting the tone for a site with an attractive image. An attractive visual design certainly helps a Web site, as does one that prioritizes information and guides the user's eye toward the most important features. However, a magazine cover doesn't need to communicate ease of use. A Web site homepage that does makes an important contribution to a company's brand reputation.

> *Splash screens must die. They give users the first impression that the site cares more about its image than about solving their problems.*

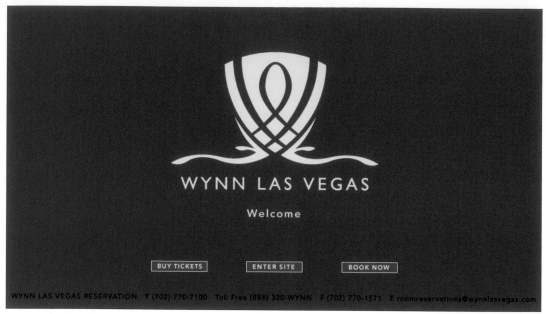

www.wynnlasvegas.com

This is not quite a splash screen because it offers users a choice of three places to go. But it's also not really a routing page because all three options should be provided on the homepage, as indeed they are. Thus, it's a waste of time to make the user see this page.

The most important difference between a magazine cover and a Web site homepage is that a magazine cover must pique people's interest enough to make them want to buy the magazine while a homepage is viewed by people who have already chosen to visit the site. Two very different roles, two very different designs. Don't put a splash screen on your Web site. Remember, you have less than two minutes with prospective customers before they decide whether to leave your site. Don't waste any of it on a splash screen.

Moving Graphics and Scrolling Text ☠

On the Web, as in life, shouting louder usually backfires because people assume you don't have anything important to say. Users tell us that text that scrolls and images that animate incessantly are likely to be useless, so they ignore them. Web sites have discovered this too. Scrolling text and frivolous animation are not nearly as common as they used to be, so we have downgraded this problem to one skull.

Custom GUI Widgets ☠ ☠

Users expect radio buttons to look like radio buttons and behave like radio buttons. The same for any other design element that's standard in graphical user interfaces. Unfortunately, some Web designers feel the urge to introduce their own design for standard dialogue elements like buttons and scrollbars.

Unless your scrollbars look like scrollbars, users might not notice them. Unless your scrollbars behave like scrollbars, users might not know how to bring the content they want into view.

Scrollbars seem to be the most commonly abused GUI widget. In our user testing, we frequently see failures due to custom scrollbars. Unless your scrollbars *look* like scrollbars, users might not notice them. Unless your scrollbars *behave* like scrollbars, users might not know how to bring the content they want into view. In either case, they can only do business with you on the basis of the few items that are visible without scrolling and they might never see the full extent of your offerings. There's no doubt that ensuring scrollbar usability provides an even higher return on investment than most other usability guidelines.

Fortunately, the prevalence of made-up dialogue controls has declined in recent years, so we now deem this a two-skull problem.

Norah Jones
Headlines: NEXT SHOW:
Check back for future tour dates
Radio
Select Your Connection Speed HIGH LOW
News Tour Media Recordings Band Store Mailing List Photos Message Board Links Contacts
48th Annual Grammy Awards
Norah has been nominated for Best Pop Collaboration With Vocals for Virginia Moon recorded with Foo Fighters, and Best Country Collaboration With Vocals for Dreams Come True recorded with Willie Nelson. The 48th Annual Grammy Awards will be held on Wednesday, Feb. 8, at Staples Center in Los Angeles and once again will be broadcast live in high-definition TV and 5.1 surround sound on CBS from 8 – 11:30 p.m. (ET/PT).
The Little Willies
Norah Jones and four friends — bassist Lee Alexander, guitarist Jim Campilongo, guitarist/vocalist Richard Julian and drummer Dan Rieser — have a band called The Little Willies that have been playing old country covers at New York City's The Living Room club for the past couple of years. They've enjoyed it so much that they decided to record an
copyright 2004 - Norah Jones
website by Fast Atmosphere

www.norahjones.com

Comply with GUI standards by using traditional looking widgets. Unique-looking scrollbars such as the yellow sun here run the risk of creating usability problems. People don't use the "home-made" scrolling designs when they deviate too far from the norm because they either don't notice or know how to operate them. Remember, having an obvious scrolling device allows your customers to see the full extent of your offerings. Scrollbars are easy to get right. The less work you do, the better your scrollbar.

Not Disclosing Who's Behind Information ☠

Trust and credibility are major issues on the Web, where even the biggest company exists only as a few words and pictures inside a browser window.

If you order from an e-commerce site, can you trust the company to ship the package? Will they take it back if it arrives in poor condition? If you register on a site, will it sell your personal information to anyone who will pay for it and expose you to endless spam about everything from similar products to offensive porn?

Trust and credibility are major issues on the Web, where even the biggest company exists only as a few words and pictures inside a browser window. The most deceitful and unethical company can look as good as one with a long history of community involvement and honest customer relationships. For a Web site to succeed, users need to know who's behind it, how it's funded, and whether it's credible.

It is now very common for sites to include a dedicated "About Us" section. Although such areas have their own usability problems, they let users know who's behind the information they see on the site. This issue is now reduced to one skull.

"About Us" Features Don't Say Enough

When we tested the usability of the "About Us" feature on 15 corporate sites, we discovered that users could find the information they were looking for only 70 percent of the time. They had particular difficulty finding basic company facts such as

Top executive or official: 59% success
Correct contact information: 62% success
Organization philosophy: 59% success

Historical timeline and milestones: 58% success
The poor score for contact information is deplorable for two reasons. First, people frequently request it and are frustrated when it is not readily available. Second, it's one of the leading markers that people use to judge a company's trustworthiness: Is it a fly-by-night operation or does it have an actual address and a phone number that it's willing to disclose?

Made-Up Words ☠

During the dot-com bubble, it seemed that every Web site had to invent its own vocabulary to describe its services. Such made-up words hurt usability because users didn't know what menu options to click. For example, calling resources "re-sauces" or food "foodile" stumps users because they don't know what the terms mean. The theory might have been to entice users to explore the site, but in practice people got lost and gave up.

Made-up words also hurt search engine optimization because users obviously won't search for words they don't use. Conversely, use of everyday language and straightforward terms increases a site's rank in search engines and the likelihood that it will be found by people who use these words as query terms.

There are still a few sites that insist on using their very own terminology, but this is getting ever more rare as such sites get less and less business. Made-up words are now only a one-skull problem.

Outdated Content ☠ ☠

In one sense, outdated information might be considered a three-skull problem because old information increases monotonically as the Web gets older. The problem is not old information per se, of course. Organized into rich archives and background information, it has an important place on the Web.

The problem occurs when users are offered outdated information as if it were new. Typically, this happens on sites that are not being maintained, which is pretty common. But bigger, professionally run sites now take reasonable care to keep their most prominent pages current, so we have downgraded this problem to two skulls.

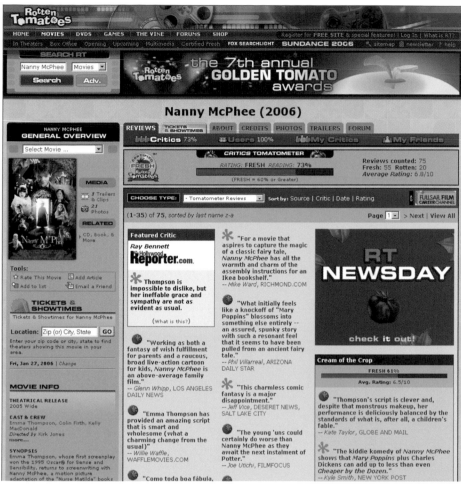

Be wary of using cute metaphors and names that people don't understand. In most instances, people on the Web want information quickly. They rely on clear and concise headings and labels to point them in the right direction. Sites that make people work to decipher "the code" turn them off. For example, the tomato theme of this film site does not communicate basic concepts effectively. Categories such as "Certified Fresh," Critics Tomatometer," and "Cream of the Crop" are unclear to users. At first glance, it's difficult to know what the tomato and green icons mean and what they have to do with movie reviews. While the site designers might have meant the green icon to denote a splat for a bad film, many users won't pick up on this subtlety and will see it instead as an asterisk.

Inconsistency Within a Web Site ☠ ☠

In the beginning, it was every page for itself. Each new page was designed for the moment, with little thought to how it would play with other pages on the site. Subsites often looked so different, you couldn't really tell they all belonged to the same company and theoretically were components of a single service.

Since at least 2000, most large companies have made a big push to present one face to the customer, and Web sites are now much more consistent than they used to be, at least in terms of main content. But most sites still have areas that were designed by a different team, and it shows.

Intranets are another matter: They are still often inconsistent, with widely diverging designs between different departments. Inconsistent design is probably still a three-skull problem for intranets, but for the public Internet, inconsistency is now a two-skull problem.

Premature Requests for Personal Information ☠ ☠

If someone walked up to strangers at a cocktail party and asked each for their telephone number, birthdate, social security number, and grandmother's medical history, he would probably find many people walking away. It's the same with Web sites. If they are too nosy too soon, people refuse to answer their questions. Web sites have to build up a bit of a relationship with users before they can start asking them personal questions.

Most Web sites used to ignore this common-sense advice. The better sites have now sobered up and deferred personal questions until after the user has decided to do business with them. Obviously, if you are going to ship a purchase to a customer, you need to know their shipping address, and people have no problem giving out this info at the appropriate stage in the relationship. But if they can't enter a site and browse around without giving out personal information, they will typically leave immediately.

Premature requests for personal information remains a two-skull problem because there are still too many sites that think it's smart marketing to ask a lot of qualifying questions of their users. But ask too much and your site will be as unpopular as a nosy person at a cocktail party.

Multiple Sites ☠ ☠

Companies used to launch new Web sites at the drop of a hat, all at different addresses. With a profusion of sites, customers never knew what services they could get from a company, and there was no hope of unified information architecture or helpful Search and navigation.

Today, most companies have recognized the need for an integrated Internet strategy, so the problem is not as bad as it used to be. We give it two skulls, however, because microsites are still too common, especially in connection with advertising campaigns. It's OK—in fact, it's pre-ferred—to have a dedicated landing page for each campaign, but the information should all be part of the same Web site, where all the elements support each other.

Orphan Pages

Orphan pages are those that have no links to anything. If you land on one, you can't go anywhere else on the site. They were pretty common in the 1990s but are almost never seen any more. This is now a zero-skull problem because virtually all designers have recognized the need to provide users with at least a minimal number of navigation options for connecting to the rest of the site.

Assessing the Fate of the Early Findings

In this chapter we have revisited 34 of the most important problem areas for Web sites in the past and given each a skull rating to indicate how important it continues to be today. Our rating scale went from zero to three skulls, so we could have awarded a total of 102 skulls if all usability problems were still as bad as when we first assessed them. However, we gave out only 59 skulls in all. This means that the usability problems we see today are 58 percent as bad as they once were—or that their potential for damage has improved by 42 percent.

The pie chart shows the current status of usability problems: the proportion of issues that remain important and the proportion that is less important now, due to improvements in technology and design, and user adaptations to various design elements.

Although many analysts are extremely enthusiastic about advances in Internet technology, it is interesting to note that technology accounted for only ten percent of the improvements. As the chart shows, changes in user behavior actually had a bigger impact, leading to 11 percent of the improvements.

The greatest amount of progress, accounting for the most skulls lost, is due to designers showing restraint in applying annoying design techniques. Better design accounts for 21 percent of the lost skulls, so that's many usability problems we don't have to face as long as designers continue on their recent good habits.

Unfortunately, there is no guarantee that they will. Future Web designers may not appreciate the damage caused to clients by violations of the early guidelines. As the problems become ever more rare on the Web, there is a significant risk that inexperienced designers will commit sins that their seasoned colleagues had to learn on.

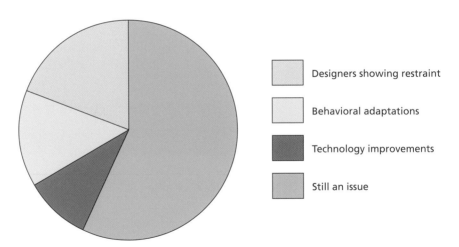

- Designers showing restraint
- Behavioral adaptations
- Technology improvements
- Still an issue

Distribution of the potential for damage from the 34 early usability problems discussed in this chapter.

More Information

Some of the first studies of Web usability mentioned in this chapter were documented in reports that are still available at www. useit.com/papers. For 1994 testing of five Web sites, see "1994 Study of Web Usability"; for 1994 studies of intranet usability, see "Sun Web: User Interface Design for Sun Microsystems' Intranet"; for 1995 studies of Web design alternatives, see "1995 Design of Sun Microsystems' Website, Using Interacticve Design and User Testing"; and for 1997 research on how people read online, see "How to Write for the Web."

For details on other reports and guidelines cited in this chapter, visit www.nngroup.com/reports, and see Flash, Teenagers, E-commerce, and "About Us" Sections of Corporate Sites.

When we think about the fact that half of the improvement in usability problems is because Web designers have decided to follow usability guidelines more often, we realize that the percentage of problems that continues to loom over us is actually larger than the pie chart indicates. The 21 percent of problems alleviated by changes in user behavior and technology is really the only share that is gone for good. The other 21 percent—usability improvements credited to better design—is not set in stone. It could change any time, so in reality 79 percent of the original issues are still worth thinking about. In other words, the majority of our usability insights from the 1990s are still valid these many years later, even if some of the pitfalls are not actively hurting users today.

In general, as we continue to research different aspects of Web usability, it's striking how often the early findings are confirmed, even as the newer studies result in a more nuanced understanding and more detailed guidelines. For this reason, we expect usability issues to continue to be of major importance for many years to come.

4 Prioritizing Your Usability Problems

Usability can be a matter of life and death. In war a soldier in a fighter plane has a critical edge if his plane's user interface for targeting and firing systems is just one second faster than his enemy's. On the Web, of course, usability does not have such a dramatic role. But it can determine whether your Web site fails or succeeds.

How do you know which usability problems have the most serious consequences for your Web site? Which ones to fix and which to let go? In this chapter, we discuss the issues that create the most trouble for users and the most missed opportunities for businesses. With this information, you can best decide how to allocate your resources.

For every usability problem on your site, you need to balance the severity of the problem against the effort required to fix it.

There is a lot wrong with Web sites today, but to improve usability, we need to prioritize our resources and fix the problems that hurt users the most. To do this, we need a systematic evaluation of the severity of Web usability problems. This chapter provides that.

When we write consulting reports for our clients, we rate usability problems very simply as high, medium, or low. We then base our recommendations on the severity of the problems: Fix everything rated high, if possible; spend some resources on medium problems; and defer fixing low issues to a later date unless they're so trivial that they can be resolved with almost no work.

For the book research, we use a 100-point rating scale for severity because numeric ratings allow us to provide more interesting statistics than a rating scale based on words. We don't recommend that you apply this more complex scale to your own design because it's too detailed for everyday development projects. Simpler ratings allow designers to focus on their priorities, which are to fix the most severe problems. A fancy scale is an open invitation for everyone on the design team to pipe up and quibble over individual points. This is not a fruitful use of time because there is no meaningful difference between something rated 62, say, and something rated 63.

There's another reason that a simple scale is best for practical projects: You need to balance the severity of the problem against the effort required to fix it. Even a high-severity problem can be fixed later if that's going to be extremely costly and time consuming. We all know that estimates of development schedules are little better than numbers drawn out of a hat, and thus overly precise usability ratings have no place opposite rough development estimates.

What Makes Problems Severe

Three factors affect how serious a problem is for users:

- **Frequency:** How many users will encounter the problem? If a relatively small number of users are hurt by it, it's a lower severity problem.

- **Impact:** How much trouble does the problem cause to those users who encounter it? This can range from almost imperceptible irritation to losing hours of work or even deciding to leave a Web site.

- **Persistence:** Is the problem a one-time impediment to users or does it cause trouble repeatedly? Many usability problems have low persistency because once people figure them out, they can overcome them in the future. Other designs are so confusing that people get lost over and over again. Design mistakes of this kind deserve a higher severity rating than those that bite once.

Scoring Severity

To calculate the total severity score of a usability problem, we multiply the frequency rating by the impact rating, then multiply that number by the square root of the persistence rating and divide that by the square root of 10. (Dividing by the square root of 10 simplifies the rating by keeping the total number of potential points under 100.)

It's obvious why we multiply frequency by impact: Essentially we're multiplying how many users are hurt by how much they are hurt, and the result is an estimate of total harm done. It may be a bit of a surprise, though, that we then multiply that answer by the square root of the persistence score instead of by the full persistence score. This is because we are dealing with Web sites, where there is not that much persistent use. Users usually only visit Web sites a few times, and if the site has sufficiently hurtful design mistakes, they won't return at all. Thus, we can't give full weight to the idea that users would hypothetically continue to be hurt on subsequent visits because for the most part they won't be revisiting

For each usability problem, we rate each of the three attributes on a scale of 1 to 10, with 10 indicating those that cause the most trouble for the most people. From these scores, we can calculate how severe the problem is. These screen shots illustrate low- and high-severity problems.

www.parks.ca.gov

A low-severity usability problem: The problem here is that the numbers on the list of checkboxes do not appear to be in numerical sequence, making them seem random. The underlying design problem is that the list looks as if it has been broken up in two columns whereas in fact it's structured by rows. This problem has a very low frequency of occurrence, because most people either click the map or click the name of the area they are interested in; very few people try to match the map and the list. For those users who do try to match them, this is still a very low-impact problem because the list is so small. You need to spend a few extra seconds scanning it, and that's all. Finally, the persistence of the problem is low because if you return to this screen, you know how to deal with it. You are not likely to spend even a few seconds thinking about the mismatch a second time. This layout problem is a minor irritation, and fixing it should not be a high priority.

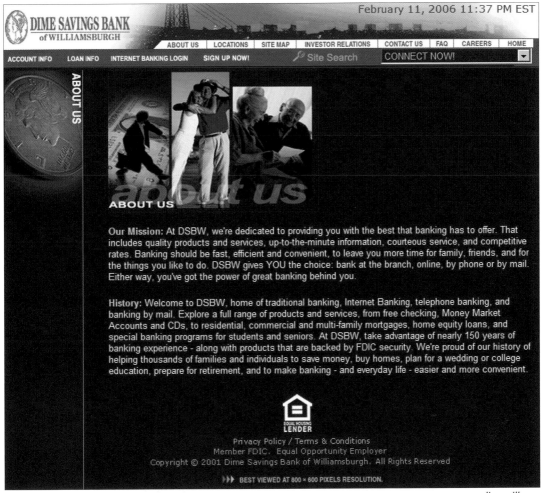

A high-severity usability problem: The problem on this bank's "About Us" page is that it does not tell enough to establish trust and credibility. Yes, the bank says that it is a "home of traditional banking," but it doesn't back that up with facts such as when the bank was founded, how many branches it has, how solid it is, or any other specific information that would make you feel comfortable handing your money over to it. This problem is high frequency because all users will want to know about a company before doing something as scary as giving it money for safekeeping. The problem is also high impact because it will cause a lot of people to simply refuse to use the site. Finally the persistence of the problem is high, because every time a new user contemplates doing business with the bank, they will want to know more about it, and every time they try to find out, they will be disappointed. This unsatisfying page significantly harms the bank's ability to attract online business.

Bad user interface can be life threatening in medical applications. In the March 9, 2005 issue of the Journal of the American Medical Association, Ross Koppel and colleagues reported on a field study of a hospital's order-entry system, which physicians used to specify patient medications. The study identified 22 ways in which the system's design flaws caused patients to get the wrong dosage of medicine. Most of these were due to usability problems.

The system screens listed dosages based on the units of medication available through the hospital pharmacy. If a rare medication is usually prescribed in 20- or 30-mg doses, for example, the pharmacy would stock 10-mg pills so that it could cover dosage needs without overstocking. When hospital staff members prescribed infrequently used medications, however, they often assumed the listed unit was a typical dosage. (Years of usability studies in many domains have shown that users tend to assume that the given default or example values are applicable to their own situations.) So a doctor might prescribe 10 mg even though 20 or 30 would be more appropriate. The usability solution here is simple: Each screen should list typical prescription dosages.

Another problem occurred when doctors changed the dosage of a patient's medication. They often entered the new dose without canceling the old one, so the patient received the sum of the old and new doses. This is similar to a banking interface error, when a customer mistakenly authorizes a payment to the same recipient twice in one day. Many bank Web sites will catch this error and ask the client to double-check their records. In general, if users repeat something they've done, the system should ask them whether both operations should remain in effect or whether the new command should overrule the last.

The article reported that at times staff had to review up to 20 screens to see all of a patient's medications. In a survey, 72 percent of staff reported that they were often uncertain about medications and dosages because they had difficulty reviewing them all. The well-known limits on human short-term memory make it impossible to remember across that many screens. Humans are notoriously poor at remembering exact information, and minimizing users' memory load has long been a top guideline. Rather than require users to remember things from one screen to the next—let alone to the next 19—the system should restate facts for users when and where they need them.

Other aspects of the system that required users to go through numerous screens placed additional burdens on some staff. As a result, they didn't always use the system as intended. For example, it was easier for nurses to keep sets of paper records that they entered into the system at the end of their shifts rather than to update it throughout their shifts. This increased the risk of errors and prevented the system from providing real-time information about the medications patients had received. In general, whenever you see users resorting to sticky notes or other paper-based workarounds, you know you have a failed UI.

The Scale of Misery

The combined severity points across all usability problems can be seen as an estimate of the total misery of the Web user experience today. We already know from Chapter 2 that the situation is pretty bad because users repeatedly fail their tasks or give up on sites. This pie chart shows what types of problems cause users the most trouble.

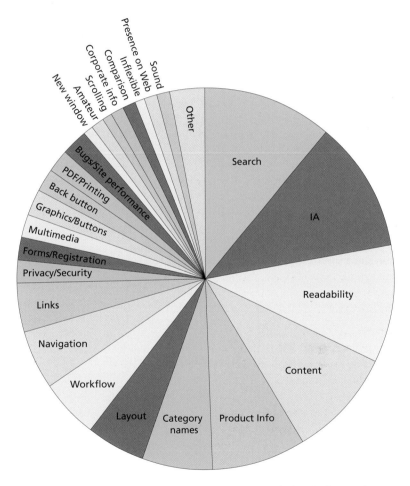

Usability problems weighted by their severity score. Each slice indicates the percentage of the total misery imposed on users by each type of design mistake. The last slice represents the 4 percent of the total score that was due to various miscellaneous issues that defy classification.

In the severity scale we prepared for this book, Search was the worst offender, sharply followed by confusing information architecture, low readability, and uninformative content. In other words, almost three-quarters of the usability issues that people encounter have to do with basic user goals: finding, reading, and understanding information. Most of these problems delayed or annoyed users, but they eventually overcome them in many cases. For example, users might get lost in a site's information architecture but still find what they want through Search.

Certainly, some very bad design mistakes are so small or infrequent that they didn't rack up enough points to account for at least one percent of the total. Aggressive, offensive, and intrusive ads, for example, accounted for only four-tenths percent of the severity score and are thus not shown in the pie chart. The low score for bad ads is based on two things. First, we didn't test very many content sites in this study, so most of the sites we used didn't have that many ads. Second, ads must be extremely obnoxious to get users to leave a site. This does not mean that users don't find them irritating. They do. But most have developed a defense strategy of ignoring anything that looks like an ad which is why we have a usability guideline advising that none of your design elements do.

To get a better grasp on the big areas of design mistakes in current Web sites, we then grouped the problems into larger categories. As this pie chart shows, Search was still such a big problem, it's literally in a category all by itself. But in this grouping, findability was the biggest issue, accounting for 26 percent of user misery. Findability—which includes design elements such as information architecture, category names, and links—is one of two ways users get to where they want to go on a site. Search, of course, is the other. When we add up the two, we see that 37 percent of people's difficulties on the Web relate to getting to the right page.

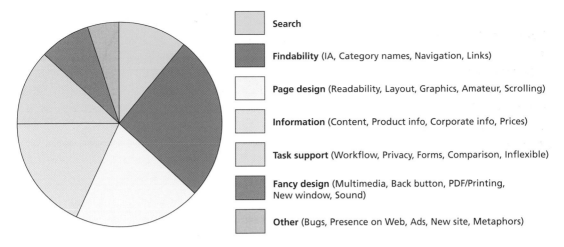

Search

Findability (IA, Category names, Navigation, Links)

Page design (Readability, Layout, Graphics, Amateur, Scrolling)

Information (Content, Product info, Corporate info, Prices)

Task support (Workflow, Privacy, Forms, Comparison, Inflexible)

Fancy design (Multimedia, Back button, PDF/Printing, New window, Sound)

Other (Bugs, Presence on Web, Ads, New site, Metaphors)

Usability problems weighted by their severity score and grouped into larger categories of design mistakes. Combining usability issues into broader categories shows the major areas that caused confusion and dissatisfaction among users.

Tip: The First Law of E-Commerce

If the user can't find the product, the user can't buy the product. The ability to get around a Web site is extremely important for usability, but the key components of Search and findability account for more than one-third of users' difficulty doing so.

Another 62 percent of user misery is caused by bad design at the page level or bad design of a progression of pages in a workflow—cases in which users arrived at the right location but it didn't meet their needs. This means that you must look beyond Search and findability to determine why your site isn't fulfilling its business potential. Much of your losses are probably caused at the page level by information that is incomprehensible, lowers trust, or simply doesn't provide a crucial answer that users want. Conversely, just one percent of users' difficulties related to issues caused by companies having multiple, inconsistent Web sites, so this is a less severe problem.

One piece of good news: Fancy design now causes only eight percent of users' misery, down from its glory days in the dot-com bubble, when it was much more commonly used. We still need to guard against the reemergence of excesses like splash screens and annoying animation, but for the moment they are mainly a thing of the past.

Why Users Fail

In the previous section, we discussed problems that primarily delay or annoy users but don't necessarily stop them from completing a task. Some problems are too severe to for average users to overcome, however. This chart shows problems that were severe enough to cause users to fail on a site either by leaving it, giving up on a task, or completing a task incorrectly.

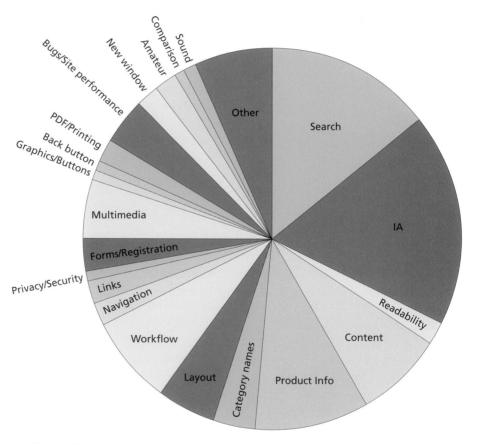

Usability problems weighted by how frequently they caused users to fail a task. These are the issues that stopped people in their tracks and prevented them from successfully accomplishing their tasks.

Comparing all types of user problems to those that cause task failures, we can see some striking differences. Most notably, Search and information architecture are larger factors in task failures. This makes sense because nothing else really matters if you can't find what you're looking for.

Conversely, readability ranked third among the problems on our misery scale, but was much less significant to user failure. It's very annoying for readers to have to squint or lean forward because text is difficult to read, but they can usually suffer through it for a few minutes until they are finished with their task. Sometimes, of course, poor readability will cause people to leave or overlook an important piece of information, but usually it's more of an annoyance than a direct cause of failure.

In the final pie chart, we grouped the design problems that cause task failure into yet broader categories. This can help you prioritize your design and make sure that you are focusing on the big areas that destroy the most business value if not corrected. Again, note that the two categories related to getting around Web sites Search and findability have assumed even more importance. Fifteen percent of task failures were caused by usability problems with Search, and a whopping 27 percent with findability problems. Difficult information or lack of information accounted for the second largest slice: 19 percent of task failures.

As much as Web designers love to discuss the importance of elements such as graphics and layout, page design is not that important for people's ability to use Web sites.

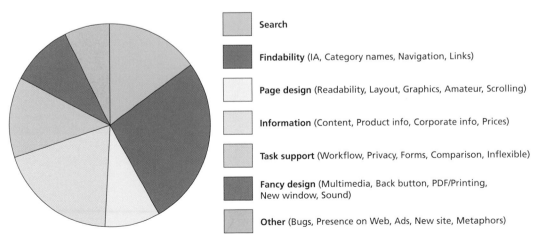

Search

Findability (IA, Category names, Navigation, Links)

Page design (Readability, Layout, Graphics, Amateur, Scrolling)

Information (Content, Product info, Corporate info, Prices)

Task support (Workflow, Privacy, Forms, Comparison, Inflexible)

Fancy design (Multimedia, Back button, PDF/Printing, New window, Sound)

Other (Bugs, Presence on Web, Ads, New site, Metaphors)

Bigger categories of usability problems weighted by how frequently they caused users to fail a task. Notice the combined dominance of findability and information.

Again comparing user failure to general user misery, it's interesting to note that page design is more of an annoyance than a direct cause of failure. As much as Web designers love to discuss the importance of elements such as graphics and layout, page design is not that important for people's ability to use Web sites. Of course, you don't want any task failures on your site, so this is not an argument for ignoring page design. But it *is* an argument for giving higher priority to improving Search, findability, and the actual information that's presented on the pages.

Is It Enough to Focus on the Worst Problems?

Should you devote all your resources to the problems that make users fail and forget those that simply cause annoyances and minor difficulties? We don't think so, which is why we analyzed the data both ways. Usability problems that are not the direct cause of a task failure can still hurt your business in many ways. Constantly annoying users with problems like low readability eventually makes them like you less, which is not good for the many sites whose main goal is marketing and promotion. Most important, when enough little irritations add up to a bad user experience, people are likely to leave and not return.

The data presented in this chapter should help you prioritize your own usability and design resources. In particular, we recommend more emphasis on content usability than what we find in most projects. Having the information users need and presenting it in an appropriate writing style are crucial for success on the Web. Of course, it's also extremely important to work on Search and findability, but most people already know this. For the remainder of this book, we will discuss these top issues that most influence people's ability to use your Web site and how you can correct them.

5 Search

In our testing, the success rate for people using external search engines was good. The success rate for people using internal search engines was atrocious. Yet Search on a specific site should actually function better than Web-wide Search.

Search is such a prominent part of the Web user experience that people have strong expectations for how it should work. Your best bet for creating good Search is to learn the guidelines that the big search engines use, and use them on your site. This chapter discusses how to make an effective search function on your site and how to optimize your hits from external search engines.

Search is one of the most important design elements on a Web site. Nineteen of the 25 Web sites we studied for this book had search engines, and people performed searches on all 19. This shows how heavily users rely on Search.

While some users went immediately to the Search box, however, others preferred locating information through methods such as navigational links. Search is particularly helpful for people who know exactly what they want and can quickly come up with good Search queries. But offering good link categories encourages people to explore your site and discover what's available, especially when they're just browsing or don't know what words to enter into a Search box. Supporting both types of behavior is important to capturing a broad audience.

The State of Search

To conduct searches, most users type one, two, or three words into the search engine. That's very little info from which to dredge up the answer to somebody's problem out of the billions of pages on the Web. But in our testing, large external search engines such as Google, Yahoo!, and MSN Search succeeded 56 percent of the time, which is pretty good. (These "big three" are sometimes referred to with the acronym GYM.) While most users in our study used one of the big three, we had a few users who preferred other search engines, mainly America Online (AOL) Search.

When people used internal search engines to search just the site they were on, their success rate was only 33 percent. Site Search should not be so much poorer than Web Search. In fact, there are many reasons why it should be better:

- There is obviously a much smaller set of pages to be considered on a single site than on the entire Web.

- Within a single Web site, you have a much better handle on the user's intent. For example, you would know whether the word "jaguars" referred to cars, animals, a football team, or a rockabilly band depending on the Web site that was being searched. Yahoo! has no such luxury.

- You know what documents are the most important on your site, so you can prioritize the hits based on their intrinsic value instead by the imputed value external search engines have to use.

- Conversely, you know which documents are old or obsolete, so you can give them a lower placement by default.

- You potentially have even more access to meta-data than big search engines do, which allows your Search software to know much more about your documents and their relationships than an external engine could discover by spidering the site.

- You have a controlled vocabulary, so you know the synonyms, misspellings, and other variants that might lead you to return a document even if the user's exact query words don't appear in the text.

- You can trust your own information, so you can use optimal, human-written summaries of each page instead of the computer-generated snippets that many search engines show because they don't trust Web sites to describe themselves honestly.

- You don't have to contend with spammers or sites that try to manipulate the search engine to achieve a higher ranking than they deserve.

Three Simple Steps to Better Search

- Buy better Search software. It's well worth the investment, considering how much users rely on Search. Also, take the time to tweak the settings to optimize retrieval on your site.
- Design the Search interface and the search engine results page (SERP) according to the usability guidelines in this chapter.

- Improve the pages on your site so that they work better with Search software. Write page titles that are easy for users to scan on the SERP. Write page summaries that succinctly describe what each page is about to help users decide which listing to click. Use the Search Engine Optimization (SEO) principles in the last section of this chapter to help the software do a better job.

The Three Things Users Expect from Search

- A box where they can type words
- A button labeled Search that they click to run the search
- A list of top results that's linear, prioritized, and appears on a new page

Tip: When Is a Search Not Search?

To the vast majority of users, Search equals keyword searching, not other types of Search. Don't use the Search button for other actions, such as Enter, Submit, or Go.

How Search Should Work

In user testing, people generally tell us that they want the Search on Web sites and intranets to work like that of their favorite major search engine. Fortunately Google, Yahoo!, and MSN all work the same: with a Search box and button, and a linear, prioritized results page. In fact, the top search engines comply with all the main usability guidelines, which is one major reason why they're on top.

So the new usability guidelines aren't just for designing *good* Search; they are for designing *expected* Search. Deviating from the expected design almost always causes usability problems.

Given how ingrained Search is, avoid invoking a user's mental model of search for other interactions. For example, don't use a Search button for a parametric search, in which the user defines certain parameters of the search. A parametric search can be helpful on e-commerce sites—searching a shoe site by specifying shoe size, width, color, brand, or style is certainly more useful than doing a keyword search. But these searches don't fit the design pattern for Search, however, so you should call them something else to avoid confusing users.

Advanced Search that combines keyword searching with other search forms can also be helpful for users, but it should be a secondary option that's only displayed when they ask for it.

Users are now forming mental models that they expect to apply across the Web, and even on their intranets. This is good. Assumptions about common tasks let users focus on their goals, not on learning the mechanics of operating the interface. All this breaks down, however, if your design conflicts with users' preconceived mental models. Don't commit this sin.

The shoe finder boxes above the photos of shoes on Zappos.com are a great example of parametric search: Why look at shoes that are not available in your size? A small quibble is that the button for the keyword search should be labeled something other than "Go!" in order to differentiate it from the parametric search button. Having a "go" button for the parametric search is great, but the Search button should be labeled Search.

In our experience, when users see a Search button, they're likely to frantically look for a box where they can enter keywords. Currently there is no single winning label for non-keyword search, but Find and Retrieve seem to work well. For winnowing, you can use labels like "Refine Results."

Search Interface

The Search interface—a text box where users can enter their queries, combined with a single button labeled Search—should usually be in the top left or, slightly preferably, top right of the page, since that's where users look for it. The box should definitely be on the homepage, but ideally it will be on every page of the site. Users turn to Search when they are lost or have given up navigating the site. You can't predict in advance where that will happen, so the only safe design is to make Search available everywhere.

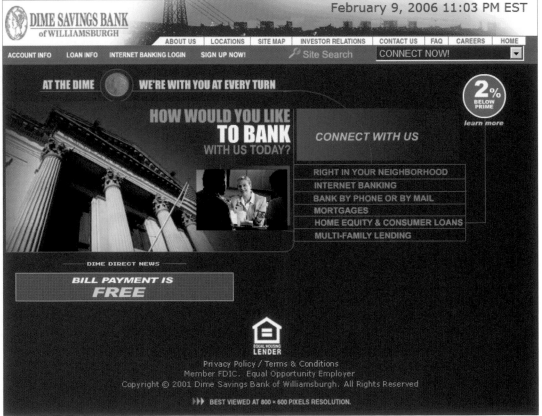

www.dimewill.com

This site has a link to a search engine but it's nearly invisible, so most users didn't know it was available. After looking in vain for some time, they concluded that the site didn't have Search.

NORDSTROM

checkout | search | help

women | men | shoes | gifts | jewelry | sale | featured

shop by: | category | trends | your style | brands | special sizes | women

your style

◀◀ Choose a category at left.

- BUSINESS CASUAL
- SPRING LINEN
- EASY CARE TENCEL
- BEACH VACATION
- WARDROBE TO GO
- MIX-AND-MATCH
- PROM TIME
- MUST-HAVES UNDER $25

beach vacation

Athena Collection Watercolor Suit
$80

Athena Collection Watercolor Pareo
$52

your account | e-mail updates | about us | our stores | site map | contact us

www.nordstrom.com

When we tested the Nordstrom Web site in 2000, users could not find the Search feature, although they frequently asked for it. Look at this screen shot for a moment. How long does it take you to find Search? When Search is not a box, users tend to overlook it.

Tip: Don't Try to Be a Search Engine

Keep the Search user interface on your site simple. Don't offer the option of searching the entire Web. Web users already have their own favorite search engines, and when they want to search the Web, they'll go to those. Searching anything beyond your own site simply clutters up your pages. The only exception is if you have multiple Web sites. If so, a multi-site Search may be in order, but beware that it will complicate your user interface and reduce usability because people expect Web sites to offer single-site Search.

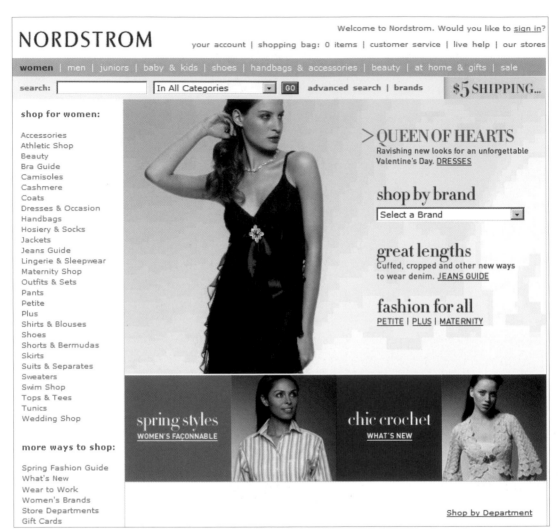

NORDSTROM

Welcome to Nordstrom. Would you like to sign in?

your account | shopping bag: 0 items | customer service | live help | our stores

women | men | juniors | baby & kids | shoes | handbags & accessories | beauty | at home & gifts | sale

search: [ ] [In All Categories ▾] [GO] advanced search | brands $5 SHIPPING...

shop for women:

Accessories
Athletic Shop
Beauty
Bra Guide
Camisoles
Cashmere
Coats
Dresses & Occasion
Handbags
Hosiery & Socks
Jackets
Jeans Guide
Lingerie & Sleepwear
Maternity Shop
Outfits & Sets
Pants
Petite
Plus
Shirts & Blouses
Shoes
Shorts & Bermudas
Skirts
Suits & Separates
Sweaters
Swim Shop
Tops & Tees
Tunics
Wedding Shop

more ways to shop:

Spring Fashion Guide
What's New
Wear to Work
Women's Brands
Store Departments
Gift Cards

> QUEEN OF HEARTS
Ravishing new looks for an unforgettable
Valentine's Day. DRESSES

shop by brand
[Select a Brand ▾]

great lengths
Cuffed, cropped and other new ways
to wear denim. JEANS GUIDE

fashion for all
PETITE | PLUS | MATERNITY

spring styles
WOMEN'S FAÇONNABLE

chic crochet
WHAT'S NEW

Shop by Department

www.nordstrom.com

Nordstrom has long since redesigned its Web site to make Search into a box and pull-down list, making it more visible than before. The company did the right thing by having the list defaulted to search "In All Categories" because that's the most widely used setting. People often leave the "All" default setting to see the breadth of their Search results. Narrowing the search too soon might shield them from meaningful results. In most instances, we warn against using Search pull-down options because they cause confusion, especially when people can't easily discriminate among the options. For example, designer jeans can fall under several categories (Apparel, Sale, and Juniors). Having to pause and guess the right category requires effort.

The fact that you can quickly spot the Search box on the busy Disney homepage is testament to the power of the open input field to draw the eye. The box is a bit too narrow and underlining makes the Search button look more like a link than a button. The difference is that links simply take you to a new page, while buttons initiate commands. Since Search is an action, you should use a button to start it.

http://disneyland.disney.go.com

Disneyland's Search box is more standard than the one on the main Disney homepage: It's placed in the upper right and the button looks like a button. However, it's not good to move important interface elements like Search around on the pages within a company's Web space. Inconsistent user experience undermines the feeling of a unified brand. A simpler way of presenting the search area would be to remove the Search label at the beginning of the text box and rename the Go button Search instead.

http://disneyvideos.disney.go.com

Following one of the other links from Disney's homepage takes visitors to yet another page design with yet another Search interface. It makes sense for Disneyland and Disney Videos to have quite different user interfaces because their services are so different (book a vacation vs. find and buy films). But keyword Search can still be presented in the same way to encourage a feeling of consistency across the user's navigation. Fortunately the most important part of Search is consistent between the two pages: It is a box and it's in the upper right. (All the more reason to have it on the right on the homepage as well.) The Search box is sufficiently wide here, at 26 characters, to accommodate most searches. A few quibbles with this design: We would advise against labels saying "Find It Fast." It's always dangerous to advertise a user interface feature as "fast" or "easy" because users will be that much more disappointed if it's not. The multiple Go buttons are inappropriate and create unnecessary clutter. Having a Search button would be appropriate for the open Search box, but the other Go buttons should go.

Query Length and Search Box Width

This chart shows the length of search strings in users' queries during our study. Half of the queries were rather short, with less than 14 characters. The other half were long, with users needing several words to express their search needs.

The distribution of Search queries in our study. For 84 percent of the queries, there is a steady increase in length up to 22 characters; the last 16 percent of queries rapidly get longer and longer. The longest query was 68 characters, or almost a full line.

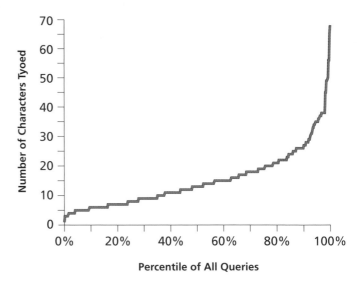

Wider Search boxes are better for two reasons. First, they encourage users to type longer queries, which usually leads to more precise and useful results. Second, typos and other errors are reduced when users can see everything they have typed.

Even so, we do not recommend that you make your Search box wide enough to accommodate every last query. Even the Web–wide search engines typically make their Search boxes about 48 characters wide, which would not accommodate every last one of the queries in our study. For a mainstream site, where Search is a utility not the goal, this would take up too much space.

In Jakob's book *Homepage Usability: 50 Websites Deconstructed*, he and coauthor Marie Tahir recommended that Search boxes be 25 characters wide. Now, just a few years later, we are recommending 27 characters. The trend seems to be toward longer query strings as people get more used to searching, and we would not be surprised if the recommendation were to increase to 30 characters in the future. In fact, if you wanted to future-proof your design, you could make your Search box 30 characters wide now.

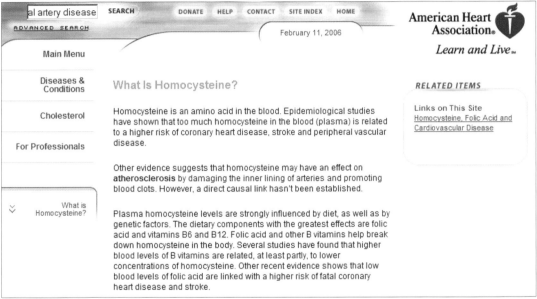

www.americanheart.org

The Search box on the American Heart Association's Web site has room for just 17 characters. This is slightly less than the average for all Web sites and it is particularly problematic on a health site because of the long and complex terms that are frequently used in medicine. "Peripheral artery disease" is simple as medical language goes, and yet it doesn't fit in the Search box, vastly increasing the risk of user errors. Just try entering "epidemiological studies homocysteine atherosclerosis" without typos.

Advanced Search

The main guideline for Advanced Search is this: Avoid it. Very few people use Advanced Search correctly, and it almost always causes more trouble than it's worth.

Unless your users are highly technically skilled (or professional librarians), they won't understand how to use features like Boolean search. In the study we conducted for this book, only 1.2 percent of queries used any form of advanced syntax (such as "and," "or," or "but"). Even worse, when people do attempt an advanced query, they usually make mistakes and don't get what they want.

The one exception is the use of quotes to indicate the search for a literal text string. In our study, quotes were used in 3.5 percent of the queries, which is enough to make this feature worth supporting.

If you do have Advanced Search features, it's usually best to relegate them to a special Advanced Search page, where there's room for all the specialized search tools and where they can be explained in some detail. Simple Search should be the default that's placed directly on the homepage and interior pages of the site in the form of a plain Search box. This approach guides average users to attempt simple Search first, which is usually best for them.

Scoped Search

Scoped Search—restricting a search to a certain range—is another advanced feature that sometimes makes sense. In scoped Search, users only search a certain area of the site and will not see results elsewhere. On a site that sells books, music, and DVDs, for example, a scoped search would help users who knows the name of the film they want. But it would prevent them from finding out if the film soundtrack is issued on CD, which potentially limits sales. Scoped Search makes sense on sites that have extremely clearly differentiated areas, and where it's common for people to only request items from one of these areas.

Scoping is dangerous for two reasons. First, if the search is scoped by default (which we don't recommend), then users may assume that they are searching the entire site. They won't know that they are not getting most of the potential hits. Users expect global Search, so sites that have scoped Search should still offer global Search as the default. Second, users may think that the item they are looking for is in a certain area of the site when in fact it's located elsewhere. In that case, they may not find the item they are looking for or whatever else the site has to offer on the subject.

If you do offer scoped Search, follow two additional guidelines besides making global Search the default: Clearly state on the SERP what scope was searched and offer one-click access to repeat the search on the entire Web site.

Search Engine Results Pages

Our No. 1 guideline for SERP design is to mimic the SERPs on the major Web-wide search engines. Provide a linear list of search results, with the most recommended on the top.

There is no need to number search results because all users start scanning from the top. There is also no need to annotate search results with relevancy rankings or other estimates of goodness. Users start scanning from the top and give up once the search results don't seem promising enough, based on the content, not where it rates in relevancy.

Each search result should start with a clickable headline, followed by a two- to three-line summary. The headline is the most important—in fact, the first words of the headline are the most important of all, since users don't even read an entire headline as they scan the search results. It's important to start the headline with the most information-carrying words that indicate what the page is about. The summary should elaborate on the headline without repeating it.

This SERP is easy to scan and has good headlines and reasonably good summaries. It is easy to page through the results because the arrow symbols at the top and bottom of the page provide nice big target links. The design of this page could be improved by removing the relevance percentages. People are focused on the titles and descriptions, not the percentages. Also, the user's query is repeated in the site's standard Search box in the upper-left corner, but on the SERP it's better to show the query in a wider Search box right on top of the results, so that the user will be more likely to spot it and use it to reformulate the queries.

www.americanheart.org

On some sites, you can add an indication of the address of the document below its summary—either the URL or the name of the area of the site that contains the document. But on most sites, this information is irrelevant and should be omitted in the interest of brevity.

You can also list the date when the document was updated, provided that this was in fact when real writing or editing was performed. If the dates only indicate when a typo was fixed or the document was moved to a different server, the feature is more misleading than useful.

This multi-national company's SERP does some things right but most things wrong. What's good: It repeats the user's query in an editable Search box and each Search hit has the expected format, with a headline, a summary that highlights occurrences of the query terms, and the URL. There's also an easy way to page through the results for those few users who want additional SERPs.

What's bad: There is no need to offer features to search for "all or any words." This should be relegated to Advanced Search instead of cluttering up the default Search page. The ability to search either all servers or regional servers is also an unwanted complication, and it should not be necessary to specify e-commerce as a special option. Often people searching for something that's for sale want the product page where they can buy it.

Because of the many extra features, the actual search results are pushed too far down the page. You can't even see the first hit in its entirety above the fold if you are using a screen with a resolution of 1024 by 768 pixels. There is no need to show the relevancy ratings, and it would be better to integrate the line for an item's location with the URL line in order to fit more search results on the screen. Finally, of course, the German headline in the fourth hit should not be used. English-speaking users are quite likely to skip this item, particularly since the summary doesn't make it clear that the article is in English.

Users rarely reformulate their queries if their first ones don't succeed. In the study we conducted for this book, users made do with a single query 83 percent of the time. In only 17 percent of searches did users try alternate queries. Still, it is helpful to make sure that users can perform query reformulation on the SERP: Include a Search box and prepopulate it with the query the user just issued so that they can modify it by simple editing.

Finally, the SERP can provide a link to the Advanced Search page. This link can be repeated at the bottom of the page, where users will see it if they scan to the end of the list and still haven't found what they were looking for.

Best Bets

Ideally Search software would always place the most important page for any query on top. In practice this doesn't happen because the computer is just a stupid machine that doesn't understand your business. It can only score pages by indirect measures, such as how frequently they use various words and how frequently other pages link to them.

In order to have your important pages rank above your secondary pages in Web-wide search engines, you have to fiddle with these secondary markers. This is known as Search Engine Optimization (SEO) and it is discussed in more depth later in this chapter.

Unfortunately you can't tell an external search engine what pages on your sites are the most important for each query—the search engine won't trust you and will try to second-guess you. But you *can* tell the search engine on your site what pages to put on top for important queries. This functionality is often known as "best bets," because you are betting that the pages you designate are going to be the best matches for your users' queries.

Construct your best bets to answer these queries:

- Product names and other brand names. When users search for these, they should get the main product page as the top hit.
- Product numbers, SKUs, catalog numbers, and other codes. Again, the main product page for the associated product should be the top hit. Never assume that users know such codes, but some users actually do.
- Category names. The main page for that category should be the top hit. Make sure to consider names that are frequently used in your industry to refer to a category, including those used by competing companies. Often each company has its own vocabulary but users don't always think of products or categories in the terms you use.
- Names of top executives and other key staff. The biography pages for these people should respond as the top hits.

When you add best bets to your search engine, you must manually construct a list of the best page or few pages for various user queries. If a user enters one of these queries, the search engine will simply place the best bets on top and then follow with its own algorithmically sorted results. It is best not to differentiate between your manually selected best bets and the computer-selected ones. Since users start scanning the SERP from the top, the best bets automatically get special prominence. If you put them in a box or otherwise highlight them, users may think that they are ads and ignore them.

A particularly fertile source of best bets is the query terms that your users enter most. Check your Search logs for the 100 or so most popular queries, enter each into your search engine, and see what comes up. If the top hit is not the most important page for that term, add it to your best bets list.

Once you have checked the 100 most frequent queries, continue down the list and check the next 100 queries. Continue until you have constructed best bets for all frequent queries.

Hewlett-Packard's SERP calls out a categorized set of related items in a column to the left of the main results. This is an interesting way of supplementing the best bet, which is the product page for the item the user searched for. For example, when we searched for a popular printer, the search engine appropriately placed the printer's product page on top of the main listings, but it also placed links to printing supplies for this printer in the left column. The page also uses the international dating convention, even though the search was performed on the U.S. area of the site. It would have been even better to spell out the name of each month.

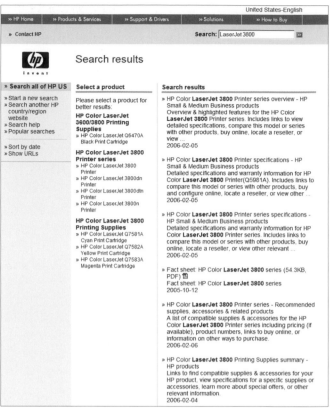

www.hp.com

Maintaining Best Bets

The best bet for a query should be the page on your site that's *currently* the most important for the query, not the one that was the most important last year. For example, if a new product model comes out, it should probably be the top hit for the model name, even if you keep pages for past models online for archival reasons and to provide continued support to your old customers.

You need an active program in place to monitor the best bets system and update the list of top pages for each query. You should also check your Search log from time to time—quarterly, for instance, to see if any new queries have become popular enough to deserve their own best bets.

　　　　　Prioritizing Web Usability

Sorting the SERP

Usually the SERP should be sorted by relevance, and no other options should be made available, since they will only confuse the user. For some types of sites, however, it makes sense to make other sorting criteria available. For example, sorting by date instead of relevance is useful for people who want to monitor recent events or find out what has changed on a site. Most people don't care about your periodic changes or updates, but for some site genres recent developments are of special importance. This is certainly true for news sites.

Giving users the flexibility to sort search results by attribute—such as price—can be very helpful. This is often the case on e-commerce sites or other product-heavy sites where users are searching for products rather than language documents.

Sorting by date can be useful on several types of Web sites beyond news sites. For example, users who want to assess the future product strategy of Yahoo! can search the U.S. Patent and Trademark Office to find out what patents the company has applied for recently.

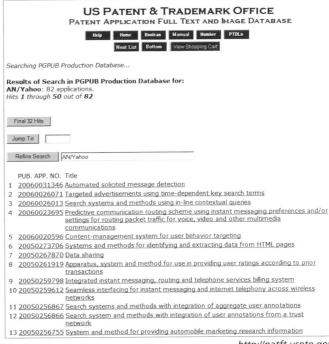

http://patft.uspto.gov

In most cases, it's best to offer users both ascending and descending views, and it's common to be able to toggle between the two. The default direction of the sort should be the one that makes the most sense to most users. For example, when sorting by date, place the newest materials on top for the search results. If the user clicks the date column, switch to showing the oldest stuff first. When sorting by price, show the cheapest items first and the most expensive items second.

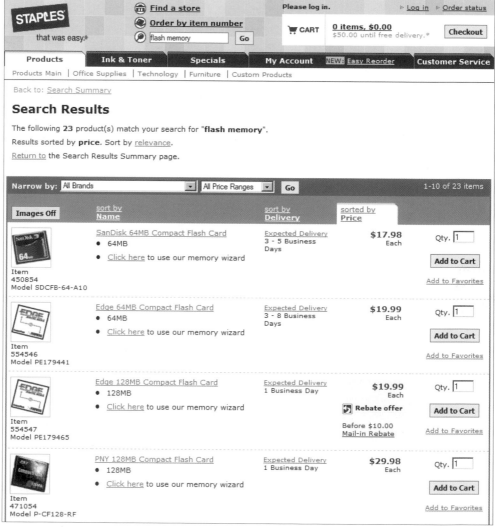

www.staples.com

No Results Found

When no results to a user's query are found, a special-case SERP is necessary. The first requirement for this page is that it clearly state that no results were found. Returning a blank page may make users sit and wait for the search to finish because there is no indication that it's already completed. Blank pages are also likely to make users think that something is broken.

Second, a no-results SERP should help users modify their queries to get better results. As with all SERPs, it should repeat users' queries in a Search box so that they can edit their queries easily, but it should also provide explicit hints for how to correct typical search mistakes. If you have a spelling correction feature—as we recommend—it should display suggestions for revised spellings prominently.

Finally, end the page with a link to your Advanced Search, if you have it. Although Advanced Search is usually more confusing than helpful, anything is better than finding nothing, and it's possible that the Advanced Search features will help users come up with a query that will work.

One Result Found

Another special case is when only one result is found. Some sites dispense with the SERP in this case and take you directly to the page that was found. We recommend against this for most sites because it violates user expectations for Search, which include seeing a SERP after issuing a query. Users can get confused when they see a content page instead of a listing of links after they have clicked the Search button.

Another reason to show the SERP even if there's a single hit is that users may want to modify their query once they see how little it found. You also need the SERP to show users alternative spellings or other features you have for query refinement.

The SERP can be skipped when users conduct a known-item query—for example, if they enter a SKU, part number, or other unique identifier that can't be considered full-text retrieval. In such cases, go straight to the page for that SKU.

(Facing page)   This SERP allows for sorting by three attributes of the products: name (which would mean brand if all products are named with the brand as the first word), delivery date, and price. Since the user in this screen shot searched for memory cards, it would have been nice if the SERP also allowed for sorting the list by storage capacity. Here the user has just clicked on the pricing column. A second click on "Sorted by Price" will reverse the sort order and place the most expensive products on top. (Why would anybody want the most expensive items? In this case, you may want to get the highest-capacity cards, and price is a way of identifying them when the system doesn't recognize capacity as a sortable attribute.)

The product thumbnails are not that useful for the type of products in this screen shot, though they do provide a fast way of scanning for brands. For items that are more visually differentiated, however, the thumbnails can be helpful. The main problem on this SERP is that the items are spaced too far apart because rebate offers and other features take up a lot of room. It is more difficult to use a SERP if users can see only a small number of items at a glance.

Search Engine Optimization

While not an exact science due to the vagaries of search engine technologies, SEO is a set of methods that is said to improve a Web site's ranking on a search engine. As we saw in Chapter 2, users almost always turn to search engines with a new problem but almost never read beyond the first page of results, so SEO should be one of the most important elements in your Internet strategy. Having a good listing on the first SERP for all relevant keywords is essential if you want to be found by people who are looking for your kind of products or services.

How do you get on the first page in major search engines? There is no sure way, and any consultant who promises to get you there is almost certainly a so-called "black-hat" SEO operator who employs unethical tricks that the search engines frown upon. In fact, search engines do more than frown: They usually remove a site they find guilty of trying to deceive them through black-hat SEO.

While working on this chapter, we serendipitously received this email. Of course, you should never buy anything from spammers. But in this case, there's another piece of basic advice that applies as well: If it sounds too good to be true, it probably is. Anybody who guarantees top placement on a leading search engine is almost certainly a black-hat SEO operator and is likely to get you booted from search engines instead.

The very first guideline for SEO is to refrain from using black-hat methods or hiring black-hat consultants. Only a few situations guarantee top placement: if you are a major company or government agency, or if you have an incredibly famous brand name that no other major organization in the world uses. In this case, you ought to be on the first SERP for your company name or brand name, and if you're not, it's usually because you are making some simple mistake on your Web site. An honorable SEO consultant can easily discover this and tell you how to fix it, and after some time you should see your site get better placement for this one keyword.

For all other query terms, it's not reasonable to expect to jump to the top of the listings in a week. If you are promised magic, you're probably getting deception, and it'll cost you dearly if you get bumped from the search engines.

Black-Hat SEO Tricks

Black-hat consultants attempt to manipulate search engines through techniques like these, all of which are considered foul play by the main search engines:

Cloaking. A Web site can send out different content depending on whether a page view is requested by a user or by the search engine's spider. This is usually called "cloaking" because the site hides its true content (what users see) behind a special page that's only made available to the search engine and is optimized to score well with that engine's software. Special pages that are created purely for search engines are called "doorway pages." It's possible (but not recommended) to have separate doorway pages with nonsense text that's optimized for each of your targeted keywords. These are not shown to users, who only see your "real" pages, which are not shown to search spiders.

Search spam: creating thousands or even millions of pages that have no real content but exist purely for the purpose of getting into search engines for every conceivable keyword. Similarly

it's considered spam to create huge numbers of duplicates of the information in the hope that it will show up more often in a search listing.

Link farms. Some black hat operators establish thousands of bogus Web sites that have no purpose other than to link to their client's Web site in an attempt to make these sites seem popular.

Comment spam: posting loads of comments on blogs, discussion forums, and other places on the Web that allow outsiders to add content. These comments invariably include a link to the poster's site in an attempt to drive up its ranking. Of course, any normal commenter will include a link to his or her homepage, but comments turn into spam when they are posted indiscriminately—often by an automated script that posts the same comment on thousands of innocent sites.

Domain repurposing: buying a Web site that has a respectable ranking in search engines, throwing out all the content that won the site its placement, and then using it for something completely different (usually pornography).

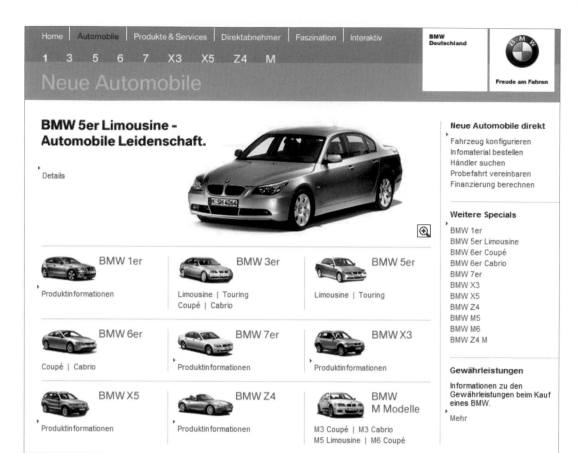

www.bmw.de

In 2006 Google banned BMW's main site in Germany for employing cloaking. (The company was reinstated after it repented and removed the offending features.) Search engines don't like cloaking because it tricks them into giving a page different treatment than the one it "deserves" based on the information that's given to regular users. Presumably BMW was moved to employ cloaking because its pages are so heavily graphical that there is not much text to be indexed by search engines. For example, the main headline about the 5er Limousine is an image of the letters and not actual text. The same is true for the category header "Neue Automobile" ("new cars"), even though these words also appear as actual text in the far right column. Two big differences between images of letters and real text: The screen readers employed by vision-impaired users can't read image-based text, and search engines can't index pixels. Search engines only understand actual text, so they are pretty much the world's most influential blind users.

SEO has a dubious reputation because of the proliferation of black-hat operators in the early years, but it's really an honorable profession, and today any major SEO consultancy will limit itself to white-hat methods that are completely ethical and well within the bounds of good Internet citizenship.

There are three major classes of "white hat" SEO techniques:

- Linguistic SEO

- Architectural SEO

- Reputation SEO

You should apply all three to your site. Fortunately almost everything you do to improve your ranking in Web-wide search engines will also improve the search engine on your site because it will give the software better data to chew on.

After that, practice patience. After improving your site to make it more findable, you shouldn't expect to get high rankings the next day. It can take months or even years to rise through the ranks. Assuming that you are still in business two years from now, you'll reap plenty of returns from your investment in SEO. Some benefits will certainly come sooner, but very few will come immediately.

Naming Names

If you are in the lucky position of naming a new company or brand, one of your first steps should certainly be to search possible names on all the major search engines. If prominent sites appear as results for a name, you should avoid it, even in cases where it would be legal for you to use it according to old-fashioned trademark law.

Consider the situation for the labor union for senior managers in British civil service, First Division Discounters Association, or FDA. With 13,000 members, all of whom are important people in the government, you would expect the FDA to get good treatment by the search engines. When searching for "FDA" on Google.co.uk, this site comes in second, which is not bad, but why isn't it first for its own name? The first listing is the U.S. American Food and Drug Administration; even in the U.K., the three-letter acronym FDA is used more often to refer to the American government agency than the British labor union. On Google.com, the British FDA comes in at number eight, and all the top seven hits refer to the American FDA in one form or another.

When the British FDA was founded in 1918, probably no one ever expected it to be confused with a major American government agency, but today it is. The British FDA will almost certainly never reach the top spot for its own name; it's a lost cause. But keeping a reasonably high position in the British search engines and a page-one listing in the rest of the world are reasonable goals.

If all else fails, run search ads. Of course, this is expensive and is expected to become even more so each year, so Search advertising is not a great substitute for having a good site that performs well on its own. But Search ads are a good short-term fix because they can usually be up quickly and results are immediate.

Search ads work so well because search engines are the one type of Web site that people visit with the explicit goal of finding someplace else to go. If they see an ad for what they're looking for, they will very likely click it. Advertisers can satisfy a user's immediate needs because they target ads based on users' query terms. (This also explains why ads on search engine homepages don't work: It's impossible to target the ad to the user's current quest until the server knows what that quest is.)

Tip: The Beauty of Using Text-Only Ads

Most search engine advertising comes as small boxes with nothing but text—no big, colorful, blinking banners. Perhaps because text-only ads are a low-end media format, users actually take them more seriously. Also, having to express a message in a few words probably leads advertisers to be more focused and communicative. The text-only format exposes content-free messages as useless, and thus might save advertisers from the bad instincts they honed on old media.

Although there is no inherent reason that you can't use text for mindless chatter—like *"where do you want to go today?"*—you won't find users clicking on such ads. Ignoring users' immediate needs is certain death on the Web.

Companies that run rich-media ads that disregard users can delude themselves into thinking that they're "promoting the brand"; in reality, they're being ignored because they don't connect with people's needs. After 13 years of watching Web users, we can clearly conclude that they are utterly selfish and live in the moment. Giving users exactly what they want right now is the way to Web success, and having to write small boxes of text encourages advertisers to travel it.

If you run paid advertisements on search engines, you should track the value of visitors who come to your site after clicking on these ads. This is the only way to determine how much to bid for clicks. Say you discover that the conversion rate for visitors from Search ads is one percent and that you make $10 profit from each converting visitor. Then you make ten cents profit from each user who clicks the ads, meaning that you can bid up to nine cents per click and still make a profit.

Avoid the following two classic mistakes when tracking the conversion rate and other return on investment data for search ads:

- Do not confuse clicks on ads that appear on a SERP with clicks on ads from the advertising network run by a search engine. Just because a search company manages a net-

work of sites doesn't mean the sites are search sites. Typically the value of ads on content pages is much lower than the value of SERP ads because readers of content pages are just browsing and may click your ad out of idle interest. You should probably pay much less for non-Search ads; if you analyze them together with the Search ads, your ROI will be messed up.

- Do not use conversion trackers or other Web analytics offered by the search engines. Remember, search engines decide how much to charge you for your advertising, so you don't want them to know how much money you make from each ad. Always use site analytics packages from independent providers who do not have a stake in how much you are charged.

Linguistic SEO

Users typing queries into search engines rarely think to use the kind of words you might employ in your latest slogans or other approved corporatese. That's why writing with the words that your audience knows and uses is very important.

Speak the user's language, especially if you want to be found in search engines. Users type queries using their own vocabulary.

There are two reasons why you should also write plain-spoken headlines that include these keywords. First, search engines tend to assign extra weight to words in page titles and other headlines; second, users scan search listings and often do not read beyond the headlines. If some of the words users type for their queries appear in your headline, they are more likely to pay attention to your listing.

In the SEO field, finding out what words customers use is usually referred to as "keyword research." There are many Web sites and software services dedicated to helping you perform keyword research. For example, Yahoo! offers a free Keyword Selector Tool that lets you enter a term and get suggestions for related terms. Yahoo! also tells you how frequently its users searched for each of the suggested terms in the last month. This allows you a first cut at prioritizing what keywords to optimize for. (However, you ought to perform your own analysis in addition, since the true importance of keywords for you depends on their use by *your* target audience.)

Tip: Keyword Overuse Backfires

One of the few times that SEO guidelines conflict with usability guidelines is in the case of keyword density. SEO consultants often want you to stuff your pages with repeated use of targeted keywords even though this can reduce readability. Usually it comes naturally to use an important term several times on a page, but if you find yourself writing convoluted sentences in order to include a keyword once more, it's time to stop. After all, it does no good to attract more searchers to your page if all they do is bounce out immediately because the page makes no sense or is unhelpful.

Google offers its advertising customers a tool that suggests keywords relevant to their products and services. How can Google know your products? Actually, it just reads what you have already written about them on your Web site and then finds related terms that users frequently search for. This screen shot shows the top keywords Google suggested for promoting this book based on the Web page we made to sell the book to the readers of our own site. The list is not perfect (for example, it includes "intranet usability" even though we cover special guidelines for intranet usability elsewhere, but not in this book), but it's a great starting point for selecting the keywords to promote the book.

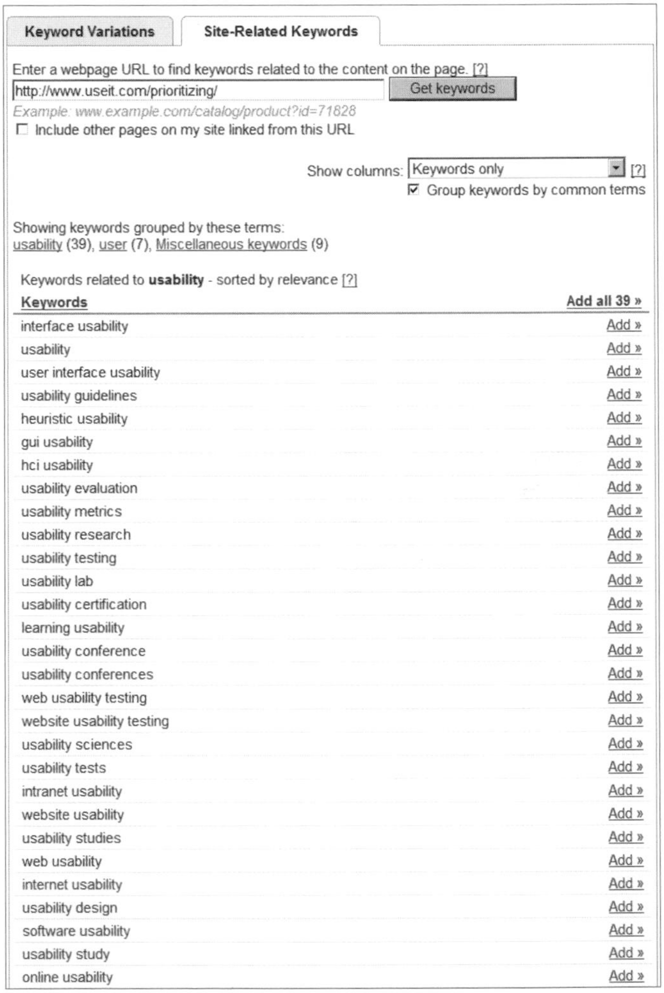

http://adwords.google.com

The two best methods for discovering your users' terminology are your own search logs and user testing. You can review the log files for the search engine on your site to discover the queries that your customers have entered. Obviously, you are not learning what people who never found your site might have typed, but your search logs are still the best source material for raw queries.

To get a broader idea of users' vocabulary, listen to what they say in user testing. How do they describe their problems and your products? Probably in completely different terms than the ones used by your marketing department. You can also use transcripts from focus groups for this, although you'll run into the problem of groupthink: Once one focus group member has started using a certain word to describe something, other members will too. This is one of the reasons we almost always prefer one-on-one sessions to group sessions for our studies.

Finally you can listen in on customer support calls and read blogs and discussion groups to get more information about users' language. One word of caution is that bloggers and people who participate in online discussion groups tend to be unrepresentative of the customer base at large. But their words are probably a better indication of customers' language than anything you'll hear inside your own company.

In thinking about what customer terminology to use on your Web pages, it is important to emphasize the words people use to describe their *problem*. It's a common mistake when you are selling a *solution* to focus on describing your features and maybe even your benefits without addressing the underlying problem. But people will often search for information about their current pain point without necessarily knowing what's out there to alleviate it.

Architectural SEO

Architectural SEO has two components: ensuring that your pages can be indexed and having an appropriate linking structure to guide the search spiders to your content.

To have a search engine index your content, that content must be actual text. Pictures of text don't work because a search engine spider is effectively blind to images. Search engines also currently can't index information that's presented in various multimedia formats such as video or audio files. It's fine to include multimedia on your Web site if it otherwise works for users (see Chapter 11 for guidelines on this), but for the information to be indexed by search engines, you must supplement the multimedia files with a textual description.

Search engines discover pages on your Web site by following the links. This means that the links must be encoded in plain HTML that can easily be decoded to tell the spider where to look next. It also means that your URLs must look like they describe regular Web pages instead of dynamically created pages. It doesn't matter whether the page is created dynamically inside your computer. What matters is that the search engine spider thinks that it's a regular page that will be there with the same content the next time a user comes around. For many spiders, this means ignoring anything after a question mark in the URL because this notation usually indicates a database query or other forms of one-time content.

Make sure that there is a clean path of links from your homepage to any page you want indexed in the search engines. The anchor text for the links should describe the most important function of each page on your site. Search engines often place extra emphasis on the text used to describe a link to a page. Having good link text is a primary usability guideline in any case because users often scan pages looking for links and need to see where they go without having to read too much.

Additionally, make sure that there are more links to the main page for a concept than to less important pages since search engines tend to give priority to heavily linked pages. If people search for one of your products and find a minor mention in a press release listed higher than the main product page, your architecture is faulty. One way to correct this is to make the press release link back to the product page. Also, if you have hierarchical information architecture, the link structure should reflect those levels, and provide more links to the higher ones. Using breadcrumbs as auxiliary navigation is one way to achieve this because a breadcrumb trail will always include links to the main pages and use their name as the anchor text.

You can initiate an active outreach effort to attract links to your site. For example, include links in your press releases and sites that carry the news will sometimes link to you.

Reputation SEO

Search engines try to give their users the best results by placing heavy emphasis on the reputation of sites. Sites that are widely considered to be good usually score higher than sites that are considered bad.

To achieve high ranking on the SERPs, you need to make other Web sites link to you. Furthermore links are given more points if they come from sites that themselves have high reputations, so you should particularly emphasize getting links from important sites. The main way to attract links is simply to have a good Web site that's worth linking to. If you have a high-quality product, people will link to it when they discuss it. If you have interesting content or helpful services, people will link to you.

Of course, other sites can only link to you if you make this possible by having simple URLs for each page and by keeping the same URLs alive forever. If you have linkrot, you lose the search engine ranking that could have come from anybody who linked to an old URL. Conversely, if you keep the same URL year after year for the same concept or service, you will gradually build up its ranking.

In addition to having a great site that others naturally want to link to, you can initiate an active outreach effort to attract links to your site. For example, include links in any press releases you issue, and sites that carry the news will sometimes link to you. Without the URL in the release, you are depending on other sites to discover the appropriate URL, which is extra work and often not done. It's also good to ensure that trade associations and other groups you belong to link to your site from their sites.

Finally, you can submit your site to appropriate online directories such as switchboard.com. Some of these directories charge money to list sites, and such paid directories are rarely as highly rated as those that are editorially determined. However, depending on how highly your site is rated, it may be worth paying for inclusion even if it only gives you a small boost in ratings.

6 Navigation and Information Architecture

Chaotic design leads to dead ends and wasted effort. Hastily thrown-up Web sites without effective information schemes prevent users from getting to the information they seek. When this happens, they may give up or, even worse, go to a different site.

A well-structured site gives users what they want when they want it. In this chapter we look at some of the most common design obstacles that stand between users and their goals— and provide guidelines on how to avoid them.

Over and over again, the people in our studies struggled to get information they wanted, cursing and complaining along the way. In fact, difficulty finding what they were looking for was the biggest problem for our users. Although Search was the single most problematic design issue, four other areas that we collectively call "findability" caused even more difficulties.

These four—navigation and menus; category names; links; and information architecture (IA), which is how the information space is structured—determine how easy it is to find things by clicking around a site, as opposed to going directly through Search. (Many people consider "category names" to be a subsidiary issue of "information architecture" because structuring and naming often go hand in hand. But because they involve different kinds of design decisions, we feel it's worth considering them as separate issues.)

Am I There Yet?

Poorly designed Web sites do more than slow users down —they can actually discourage them from using the site. When people can't find what they need, they often assume that the information isn't available there. In frustration, they may go elsewhere.

With a sympathetic design, people find and manage information effortlessly; the labeling, layout, and relationship between individual pages are clearly represented. Good navigation design shows people where they are, where things are located, and how to get the things they need in a methodical way. An appropriate IA makes people comfortable to explore and confident that they can easily return to previously viewed pages.

One of the biggest compliments a site can get is when people *don't* comment on its structure in user testing. On well-organized sites, users can freely move along, focusing on their task, without having to worry about the site's structure. It's the designer's job to worry about the site's structure, not the users'.

One of the biggest compliments a site can get is when people don't comment on its structure in user testing. It's the designer's job to worry about the site's structure, not the users'.

Trying to design your site's structure without the input of your custom-ers is a huge mistake that can cost you thousands to millions of dollars. Design for their convenience, not yours.

Match the Site Structure to User Expectations

The most effective sites at directing people to the right place are those that match user expectations. We know that users won't spend the time to memorize or learn the navigation of different Web sites. Allocating adequate resources to design the best IA for your site ensures that customers find answers they need in the places they expect. The more natural the design feels, the more likely users will return to it.

People don't like to wade through many ambiguous links to get to content. They expect sites to organize information in a way that makes sense to them. Use a navigational structure that reflects their view of the site and its information and services. Remember, the operative word is "them," not "you."

You might think that your site's organizational structure is intuitive. One of the biggest mistakes organizations make when categorizing components is to use schemes that are familiar to them, such as arranging products by brand or mirroring sites' content to their organizational charts. As a result, it's common for sites to make perfect sense to the creators but not to their end-users.

Why? Because how you and your company structure and organize information may be very different from how your users envision it. If you're selling flashlights, for example, it's better to organize by attributes that users may be looking for, such as travel size, than by brand names, such as Xeon. While Xeon may be a familiar line of flashlights within your organization, it may not be to your customers.

Trying to design the structure of your site without the input of your customers is a huge mistake that can cost you thousands to millions of dollars. No matter how good and fancy your site may look, it's useless if it doesn't make sense to your target audience. Design for their convenience, not yours.

(Facing page, top) This site is too brand centric. To figure out what billiard table best fits their needs, people who are unfamiliar with the brands must click each of the three options: Mizerak, Murrey, and Mosconi. This is a waste of their time. And the marketing descriptions for each brand don't provide the kind of information that might help people get closer to finding what they want.

How should your site be organized? Although we strongly advise you to design your structure to reflect your users' thinking and tasks, we can't offer you a cookie-cutter method for doing so. What people need from different sites varies, so each site's optimal IA is dictated by the unique purposes and goals of the organization and its users. The topic of creating usable IAs and navigational schemes can—and does—fill entire books. We bring it up here simply to stress its importance. When users can do what they set out to do on your site, you will reap the benefits.

(Facing page, bottom) Even though the Escalade site does provide information about different types and styles of equipment, users missed it because the prominent logos and branding overshadowed links to that material:

"I found that it was difficult. Once you got to the manufacturer, that was the end of the road. You couldn't look at the product individually.... I didn't particularly like that."

"Each individual product label is selling the company that sells the product, instead of the product."

"I can't find it. I would go to a different Web site. I would go to Google."

Intranet IA

The guideline to avoid structuring a site around a company's internal structure only applies to Web sites targeted at an external audience. When designing for an internal audience of employees, other rules apply.

A company's employees often do know how the company is structured. Also, many of the tasks that employees do are naturally related to the company's structure. Employees often need to look up the organizational chart to find out who runs a department and how various departments are connected.

It is a good idea to have an explicit representation of the company's structure on the intranet. But it is still best even for intranets not to structure their IA around the org chart. Most of the best intranets we have studied use job performance, workflow, and frequent employee tasks as the foundation for their IA.

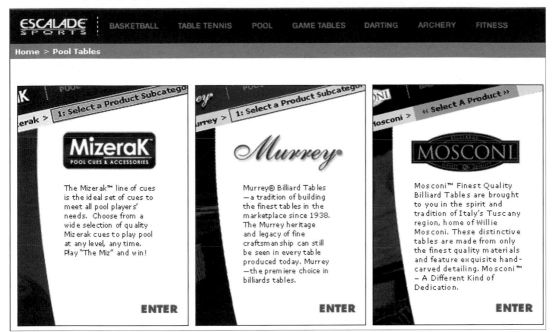

The Mizerak™ line of cues is the ideal set of cues to meet all pool players' needs. Choose from a wide selection of quality Mizerak cues to play pool at any level, any time. Play "The Miz" and win!

Murrey® Billiard Tables — a tradition of building the finest tables in the marketplace since 1938. The Murrey heritage and legacy of fine craftsmanship can still be seen in every table produced today. Murrey — the premiere choice in billiards tables.

Mosconi™ Finest Quality Billiard Tables are brought to you in the spirit and tradition of Italy's Tuscany region, home of Willie Mosconi. These distinctive tables are made from only the finest quality materials and feature exquisite hand-carved detailing. Mosconi™ – A Different Kind of Dedication.

ENTER   **ENTER**   **ENTER**

Harvard game tables offer a wide array of quality built games to meet all your family needs. Whether you're looking for the most durable foosball games, the fastest action table hockey games, the many choices offered by multi-game tables or the latest in interactive electronic sports games, Harvard game tables has the right choice for everyone in your family.

www.blackmountainbicycles.com

This site tries to meet the needs of a broad audience by categorizing bicycles by both brand and type. Those who are already familiar with a brand can access it by name, and those who are looking by function or other features can search by type. Unfortunately, this site doesn't make the latter option readily apparent. Users must select a brand before they're offered a place to search products by features such as type and price.

(Facing page, top) **Proper categorization:** In our testing, people using the City of San Diego site didn't mind the massive number of links on the homepage because it is organized with short, meaningful headers; users prefer short descriptive links to long, detailed descriptions. Notice how the subcategories help define the larger categories by providing specific of the content found inside each. For example, it's not always obvious what a category such as Community would encompass and we would usually advise against it. But on this site, it's clear what's inside this area because its six subcategories tell you. The site also uses the generic subcategory *more,* however, which we don't recommend because it isn't self-explanatory.

www.sandiego.gov

www.cummins.com

Improper Categorization: Users who tested this site expected to find information on fuel cell technology under Products, not under Who We Are, where it is the last option on the menu. This miscategorization made people struggle or think that the information didn't exist here:

"Now I'm lost…. It doesn't help me. I don't feel like I have options. I have to browse around. It's not easily found in the upper columns [the global navigational choices]."

"I'm looking for a fuel cell category. I don't see it under Products."

"That took a little too long!"

Navigation: Be Consistent

Consistency is a fundamental concept in navigation. Keeping a consistent navigational structure helps people visualize their current location and options, and minimizes guesswork. Navigational elements act as stepping-stones to help people traverse from one area to the next.

Changing navigation is like removing stepping-stones while users are still in midair; when they land, it's not where they expected. Navigation that was on the left on the previous page may now be in the middle; the categories have changed. The back button doesn't work and there's no easy way to return to the previous pages.

When navigation changes drastically from one page to the next, people must shift their attention from using the site to figuring out how to use it. Web sites with unreliable navigation make users uncertain and hesitant.

Large Web sites comprised of subsites or affiliated sites are notorious for committing this crime. Each subsite is usually created by a different group and has its own organization and look-and-feel. When the subsites are linked together haphazardly, user experience is atrocious. People must often request the same thing multiple times because each subsite acts independently. Corporate Web sites, for example, feel disjointed when investor relations, press relations, and product sections have their own navigational schemes and look completely different.

Good navigation is predictable and makes people feel comfortable exploring the site. It doesn't need to be studied or memorized because it reflects their impression of how information should be represented in Web space. It has sense and order, and there's little or no ambiguity about where items are. Users can move forward, backtrack, explore, and feel confident that they will not lose their way.

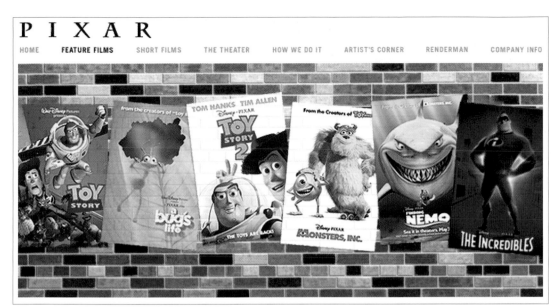

www.pixar.com

The simple global navigation area at the top of the Pixar site stays visible and consistent throughout the site. Whether people are on Feature Films or About Us, they know where to look for various navigational options. Our users felt that they could confidently explore the site and easily return to an area at any point:

"It just states everything on top. You don't have to look around. It was set up and laid out very well. Your eyes don't have to wander all over the screen."

"Everything you click is connected to each other. It seems like an easy Web site to use."

Social Security Online
www.socialsecurity.gov

Retirement & Medicare

Home   Questions?   How to Contact Us   Search

Plan Your Retirement

I want to...

Find my retirement age

Learn about factors that may affect my retirement benefits

Calculate my benefits

Learn about Social Security programs

Decide when to retire

Apply for retirement

Find out what happens if I work after retirement

Social Security's retirement program has been a basic part of American life for more than 68 years. In addition to benefits for retired workers, Social Security also provides financial support to younger workers and their families who face a loss of income due to disability or the death of a family wage earner.

Because we're living longer, healthier lives, we can expect to spend more time in retirement than our parents and grandparents did. Achieving a secure, comfortable retirement is much easier when you plan your finances. Most financial planners recommend you prepare for the future with a combination of Social Security, private pensions and personal savings.

If you're getting Social Security benefits when you turn 65, your Medicare Hospital Benefits start automatically. If you're not getting Social Security, you should sign up for Medicare close to your 65th birthday, even if you aren't ready to retire.

Depending on what you own and how much income you have, you may be eligible for Supplemental Security Income (SSI) when you are 65 or older. You may be eligible for SSI prior to age 65 if you are disabled or blind.

Plan your retirement here

Get an estimate of your retirement benefit using our calculators

FirstGov

Privacy Policy | Accessibility Policy | Linking Policy | Site Map

Benefits.gov

Social Security Online
www.socialsecurity.gov

Retirement Planner

Home   Questions? ▾   Contact Us ▾   Search [   ] GO

Planners Home

Decide When to Retire

Retirement Planner Home

Benefit Calculators

Eligibility Issues

Near Retirement?

Apply for Benefits Online

Frequently Asked Questions

Other Resources

A secure, comfortable retirement is every worker's dream. And now because we're living longer, healthier lives, we can expect to spend more time in retirement than our ancestors did. Achieving the dream of a secure, comfortable retirement is much easier when you plan your finances.

Your Social Security benefits are the foundation on which you can build a secure retirement. Most financial advisors say you'll need about 70 percent of your pre-retirement earnings to comfortably maintain your pre-retirement standard of living. Under current law, if you have average earnings, your Social Security retirement benefits will replace only about 40 percent. The percentage is lower for people in the upper income brackets and higher for people with low incomes. You'll need to supplement your benefits with a pension, savings or investments.

How the Social Security Retirement Planner can help you now

This planner provides detailed information about your Social Security retirement benefits **under current law** and points out things you may want to consider as you prepare for the future. You can use the calculators to test out different retirement ages or different future earnings amounts. If you are already near retirement age, you'll find instructions on how to apply for benefits and what supporting documents you'll need to furnish. There is also information about how members of your family may qualify for benefits with you.

Use the buttons on the side or click on the links below to check out the information you need:

- Calculate your retirement benefits using different retirement scenarios.

www.ssa.gov

(Facing page) The overlapping content areas and inconsistent navigational options on the U.S. Social Security Web site invite errors. Selecting different but similar sounding paths yields different results. For example, finding your retirement age is easy if you select Plan Your Retirement from the homepage. However, if you opt for a different route and enter the Retirement Planner, it's more difficult to find your retirement age. The "Find my retirement age" link is prominent in the first example but not available in the second, even though both appear to be retirement planners. Compare the two screens and notice the overlapping choices between them. Such unstructured IA causes people to forget what they clicked on and what their remaining choices are, leading to comments like these:

"I would think the retirement age would be easy to find, but I didn't locate it. It makes me feel stupid."

"It could be more user-friendly. It needs to think like a new user."

www.ssa.gov

When visitors to this site click Learn About Factors that Affect Your Retirement Benefits, the choices on the previous screen disappear and are replaced by ones that are different but somewhat related. This caused confusion among our test users. For example, it was not clear to them whether Calculate My Benefits on the previous screen is the same as Benefit Calculators. The burden is placed on users to sift through the various links and determine which are the same and which have new information.

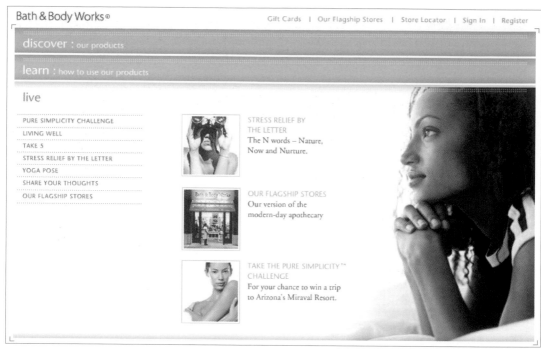

www.bathandbodyworks.com

The topics under the main categories on this site expand and contract depending on which category the user selects. Each of the three panels has different topics and navigational styles. The extreme changes in navigation disoriented our users:

"I'm getting myself lost. I don't know where I was now."

"It has three different bars; it would be easier if it were on one homepage, rather than clicking on three places to get more information."

"This is a frustrating because you can't find what you want."

"I don't even remember: Did I click on fragrance? Where am I?"

"It wasn't obvious where things are. You had to search and hunt more than on other sites."

(Facing page) The inconsistent navigational scheme on Nestlé's site made it difficult for our users to find their way. The global navigation changes for different sections. For example, the main navigation on the All About Nestlé page appears on top and on the side. The main navigational elements on the Nutrition page, however, are only on top, but in two levels. Here's what users said about this site:

"It's not something that I will go back to because it was difficult and awkward to navigate. I like a different style of Web site—I like a side bar where you can see things. Here you have a couple top bars and other things going on. I'm all over the place."

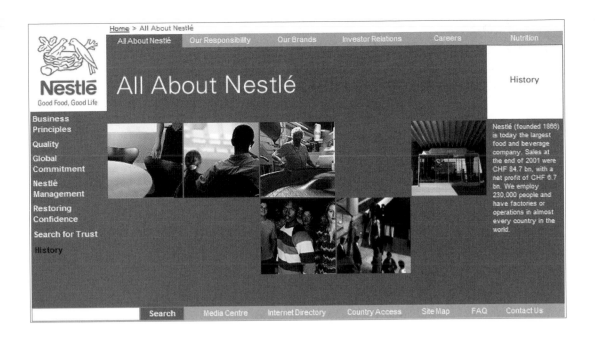

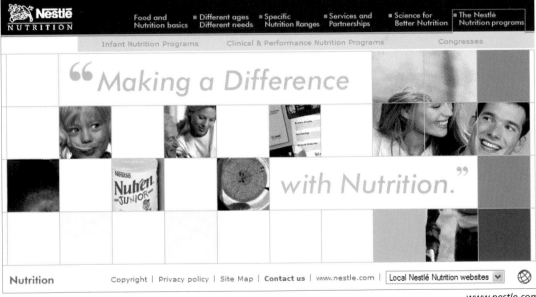

"I'm not finding what I'm looking for on this site. If I were going to look for a snack food, I would leave because I'm not seeing it."

"I ended up wasting a lot of time trying to find what I need."

"There is so much information. And trying to complete the tasks took a little longer than I would have thought. It got confusing trying to find a few simple things."

Navigation: Beware the Coolness Factor

Navigation is a means to an end: Its purpose is to get people where they need to be quickly. The more efficient you make it, the more likely people will stay interested.

Main topics should be static and appear at once so people can quickly skim through the choices. Waiting for navigation to slowly load or rotate is a waste of their time. Any type of dynamic navigation needs to be easy to operate. Menus that are too sensitive and change even at the slightest mouse movement may be more cumbersome than they're worth—and they'll kill your chances of getting any business from senior citizens, people with disabilities, and novice Web users.

Users are not looking for a scavenger hunt, so don't hide main navigational items. It's not enjoyable to chase moving targets or move the pointer around a site ("minesweeping") in hopes of finding something clickable. It is even more difficult for a person with reduced manual dexterity or motor impairments who has a hard time controlling the mouse. It's much faster for everyone to survey options when they're simply visible.

In sum, avoid cute and fancy navigation. People despise it. Save your creative juices for those areas of your site that users actually care about.

Kids Like Minesweeping

In user testing, we have found that children aged 6 to 12 enjoy the minesweeping that we otherwise warn against. Kids often view Web sites as a game and appreciate the opportunity to explore an environment and make it reveal its secrets. In particular, they don't mind moving the mouse across a well-drawn graphic to see what's behind it.

By their teens, however, kids have lost their appetite for minesweeping. Teenagers are impatient and want fast results when using Web sites.

In general, the usability guidelines for teens are somewhat different from those for adults, and the guidelines for young children are very different from those for adults. There are certainly many similarities, but if you are targeting younger users, we recommend that you conduct separate user studies with people from that age group. Except when otherwise stated, the guidelines in this book relate to adult users.

BOOK NOW
BUY SHOW TICKETS
SIGN GUEST BOOK
INVESTOR RELATIONS
CONTACT
ABOUT

WYNN LAS VEGAS

ROOMS & SUITES | DINING | THE SHOWS | FIGHT NIGHT | SHOPPING | GOLF | RESERVA

© 2005 Wynn Resorts, Holdings.

www.wynnlasvegas.com

The main menu on this site automatically moves across the page at a slow and steady pace. If you want Reservations, for example, you wait for it to appear. You could increase the speed by moving the pointer over the arrows, but who wants to mess with that? Web sites should be able to maintain an elegant design without sucking up people's time.

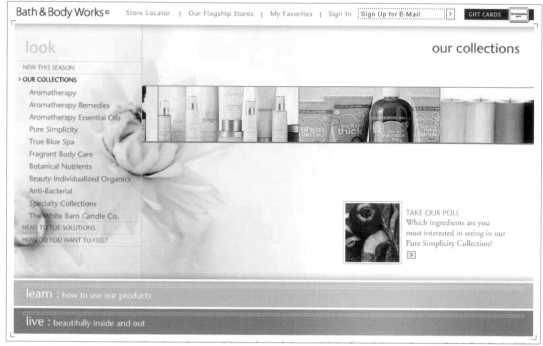

www.bathandbodyworks.com

Old design: Our users were frustrated when the product offerings on this site moved as they moved their mouse over the page. Some had no idea that they were controlling the movement! In general, people resent having to scrub their mouse over one area at a time to get information. Some of our users didn't have the patience to hunt for products in this manner and said they would give up:

"It moves around too much. When you try to get to an item, it moves. It makes you dizzy. I don't like it."

"It's frustrating that it goes away when I'm trying to get to it."

New design: This Bath & Body Works redesign is better and eliminates several of the usability problems we found in our user testing. Static pages have replaced the fancy dynamic interaction model. People no longer have to move their pointer over pictures to get product descriptions.

We have included screenshots from the previous design because its flaws still appear on other sites. Just as Bath & Body Works learned its lesson, you can too. And unlike them, you may not have to lose business first!

www.dimewill.com

www.atlantis.com

(Facing page, top) Hidden navigational labels trip people up. For example, this page doesn't appear to have anything to click until users hover their pointers to reveal text labels. Some of our users didn't realize this and wondered what they were supposed to do on this page. People prefer visible choices so they can be reviewed in a single glance.

(Facing page, bottom) The navigational panel on this site appears only after people move their pointers over the graphical areas in the center. Our users balked at having to conjure the navigational menu each time they needed it.

Reduce Clutter and Avoid Redundancy

Don't provide multiple navigation areas for the same types of links. Categories that are duplicated or indistinguishable complicate the interface, making users work hard to create order. People must expend effort to figure out the difference between links with similar names. And overemphasizing links by sprinkling the same ones all over the page actually decreases the likelihood that viewers will see them. In fact, the fewer objects on the page, the more likely people will notice them. With many competing elements, all items lose prominence.

It's best to clearly feature something in one place. Reducing redundancy minimizes clutter, making it easier for people to find information.

Don't Be Duped by Duplicates

Clients often tell us that they would like to retain redundant links on their homepage or elsewhere on the site because each of the links attracts substantial traffic. Sometimes they even quote statistics showing that traffic to a page increased when the links were duplicated.

While such statistics may sound compelling, they are often deceiving. Yes, it's true that each link gets clicks, but that doesn't mean that users wouldn't have found the destination if there had been only one link. Say the same links are at the top and bottom of a page. Users often consider the link at the top but decide to check out the rest of the page before they click it. Reaching the bottom of the page, they may click the second link instead, but if it wasn't there, they would have scrolled back up and clicked at the top.

It's also true that duplicating a link can increase overall traffic to a destination, but that's simply because you are promoting that item more heavily than others and giving it more screen space. Making a link bigger or placing it more prominently on the page can yield the same result without creating confusion. Furthermore, any time you promote one item, the net result is *less* traffic to other items on the page. Users only have so much attention to give you, so when you grab more of it for one link, you lose it for the others.

In the end, you usually lose more than you gain by using duplicate links. Even if you increase traffic to a specific page, you may lose return traffic to the site from users who were confused and couldn't find what they wanted.

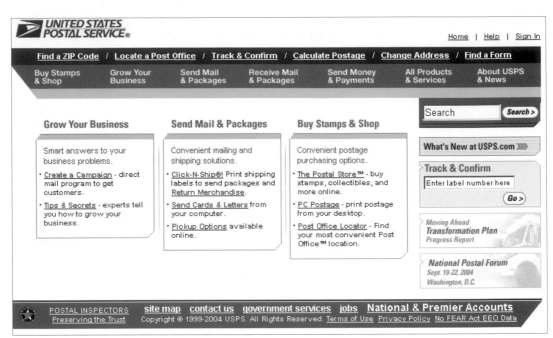

www.usps.com

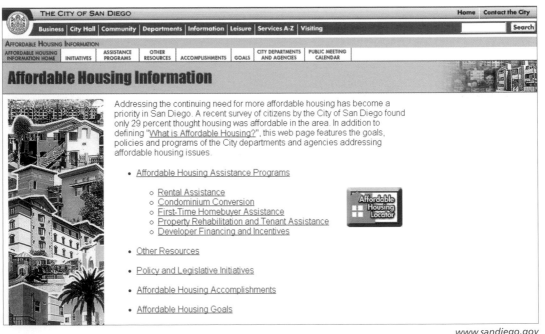

www.sandiego.gov

(Facing page,top) Duplicate links unnecessarily complicate the United States Postal Service site. The options in the middle of the page are identical to the links in the blue area at the top.

(Facing page,bottom) The City of San Diego repeats tabs at the top that are already in the main content area of the page. It would be better to show the navigation in one obvious place and reserve the remaining area for other relevant content or leave it as white space.

www.escaladesports.com

The Escalade Sports Web site offers redundant navigational methods: the text list method and a graphical method (with circular dial). Most of our users opted for the text method because it is easier to scan. As a last resort, others used the graphic but were disappointed to discover that both methods led to the same information. What a waste of time!

Links and Label Names: Be Specific

Make sure users can easily understand your navigational labels. When people are in navigation mode, they usually ignore large blocks of content and home in on links to glean the site's meaning. Keep link names as brief and specific as possible to maximize scanning. Clever made-up words or category names are problematic because people don't understand them. If you must have clever names, always explain their meaning. People tend to skip over meaningless words.

Tighten up your links by starting with keywords or an information word. Remove extraneous words, such as repeating your company name in each link; this adds unnecessary complexity to the interface. Links that start with identical or redundant phrases require people to carefully read all of them to glean the differences.

Don't use generic instructions such as Click Here as link names. Instead, help people quickly differentiate links by giving them informative names. Rather than just linking to More, for example, tell users specifically what they'll get *more* of.

(Facing page, top) Old design: Vague words and category labels such as discover, learn, and live annoyed our users. Some wondered what "live: with our products" meant. Even with the description, the wording is trite and unclear. A label such as "how to have a healthy lifestyle" would provide more useful information. Catchy names are useless if they don't help people predict what's behind the link:

"The topics aren't what I think they're going to be—like Head to Toe Solutions should be Body Wash or something like that."

"I think this is hard to do. There aren't enough categories to quickly find what I'm looking for."

(Facing page, bottom) New design: After we had completed the test described in the previous figure, Bath & Body Works redesigned its site. This homepage replaces vague category names such as learn and live with more direct ones, such as Face, Hair, and Articles & Advice. Good move.

www.bathandbodyworks.com

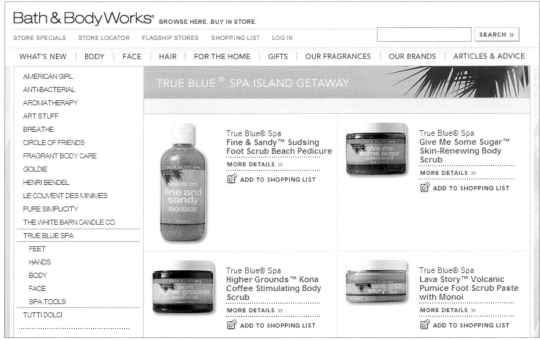

www.bathandbodyworks.com

BBW never stops. As we were finishing this chapter, the company launched yet another redesign, this time with more descriptive navigation labels. Even though the label Face would be too obscure on most Web sites, we thought that it was acceptable here. Yet even on this site, the new, more explicit label Facial Skincare has stronger information scent and thus works better at directing users to the products they want to buy.

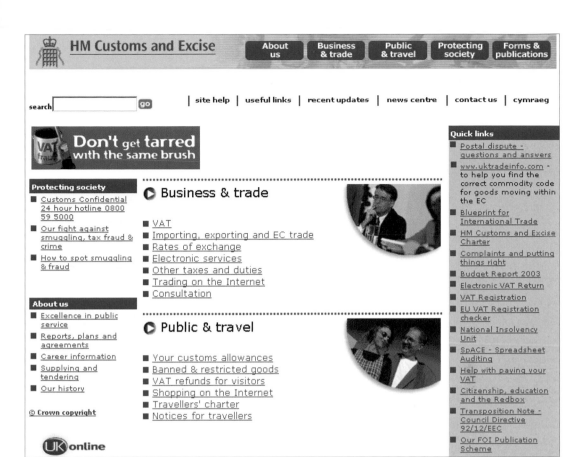

www.hmce.gov.uk

Old homepage: The British government's revenue and customs site homepage provides facts about Value Added Tax refunds and other information of interest to travelers with descriptive links such as "Your customs allowances" and "VAT refunds for visitors," which tell users exactly what information is behind them. The site smartly places commonly used links in the main area of the page, free from many other distractions.

www.hmce.gov.uk

New Homepage: Unfortunately, this redesigned homepage is a definite downgrade in usability because the headers, links, and navigation don't say exactly what they mean. For example, what is "eVat Services"? If you just traveled to the U.K. for vacation, what would you click on to see how you can get your Value Added Tax refund? There are many places that say VAT, but which one is the best choice? In the old design, there was an obvious link that said "VAT refunds for visitors," but this no longer exists. Bad move.

In general, it's almost always a warning sign when you find yourself using names that start with "e" or "Internet." Users know that they are online when they are accessing a Web site, and there's no need to call further attention to this fact by cyberfying the names of your services.

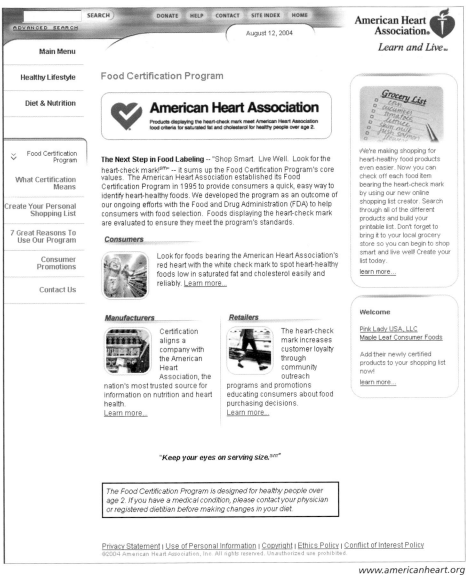

www.americanheart.org

The generic "Learn more" links sprinkled throughout the American Heart Association site don't help guide users to the areas of interest. People can't quickly scan the links to get the gist of their meaning. Instead, they are required to read the caption, which unnecessarily slows them down. It's better to explicitly tell people what they'll learn more of than to tease them with links that don't contain pertinent information.

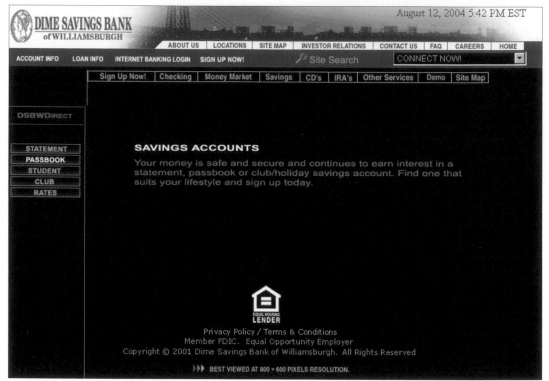

People find it difficult to differentiate between meaningless category names such as Club and Passbook. It's nearly impossible to glance at the options and decipher their meaning without clicking on each. This type of navigation requires too much work.

(Facing page, top)   Old design: This car site stumps users because its vehicles are organized by model name. This is fine for people who are familiar with Honda models but not for those who aren't. Users in our testing wondered what kinds of vehicles the different models were and didn't know, for example, the difference between an Odyssey and an S2000. While there is an All Models link at the bottom of the list, many people overlooked it.

(Facing page, bottom)   New design: Honda improved its navigation categories slightly in this redesign. Note that the link previously labeled Odyssey is now Odyssey Minivan and that S2000 has been changed to S2000 Roadster. These changes are not much better than band-aids, though: They dress the wounds without curing the disease. It would have been better to design a navigation system that clearly explained the difference between the models rather than still requiring users to navigate by model.

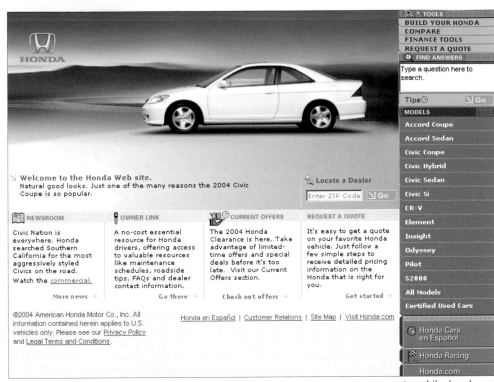

Welcome to the Honda Web site.
Natural good looks. Just one of the many reasons the 2004 Civic Coupe is so popular.

TOOLS
BUILD YOUR HONDA
COMPARE
FINANCE TOOLS
REQUEST A QUOTE

FIND ANSWERS
Type a question here to search.

Tips   Go

MODELS
Accord Coupe
Accord Sedan
Civic Coupe
Civic Hybrid
Civic Sedan
Civic Si
CR-V
Element
Insight
Odyssey
Pilot
S2000
All Models
Certified Used Cars

Honda Cars en Español

Honda Racing

Honda.com

Locate a Dealer
Enter ZIP Code   Go

NEWSROOM

Civic Nation is everywhere. Honda searched Southern California for the most aggressively styled Civics on the road. Watch the commercial.

More news →

OWNER LINK

A no-cost essential resource for Honda drivers, offering access to valuable resources like maintenance schedules, roadside tips, FAQs and dealer contact information.

Go there →

CURRENT OFFERS

The 2004 Honda Clearance is here. Take advantage of limited-time offers and special deals before it's too late. Visit our Current Offers section.

Check out offers →

REQUEST A QUOTE

It's easy to get a quote on your favorite Honda vehicle. Just follow a few simple steps to receive detailed pricing information on the Honda that is right for you.

Get started →

©2004 American Honda Motor Co., Inc. All information contained herein applies to U.S. vehicles only. Please see our Privacy Policy and Legal Terms and Conditions.

Honda en Español | Customer Relations | Site Map | Visit Honda.com

www.automobiles.honda.com

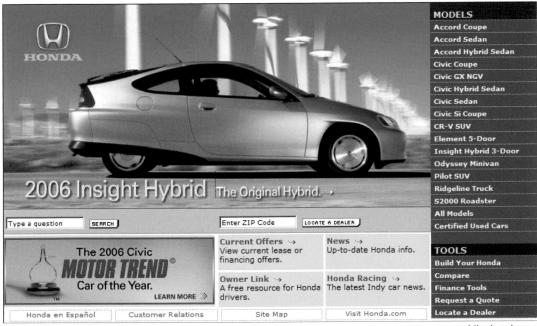

2006 Insight Hybrid   The Original Hybrid. →

Type a question   SEARCH

Enter ZIP Code   LOCATE A DEALER

The 2006 Civic
MOTOR TREND©
Car of the Year.
LEARN MORE »

Current Offers →
View current lease or financing offers.

News →
Up-to-date Honda info.

Owner Link →
A free resource for Honda drivers.

Honda Racing →
The latest Indy car news.

Honda en Español | Customer Relations | Site Map | Visit Honda.com

MODELS
Accord Coupe
Accord Sedan
Accord Hybrid Sedan
Civic Coupe
Civic GX NGV
Civic Hybrid Sedan
Civic Sedan
Civic Si Coupe
CR-V SUV
Element 5-Door
Insight Hybrid 3-Door
Odyssey Minivan
Pilot SUV
Ridgeline Truck
S2000 Roadster
All Models
Certified Used Cars

TOOLS
Build Your Honda
Compare
Finance Tools
Request a Quote
Locate a Dealer

www.automobiles.honda.com

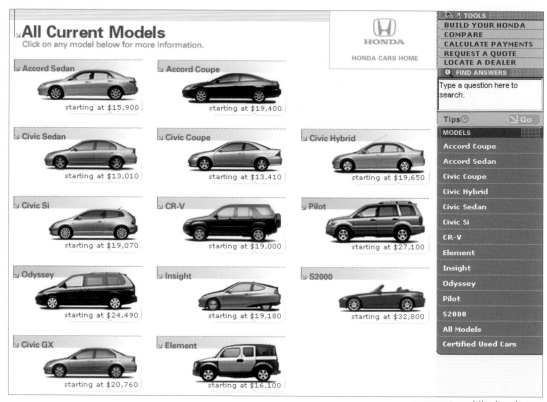

This page does a better job of depicting the various models by including prices and photos. The images help provide an indication of the vehicle type. However, the photos are relatively small and many of the models look very similar, making it difficult to ascertain, for example, if the Civic Si is a minivan.

(Facing page, top) This site does a good job of classifying vehicles because it employs terms that people understand. Rather than assume that users are familiar with Ford model names, it uses simple and familiar terms such as Pickup Trucks and Minivans/Vans, which are more helpful than model names.

(Facing page, bottom) Flooring types on this site are organized by product line, and not by traits. This structure might make sense for Anderson employees, but not for potential customers who search products by attributes. Names like Appalachian and Biltmore may be meaningless to users. When site designers feel it's necessary to provide instructions for how to navigate their site, it's a sign that the interaction design doesn't work. Better to meet people's expectations than expect them to meet yours.

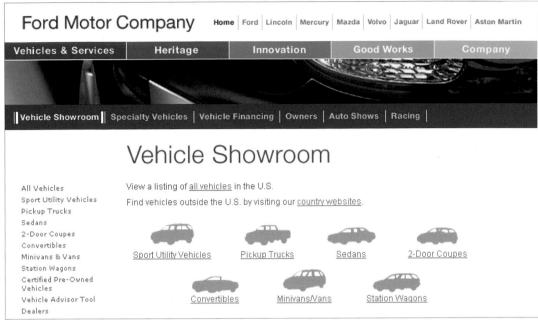

www.ford.com

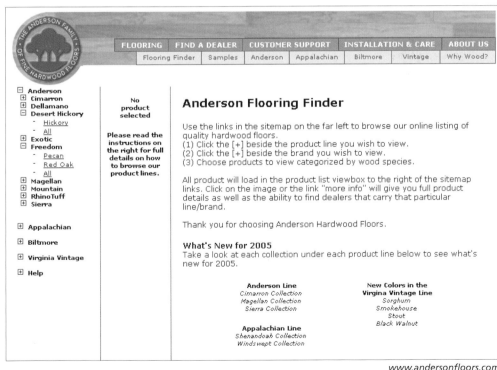

www.andersonfloors.com

Vertical Dropdown Menus: Short Is Sweet

Vertical dropdown menus have become a widely used navigational tool, mainly because they save space on screens with limited real estate. Over the years, users have learned to adapt to them. While dropdown menus have their advantages, they can also be problematic, especially if they are long. The longer the menu list, the more difficult it is to control. The further users must travel down the list, they more likely they are to lose their place.

It's often better to present long lists in standard hypertext format, where there's more room for descriptions that help people differentiate between the choices. Dropdown menus tend to be narrow and allow little space for descriptive category names. Rather than risk the chance of providing a long list of items whose meanings overlap or are unclear, let people click on the main heading and then take them to another page that clearly lists their choices with proper descriptions.

Multilevel Menus: Less Is More

Use fly-out horizontal menus sparingly and keep the levels to no more than two. Any more than that covers up the page and is difficult to use. A third level is usually a sign of trouble, and a fourth level virtually always makes a menu impossible to operate. With too many levels, it becomes a navigation problem in its own right to locate the desired option in the constantly expanding and hiding submenus.

People generally operate under the assumption that the shortest distance between two points is a straight line. So with multilevel menus, they tend to drag their mouse diagonally to get to the sublevels. When this happens, they usually lose their position and become frustrated at having to reselect their options. The problem is worse on laptops because touch pads make drag-and-click manipulations even more cumbersome.

Make sure that dynamic menus remain on the page long enough for people to make their selections. Temperamental menus that require precision and open and close at the

(Facing page, top) The multilevel menus on this site annoyed users because they were difficult to control. Accidentally moving the pointer just outside of the product category area caused a different menu to appear unexpectedly.

(Facing page, bottom) The American Heart Association Web site incorporates fly-out menus judiciously by restricting them to two levels. Also, the design accommodates the tendency for people to drag mouses diagonally when making a selection. The menu persists even if people veer slightly outside of the menu area.

slightest mouse movements are difficult to control. Power users might have the experience to control dynamic menus without much difficulty, but the average person will struggle.

www.escaldesports.com

www.americanheart.org

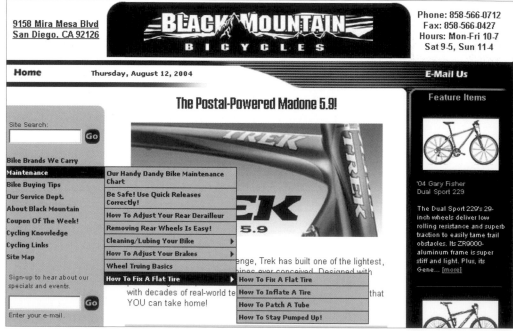

www.blackmountainbicycles.com

Make sure that people can easily tell what is clickable and what is not. Don't force them to click everything on the screen to figure out where the links are.

Can I Click on It?

When people don't know what's clickable on a site, they must work harder and guess. They can easily miss what they are looking for, give up prematurely, or think that they have explored all options when they haven't.

The standard paradigm of underlining links and using blue link color provides a strong visual cue to their functions. Don't use blue for nonlink text because blue is still the color most strongly associated with clickability.

That said, blue is *not* always the desired color for links. For reasons such as branding and aesthetics, blue links may be unsuitable. Bolded text also indicates clickability. Highlighting text when the pointer hovers over it to indicate links is also helpful, though it should never be the only indication of clickability because users would then need to minesweep the screen to find the links.

Graphical interface elements that appear raised or otherwise stand out also imply clickability. Users usually perceive standard button shapes as clickable, as well as anything else that can be clicked in other popular user interfaces.

In sum, make sure that people can easily tell what's clickable and what's not. Don't force them to click everything on the screen to figure out where the links are. Give links visual treatments that are commonly associated with clickability: mainly colored text and underlining. Don't depend solely on the hand cursor to indicate links. Even experienced users don't always notice when the pointer changes to a hand, and to novice users, the pointer and hand mean the same thing.

"Affordance" was originally a psychology term used to define the possible actions between a person or animal and the world. Our colleague Donald A. Norman applied the term to the user-experience world in his classic book *The Design of Everyday Things.*

Basically, in design an "affordance" is whatever can be done to an object. For example, a chair affords sitting, a button affords pushing, and a handle may afford turning or pulling, depending on how it's designed. Don's great insight was that *perceived* affordances are even more important than *real* affordances in terms of usability. His most famous example is a door: A door may afford pulling or pushing, depending on which way it opens. When a person can see in advance whether to pull or push the door to open it, that's a good user interface. In other words, the person can perceive the door's affordance simply by looking at it—he doesn't need to struggle with it to discover its actual affordance. (And he certainly shouldn't need a manual to operate a door; any door that comes with explicit instructions to "push" or "pull" is a poorly designed door.)

In screen-based user interfaces, we need to twist the concept of affordances a bit more.

In some sense, every dot on the screen affords clicking because it's possible to point at anything and click the mouse. In practice, however, we say that a screen element affords clicking only if something happens when you click it. The key issue, then, is whether a clickable element has the *perceived affordance* of clickability—in other words, can the user predict simply by looking at an element that something will happen if she clicks on it? If so, the design usually has a much higher level of usability than one that makes users guess what's clickable.

When we discuss this concept, it is usually in relation to whether clickable objects have a perceived affordance of clickability to the user. This determines whether users can easily recognize their choices on any given screen. But there's the opposite side as well: Do any nonclickable screen elements have a perceived affordance of clickability? If so, users will believe they have choices that they don't have, and they will be confused when they click and nothing happens. To avoid this problem, do not use confusing design markers. For example, don't use a graphic that looks like a button if it is not clickable—and don't make text blue or underlined unless it is a link.

(Facing page, top)   In our user testing, people on this site complained that there wasn't a way to apply for an account online and thought that they had to contact a bank representative. They didn't realize that the orange rectangular box was a button. Because of its flat appearance, people thought that it was simply a static graphic used to call attention to the Contact link next to it. When comparing these two links, the underlined colored text has a strong perceived affordance of clickability, while the flat box does not—it seems to be purely decorative. Most users would probably ignore the Apply graphic even without the underlined text next to it. But when the box is paired with something with a strong perceived affordance of clickability, their attention will almost always be drawn to the latter.

(Facing page, bottom)   The blue bulleted list on this site looks like links and the users we tested were perplexed that clicking on them didn't take them to a new page. When nothing happened, a few people even thought that the site was not functioning. The color blue has a strong perceived affordance of clickability. Don't use it for nonclickable items.

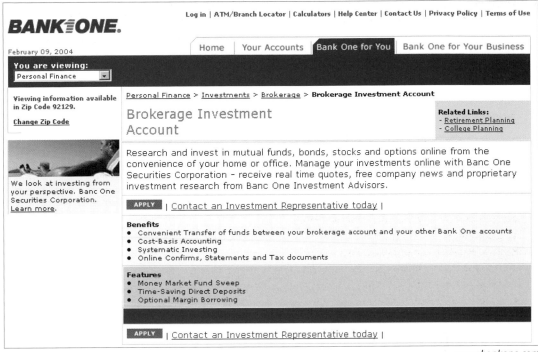

www.bankone.com

www.san-diego-vision.com

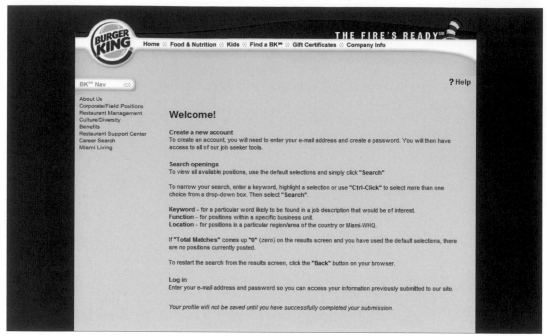

www.bk.com

The users in our tests didn't know that the headers on this site were active because they lacked the perceived affordance of clickability. They were not underlined, so people simply thought the bolded text was headers. The instructions say to click Search to get job openings, and people were perplexed when they didn't see a button to activate the request.

(Facing page, top)   This is an example of the misuse of visual metaphors. While the rectangular boxes with beveled edges look like buttons, they are not. The instructions say to click something else.

www.bk.com

Can you tell which elements here are clickable? If you guessed any of the graphics or bolded headers, you are wrong. The only thing active is the "Read more..." text. It's good that the clickable text is blue, but what about the other blue bolded items? It's important to use color and graphical treatments consistently to denote different things.

www.hmce.gov.uk

The week Mozilla launched its Firefox browser, it was a safe to assume that the vast majority of visitors to the homepage came to download the new software. So Mozilla wisely featured a direct link to this task as the most prominent design element on the homepage. Unfortunately, the arrow that looks like a download icon is not clickable. This is only a very small usability problem, however, because most people would click the text link below it. The site also presents direct links to other high-priority tasks through its other three main products.

Another good element of this homepage is the featured quote from Walt Mossberg, a respected software reviewer. It's much more credible when someone outside of your organization praises your product—and it's certainly more credible when someone else speaks badly of the competition, as in this case. Finally, it was smart to link to Mossberg's full article on the *Wall Street Journal*'s Web site. It shows others that Mozilla is not afraid to let users read the full review for themselves. This strategy is effective regardless of whether users actually follow the link or not.

Direct Access from the Homepage

One of the most successful design strategies we encountered in our testing is the placement of direct links on the homepage to a very small number of high-priority operations. No matter how well you structure your information architecture or how transparently you represent it in your navigation system, users may get lost or impatient if they must navigate through multiple levels. Direct links shortcut and simplify this.

Unfortunately, you can't present direct links to a large number of features on the homepage. Doing so defeats the purpose because users are more likely to click the wrong link. Also, a long list of direct links defeats other homepage goals, such as setting the stage for the site and informing users about the full scope of their options. The details drown the big picture, paradoxically giving users less of an overview.

www.mozilla.org

More Information

For more details on studies mentioned in this chapter, visit www.nngroup.com/reports and see "intranet," "children" and "teenagers."

Reserve direct links from the homepage for a small number of the most important user tasks. For any individual area of the homepage, you probably need to restrict the number of direct links to three to five. Three or fewer is most appropriate for multiple areas that each feature their own direct links.

www.mozilla.com

For the next major release of Firefox, Mozilla simplified the homepage even more and better highlighted the task of most visitors: to download the new version. Moving the link Other Systems and Languages outside the big button for downloading the main version was another marked improvement on the site. In the previous design, the link for these was inside a big shaded area that clearly was intended primarily for people who wanted the English version for Windows. Anyone who wanted a different version was likely to look elsewhere on the screen.

7 Typography: Readability & Legibility

Artistic elements such as typography and color schemes play an important part in making a good first impression with your Web site. Typography gives people a feeling for your company and conveys information about what they can do on your site. Different fonts can signify whimsy or gravity, and point size and color can emphasize content. Sustaining positive impressions throughout the site means choosing the type and colors that work best on the Web.

Sound rudimentary? It's not.

> *The primary goal of communication design is to convey information. Choose typography that communicates.*

Legibility is still a problem on Web sites today. Regardless of how good your site looks, if people can't easily read the text, it's destined for failure. In our studies, we repeatedly saw people of all ages and visual capabilities strain to read text on the sites we showed them. Some people had to stop what they were doing to put on reading glasses while others needed to lean in close to the screen and squint. This is uncomfortable for users and should not be necessary.

The right typography and color schemes are essential components of good visual design, but we've seen decisions based solely on branding, personal preferences, aesthetics, or just pure ego—at the expense of the users' needs. The results:

- Text appears too small or fuzzy
- Text is not easily resizable
- Text color provides inadequate contrast with the background
- Text is overshadowed by surrounding design elements

We want to say that it's not a pretty sight, but we have to admit that some of these sites are truly beautiful, created by very talented designers. If they were to be showcased as visual art, they would be lauded. But unlike masterpieces hung on museum walls, Web sites are to be used by large numbers of people. To be most effective, they must adhere to some practical guidelines.

Tip: The Downside of Dummy Type

Why do so many Web sites have illegible text? Didn't anybody read the text while designing the site?

The unfortunate answer is "no." It's quite common for Web sites to be designed without real content. Instead the designer fills the pages with dummy text that begins with "lorem ipsum." (Paradoxically this is known as "Greek text" even though the words and the character set are pseudo-Latin.)

It often makes sense for designers to use placeholder text while they work on visuals before the content is finalized. However, legibility problems can easily be underestimated when all you see is "lorem ipsum." When reviewing screens with nonsense text, you simply think to yourself, Text goes here. If you are not trying to read it, you won't notice if it's unintelligible.

Our guideline: If you don't have the final content available while designing a Web site, at least insert representative text from the current site instead of nonsense text.

People use print and Web media differently, and designers must adjust their Web sites accordingly. A billboard or magazine cover is static; a reader understands it simply by looking at it. But the Web, of course, is interactive: People need to *do* things on it, and typography can help or hinder this process. The primary goal of communication design is to convey information. Choose typography that communicates. The typfaces you select should be legible and reflect the character and tone of your site.

www.sandiego.gov

The nice font size and high contrast between the text and background colors on this Web site made reading comfortable for people of all ages in our testing:

"I find it easy to read. Even the print is big enough for me to read. In the past couple of years, I find that I do this more, more, and more [leaning back further from the screen]. I'm 43 and this is something new to me."

www.pixar.com

The small white text on this page was difficult to read. Some people had to lean forward in their chairs to make out the words. The main problem is the small font size, but the low contrast between the text and the background compounds the problem.

"It's kind of hard to see, pretty small print."

Even younger audiences complained about the tiny text and lack of contrast on this site. Light blue on white is not a good color combination if you want people to actually read the text:

"It would help if all the words were bigger and not blue. It's like trying to read yellow."

Cramming more content on a page by shrinking the text size backfires because it makes the page busy and difficult to read. Who wants to stay on a Web site that causes eyestrain when other sites with the same information don't?

"I don't like small writing. It bugs me. It gives me a headache after reading it for a while."

Even though this site has good contrast overall, people still complained about the font size. They didn't understand why the page couldn't be expanded to increase the text size and felt that the white areas on each side of the page were wasted space. When viewing Web sites on a 1024-by-768-pixel monitor (the most common screen size and the one we used in our studies), the user can see about 570,000 pixels of information inside a browser window. On this page, only 119,000 pixels are dedicated to the main content in the description of the "spring break escape" package and the links to start booking it. In other words, only 21 percent of the visible space is utilized for the primary content, and 79 percent is used for filler images or left unused. This irritated some of our users:

"I wouldn't want the print to be smaller. It bugs me. I have average eyes, so this would be the minimum amount. There is quite a lot of wasted space here; I would have gone up a size or two. If it doesn't cost [the site] money, then it's good to do."

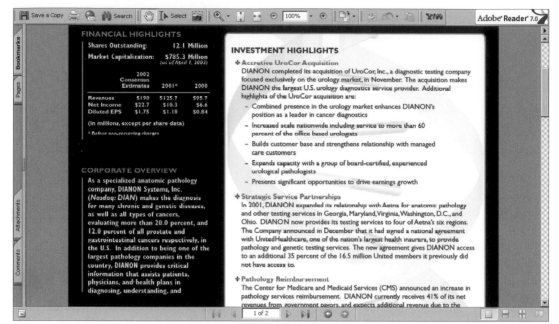

www.dianon.com

This Adobe PDF didn't display well onscreen. The text appeared jagged, making it difficult to read, even at 100 percent. The presentation looked unprofessional, which turned people off. In general, PDFs look bad on Web sites because the information is designed for the printed page and not for the screen.

"I'm thinking that it looks busy. A lot of little things. None of the fonts and script on this page is clear. It's blurred. I wouldn't use this site unless I had to, because it's difficult to make out."

Body Text: The Ten-Point Rule

Is bigger better? There isn't a single text size or typeface that appeals to all audiences or fits all situations. Some people simply prefer small fonts to large fonts and can read the text in both equally well. For people with diminished eyesight, however, large text is a necessity.

When choosing font sizes, it's best to go larger to avoid alienating some of your readers. At a minimum, make sure that body text is at least ten points. Smaller text quickly diminishes readability because smaller letters simply don't look as distinct, even for people with normal vision. Minuscule characters tend to lose their characteristic shapes on the screen, especially when bolded or italicized.

Recommended Text Sizes

Audience Type	Point Size
General audience	10 - 12
Senior citizens & people with visual impairments	12 - 14
Young children and other beginning readers	12 - 14
Teenagers/young adults	10 - 12

A small font size is not a solution for fitting more content on a page. And having more content doesn't mean that people will read more. In fact, they will probably read less. Dense text drives people away. This is a true example of the "more is less" dictum for design: More text often means less reading.

It's better to choose your content wisely than to cram everything on one page. If your Web site is truly hurting for space, it's fine to bend the rules a bit and use smaller text in areas most people don't care about, such as terms of use, affiliate network, copyright, and legal notices. Otherwise, stick to text sizes that people can read comfortably.

When faced with space issues, first try to cut the text. If this is not possible, put the least important text on secondary pages that can be accessed through hyperlinks. Focus the initial page on the information that everybody needs and there's a chance that they may actually read it.

Anti-aliasing is an action that smoothes jagged edges of vector-based shapes and text. Designers often use anti-aliasing to make objects appear more polished and refined, but this can create new problems such as blurred text. Avoid anti-aliasing for text sized smaller than 12 points. Otherwise use it sparingly, as it bloats the size of image files and increases downloading time, irritating users.

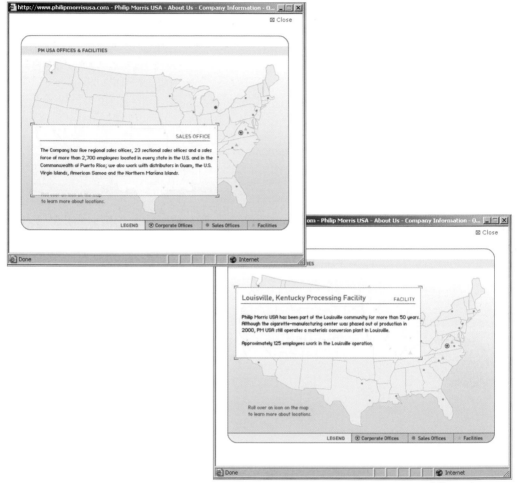

www.philipmorrisusa.com

Compare the difference in readability between these two examples. Notice that the text in the first example appears crisper than the text in the second example. This is because the first screen shot is the alias version and the second has been anti-aliased.

Age Is Not the Issue

Small, faint text is not only a problem for middle-age people and senior citizens. In a recent study conducted with teenagers, we found that they don't like inconspicuous text any more than their aging parents do. Teenagers scan quickly and want important elements to grab their attention. Even with perfect vision, they prefer to skim a page without having to strain.

Glasses, contact lenses, and environmental factors such as illumination levels can affect people's ability to read text, regardless of age or visual level. Having text that is legible under various environmental and physical conditions ensures that your audience can comfortably use your interface in the way you intended.

www.pg.com

Can you read this? Even teenagers with perfect vision had difficulty reading the tiny text on this site. The italicized light blue text blends with the background, making it difficult to make out the words.

Young people complained about the tiny font sizes on this site. One user in particular explained that being seen squinting at small fonts tarnished her image: It's cool to lean back in your chair and use the Web, but uncool if it looks like you're straining.

"You look at this stuff and it's hard to see. You have to squint. These are really small and you can't see. It needs to be a little bigger."

"The writing is kind of small."

Tip: When the Same Size Appears Smaller

Test different typefaces and make sure to account for size differences. The same size font may appear smaller or larger depending on the typeface. For example, the same text in 12-point font appears larger in Georgia than in Times New Roman.

This is how text appears in 12-point Georgia.

This is how text appears in 12-point Times New Roman.

Planning for Differences in Hardware

Typography decisions should allow for a wide range of computer systems, from top-of-the-line to very old. Web sites appear differently onscreen depending on the hardware. Text that appears reasonably crisp on new, fancy monitors can look fuzzy on outdated ones, especially in small sizes.

Just because you can see text well on *your* screen doesn't mean that your audience can on theirs. People who work in the computer technology industry tend to have the most up-to-date systems. Web sites are often created and tested on powerful machines with big monitors and high resolution, making it easy to forget that the rest of the world doesn't have the same equipment.

Unless you're designing for high-end users, assume that a significant percentage of your audience is using old machines with poor monitors. Senior citizens, teenagers, and young kids often use donated or hand-me-down equipment and low-performance monitors. People in offices work on laptops with small displays and on surprisingly old computers. If you know that a significant portion of your audience uses older equipment, it is worth the effort to use crisp font styles and larger font sizes so that they can easily make out the words.

Common Screen Resolutions

Current statistics show that most people's computers have screen resolutions of 800 by 600 pixels or 1024 by 768 pixels. The larger screen size is the most popular, and trends indicate that 1024 by 768 will be the smallest common screen in the future.

The chart on the next page shows the trend in monitor sizes used by a broad sample of users during a seven-year period. While the use of small monitors has been declining rapidly, big monitors have still not seen explosive growth. But monitors with screen resolutions of 1600 by 1200 pixels or greater are already in common use in high-end businesses. Large monitors will gradually become more common for home users as well because they allow for much more efficient use of both the Web and many common applications.

Trends in Screen Resolution

Note: The figures for 1999 to 2005 are empirical data while those for 2006 to 2009 are estimates. (Source data: TheCounter.com (1999-2001), OneStat.com (2002-2005), and W3Schools.com (2002-2005). All sites sampled a wide range of users.)

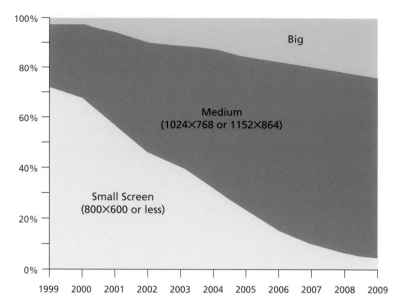

Remember, it pays to know your audience. These general trends may not accurately reflect your readership. While it's impossible to know exactly what equipment most of your audience is using, you should have a good idea. If your design is rigid and requires a specific screen resolution setting, some viewers might not be able to use your Web site.

Accessibility Affects All of Us

Interface design can either cripple or empower users. People with normal capabilities can be hobbled by cumbersome interfaces just as those with disabilities can be liberated by well-designed sites. To be accessible, a site must be approachable by audiences with varying levels of abilities.

An accessible site is one that removes obstacles that get in people's way; removing the obstacle overcomes the disability. For example, allowing visually impaired people to resize text results in better readability, thereby eliminating the visual impairment even though the person's sight remains the same.

Don't assume that all people who are visually impaired use assistive technology. Visual impairments run a wide gamut, from diminished vision to no perception of light. Users on the milder end of the spectrum might not require assistive technology but need resizing capabilities to read. Even people with good eyesight sometimes need to boost up the text size, especially when using displays with low-resolution settings.

The severity and level of visual impairments generally increase with age. As our population ages, this will become a more common issue in Web design. All of us at some point in our lives will have some degree of visual impairment.

Relative Specifications

We recommend setting text size using a relative size scheme (such as percentages or em values) instead of fixed type sizes. For example, don't specify that a headline should appear in 14-point type. Say that it should be 140 percent of the size of the body text. Then if users enlarge the text, the headline will still look bigger than the rest of the text. A liquid design allows text to be scaled relative to the viewer's browser settings and screen resolution while still letting designers dictate the structure of the page.

In poorly conceived attempts to control how a Web page looks, many designers use absolute units of measurements to set the size of text. Absolute text properties make it almost impossible for users to change text size. This is a big problem for viewers, especially users with impaired vision.

Trying to control what users see by using the "one size fits all" approach usually backfires. People resent sites that appear prescriptive, preventing them from making the necessary adjustments to use the site comfortably. It's like owning a car and not being able to adjust the seats. It's their screen—let them control what they see.

Even if there is a way to disable cascading style sheets (CSS), the average user doesn't know about this or how to do it. To make matters worse, Microsoft has removed the resize button from the Internet Explorer, version 6 toolbar. Technically, people can put it back, but the option is so hidden that most users wouldn't even know it's there.

Designing for Vision-Impaired Users

If your site caters to senior citizens and people with low vision, provide an obvious way for them to adjust the text size. Don't count on people using the preference settings in their browser; most people are afraid to mess with browser settings. Have a visible resize button within your pages so that people can easily adjust the text size.

We don't recommend having a resize text button on all mainstream Web sites, as it increases development and interface complexity with insufficient payoff. In most cases, it is sufficient to use a carefully chosen typeface that displays well but is also scalable by end-users.

The Rule of Relative Size

Creating pixel-perfect layouts is futile. Define what the default should be but allow people to override your preset. Maintaining control means relinquishing some of it.

The Social Security site caters to a mature audience and appropriately uses large font sizes and allows readers to adjust the text size.

(Facing page, top) Unfortunately, changing the text size on the Social Security site isn't straightforward. Instead of providing onscreen controls, the site requires that users change text size from the browser menu, which is too complex for many elderly people to understand.

(Facing page, bottom) **Old design:** This site provides text-resizing options, but the icons are so small and obscure that many people in our study didn't notice them. It's better to offer a more comfortable default font size than to require people to make adjustments. The preferred icons for text resizing contain the letter "A" in different sizes (for example, a smaller A for making text smaller and a bigger A for making text larger).

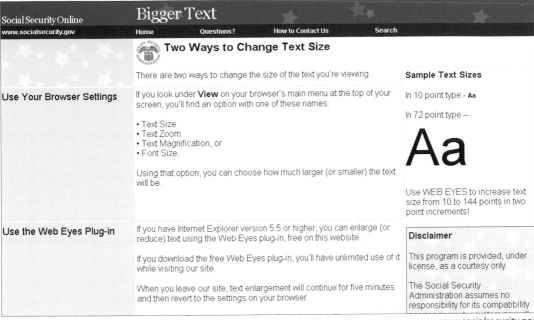

www.socialsecurity.gov

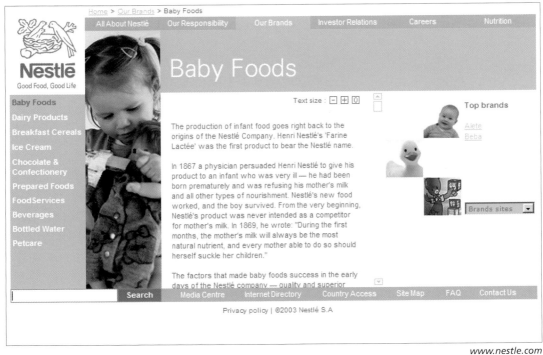

www.nestle.com

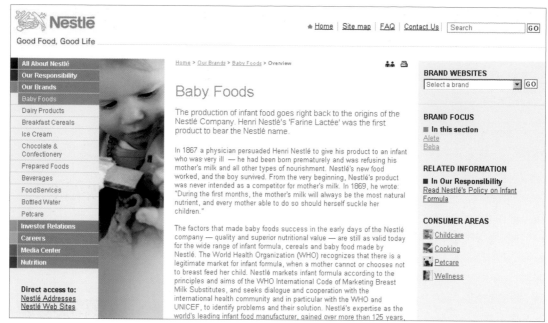

www.nestle.com

New design: The default font size on the redesigned Nestlé site is an improvement over the previous version. The larger size text is much easier to read.

(Facing page, top)   This Web site caters to a broad audience by using relative fonts. Even though the text size is appropriately set for general users, the site offers an additional text resizing option for those who need larger text. Note the use of progressively larger A's as the resize controls. This notation works well for most users.

(Facing page, bottom)   This site uses typefaces that are appropriate for its main target audience. The legible text works not only for senior citizens but also for users of all ages. The site even has contrast and speech options for people with special needs.

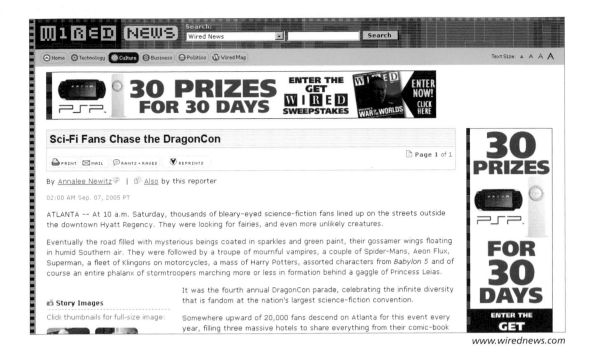

www.wirednews.com

NIH SeniorHealth.gov

Featuring Health Information from the National Institutes of Health

● Click to Begin

This website for older adults was developed by the National Institute on Aging and the National Library of Medicine, both part of the National Institutes of Health.

National Institute on Aging, U.S. National Library of Medicine
National Institutes of Health, U.S. Department of Health & Human Services
Contact us, Accessibility, Copyright, Privacy

www.nihseniorhealth.org

Choosing Fonts

All fonts are not created equal. When choosing a font for your Web site, make sure to opt for those that are available on your customers' computers and browsers. Otherwise their systems might use a default typeface that's not optimized for online viewing and the site will not appear as you intended.

Since you can't know what system each viewer has, you should create a flexible design and still maintain some control over your Web pages' appearance. Always supply a list of font alternatives, in order of preference.

The two most common font families are serif and sans serif. Serif fonts have cross-lines at the tips of each letter or other embellishments, and fine variations. Sans serif fonts are plain and don't have the decorative embellishments. They vary between thick and thin strokes, compared to fonts from the serif family. Because serifs rely on fine detail, they work well for the high-quality typography of books and magazines. In fact, readability studies have found that most people read serif text faster than sans serif text in print. Sadly, computer screens don't offer the typographical quality of print, so the fine details in the serifs end up not looking so fine after all. As a result, studies of onscreen reading find that sans serif text is the fastest to read, exactly the opposite of the finding for print.

This table outlines the fonts that come preinstalled on most browsers. It's wise not to stray from this list.

Common Fonts and Their Families

Font Name	Generic Font Family
Arial	Sans serif
Arial Black	Sans serif
Comic Sans MS	Cursive
Courier New	Mono Space
Georgia	Serif
Impact	Sans serif
Times New Roman	Serif
Trebuchet MS	Sans serif
Verdana	Sans serif

When in Doubt, Use Verdana

Even with current technology, screen resolution is much lower than print resolution. Fonts that are ornate or detailed might look fine in print but don't render clearly on the screen, resulting in jagged and degraded text formations.

Using typefaces that are not intended for online reading can be detrimental to your Web site, especially at smaller sizes. Typefaces that are optimized for online viewing tend to be unadorned and crisp, making them easier to read on screens. This table describes the characteristics of the most common fonts.

Characteristics of Common Fonts

Font Name	Online Readability	Character/Tone
Arial	Readable at reasonable sizes. Good at font points 10 or above.	Modern, clean basic, no-frills. Generally liked by people of all ages.
Comic Sans MS	Fancy lettering makes it difficult to read online, even at large sizes.	Friendly, youthful, fun, and informal. Not appropriate for more serious or professional Web sites.
Georgia	The best serif font designed for online reading. Generally good at font sizes 10 and above.	Traditional-looking, but more modern-looking and readable than Times New Roman. Good online serif alternative.
Impact	Generally used for print. Not recommended for online viewing. Poor readability even at large sizes.	Bold. Not suitable for blocks of content. Can be used sparingly for short headlines.
Times New Roman	Good for printed materials. Onscreen, readability quickly diminishes at small point sizes. Only good at font sizes 12 or higher.	Traditional-looking. Not recommended if you want to appear professional. Generally not preferred by audiences of any age.
Trebuchet MS	Readable at reasonable sizes. Good at font points 10 or above.	Modern, simple, edgy.
Verdana	The most readable online font, even in small type.	Modern, simple, professional. The recommended font for use in body text, where readability is critical. High in user preference.

Both the serif and sans-serif families have a font that is designed for online reading: Georgia and Verdana, respectively. In general, sans-serif fonts appear more modern than serifs and are more legible at very small sizes. If you're not sure which to use, it's safer to go with Verdana. This sans-serif font is common on all computer systems, works especially well at smaller sizes, and is most pleasant to read on screens. If you're inclined to use a serif typface, Georgia is a good alternative because it also works well for online viewing, although many people prefer Verdana—especially younger users, who seem to feel that Georgia doesn't match their sense of style. But remember that serif fonts are slightly worse than sans serifs for on-screen reading, so only use Georgia (or other serif typefaces) if your style or banding absolutely requires it.

When Will Screens Read as Well as Print?

Current computer monitors typically display around 80 to 100 dots per inch (dpi) while paper can display from 600 dpi for a laser printer to 3000 dpi for a glossy magazine. The dpi rating translates directly into crispness of characters. Because of their drastically lower resolutions, computer monitors are inherently fuzzy, which is the main reason to avoid serif typefaces.

Screens have already gotten somewhat better since the 72-dpi resolution found on the first Macintosh in 1984. But they haven't improved as fast as other PC components. An average PC computes at a speed that's about 16,000 times faster than the first Mac and has about 8,000 times more memory. But the average computer screen is only about four times bigger than the Mac screen in 1984 and doesn't even come close to having twice its dpi.

By 2025 we should finally get decent computer screens that approximate the typographic quality of paper. Specialized applications are probably going to get good screens earlier than that. Once computer monitors get to be as good as paper, it's likely that the usability recommendations for online typography will change, and we will recommend the same guidelines as those developed for print long ago, including a change to serifs as the preferred fonts.

Limit the number of font styles and colors on your site and apply them consistently. People don't trust sites that look like ransom notes.

Mixing Fonts and Colors

Limit the number of font styles on your site and apply them consistently. Use font styles as a subtle and effective way to create order and communicate hierarchical elements on your site. Items that appear graphically similar have the same level of emphasis.

Varying fonts and font attributes can help people differentiate between the relative importance of headings and information. Assign different attributes—such as boldface, color, and size—to a specific typeface for emphasis. But do this sparingly; when everything is highlighted, nothing is emphasized.

The same rules apply to color. We recommend having no more than four different colors and three typefaces in the main areas of your site or it will appear unstructured and unprofessional. People don't trust sites that look like a ransom note.

This is an example of the overuse of typeface attributes. It's not clear why some typefaces are bold and in different colors. Colors and attributes should be used sparingly and for a reason.

www.nestle.com

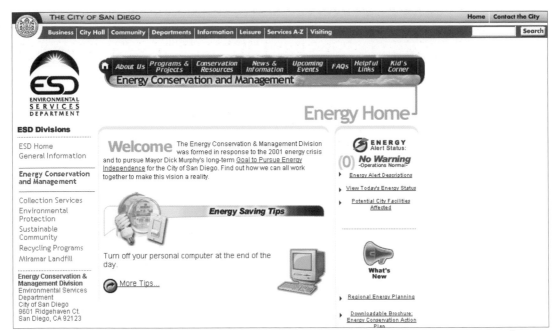

www.sandiego.gov

Count the number of different typefaces on this page. With so many labels calling for your attention, it's difficult to know which to give it to.

(Facing page, top)   The number of colors and font styles combined with the pictures and graphical and background elements make this page too busy. Use visual design elements wisely, to help communicate and create order, not just to decorate the page.

(Facing page, bottom)   The Terms and Conditions on this site are written in all capital letters, creating an illusion of a wall of text. We know that people tend to skip over Terms of Use agreements, and showing them in all caps makes them even less appealing to read.

www.money.cnn.com

www.bedbathandbeyond.com

The blue text in all caps forms compact blocks of text that are difficult to scan. The three-column format results in awkward word wrapping, and starting links with "CLICK HERE FOR" is superfluous. People know that lnks are meant to be clicked.

The Case Against Caps

ALL-CAP TEXT REDUCES READING SPEED BY ABOUT TEN PERCENT. MIXED-CASE LETTERS HAVE VARI-ATIONS THAT BREAK UP THE TEXT INTO RECOGNIZABLE SHAPES, WHEREAS A PARAGRAPH IN ALL CAPS HAS UNIFORM HEIGHT AND SHAPE, MAKING IT APPEAR BLOCKY AND RUN TOGETHER. ALSO, THE USE OF ALL CAPS CAN SEEM CHILDISH AND AMATEUR, OR AGGRESSIVE OR UNPROFESSIONAL. RESERVE ALL-CAP TEXT FOR SHORT HEADINGS AND TITLES, AND FOR SHOUTING.

The Home Depot, Inc.

Site Map   Store Locator   Contact Us

About The Home Depot
Corporate Responsibility
■ Investor Relations
   Stock Information
   Corporate Governance
   Financial Reports
   Shareholder Services
   News Releases
   Events and Presentations
   Investor Facts
   Contact Investor Relations
Careers
Media Relations
The Home Depot Companies

Home > Investor Relations

Investor Relations

Founded in 1978, The Home Depot, Inc. is the world's largest home improvement retailer, the second largest retailer in the United States and the third largest retailer on a global basis, with fiscal 2003 sales of $64.8 billion. The Company's common stock has been publicly traded since 1981, and is listed on the New York Stock Exchange under the symbol "HD."

RECENT FINANCIAL NEWS RELEASES

02/18/05
THE HOME DEPOT TO HOST FOURTH QUARTER AND FISCAL YEAR 2004 EARNINGS CONFERENCE CALL ON FEBRUARY 22, 2005

01/13/05
THE HOME DEPOT ANNOUNCES SALES AND EARNINGS TARGETS FOR FISCAL YEAR 2005

01/03/05
THE HOME DEPOT ANNOUNCES INVESTOR AND ANALYST CONFERENCE JAN. 13, 2005

View archived news releases

EXECUTIVE PRESENTATIONS

02/22/05 - 9:00 AM ET
HOME DEPOT INC. 4TH QUARTER 2004 EARNINGS

View Annual Report »

Proud Past,
Bright Future

View **Proxy Statement**
Order an **Annual Report**
Sign up for **Electronic Delivery**

HD Current Stock Price »

Date: Feb 18, 2005
Time: 12:58 PM ET
Price: 42.14
Change: + 0.33
Daily High: $42.23
Daily Low: $41.74

www.homedepot.com

There's no need to show the title of financial releases in all capital letters. Mixed-case words are easier to read, especially with low-contrasting text and underlined links.

Text and Background Contrast

Along with the right typeface and size, the right color contrast ensures legibility and readability on your site. Remember, reading online is much more difficult than reading on paper. Highly contrasting text and background colors make it easier.

Black text on a white background or something similar is easiest to read. In general, dark colors are best for text, and cool, desaturated colors are best for backgrounds.

Even though white text on a black background has the same contrast as black text on white background, readiblity isn't as high, especially at small sizes. When the colors are reversed, the white edges appear blurred. To overcome this effect, you must increase text size to at least 12 points for some fonts. If dark backgrounds can't be avoided, you can alleviate the problem by choosing a dark color other than black. Even though the contrast is slightly lower, it is less blurry.

Avoid using similar colors such as light gray on white backgound. Low contrast can cause eye strain and discomfort. This problem is intensified for people with poor vision, who have more difficulty seeing letters or pictures against backgrounds that have a similar hue or intensity.

Be careful about using vibrant color combinations such as purple and yellow. While such colors are technically high contrast, bright colors cause a vibrating effect on computer text that can make it difficult to read.

Nothing screams out amateur more than a busy background. Don't do it. Not only does it look bad, but text set in a busy background decreases readabilty. Save yourself and your audience the headache. As one of our test users bluntly put it: "They picked the wrong color for words. The background is bright and the text is bright, so it's difficult to see. Sometimes your eyes blend the colors. It ruins your eyes. It gets tedious when you have to highlight the text to read."

Dark colors are best for text, and cool, desaturated colors are best for backgrounds. Low contrast can cause eye strain and discomfort.

Readability Level of Different Color Combinations

Color combinations	Readablity Level
Black text on white background	High: Highest value of contrast. High perceptable difference.
Blue text on white background	High: High perceptable difference, as long as you use a dark blue.
Black text on grey background	Med: Medium to high perceptable difference depending on the color combinations and saturation level.
White text on blue background	Low: Difficult to read as the dark background is percieved to over-power the white text.
Gray text on white background	Low: Low value of contrast. Low perceptable difference.
White text on grey background	Low: Low value of contrast. Low perceptable difference.
Red text on white background	Very Low: Certain bold color combinations create a vibrating effect, tiring on the eyes.
Red text on black background	Very Low: Certain bold color combinations create a vibrating effect, tiring on the eyes.

(Below) This homepage contains a large number of links. However, the careful organization and clean design facilitate scanning. The sparing use of color to denote headings and links draws people's eyes to areas they care about. There is a background "watermark" image behind the text, which we usually warn against, but it's subtle and not overly distracting.

"The colors are great because I can find things easier."

www.socialsecurity.gov

Maria Sklodowska-Curie
1867-1934

Deutsch Version

Maria (Marie *Fr.*) Sklodowska-Curie (born in Warsaw, Poland, on November 7, 1867) was one of the first woman scientists to win worldwide fame, and indeed, one of the great scientists of this century. She had degrees in mathematics and physics. Winner of two Nobel Prizes, for Physics in 1903 and for Chemistry in 1911, she performed pioneering studies with radium and polonium and contributed profoundly to the understanding of radioactivity.

A truly remarkable figure in the history of science !

Perhaps the most famous of all women scientists, Maria Sklodowska-Curie is notable for **her many firsts**:

- She was the first to use the term radioactivity for this phenomenon.
- She was the first woman in Europe to receive her doctorate of science.
- In 1903, she became the first woman to win a Nobel Prize for Physics. The award, jointly awarded to Curie, her husband Pierre, and Henri Becquerel, was for the discovery of radioactivity.
- She was also the first female lecturer, professor and head of Laboratory at the Sorbonne University in Paris (1906).
- In 1911, she won an unprecedented second Nobel Prize (this time in chemistry) for her discovery and isolation of pure radium and radium components. She was the first person ever to receive two Nobel Prizes.
- She was the first mother-Nobel Prize Laureate of daughter-Nobel Prize Laureate. Her oldest daughter Irene Joliot-Curie also won a Nobel Prize for

www.staff.amu.edu.pl/~zbzw/ph/sci/msc.htm

People disliked the use of red text on this page because it was glaring and difficult to read, especially against a yellow background. The difficulty of reading bright colors can cause eye fatigue.

(Facing page, top) This site is visually appealing, but the text is too small and the contrast insufficient. The white text on dark background appears fuzzy even for people with normal vision.

(Facing page, bottom) Users didn't like the navigational areas because the text and background colors are too dark and low in contrast. Even the dropdown list has low contrast. Not only is it difficult to read; it is aesthetically unappealing.

"This dark color is very annoying. Because it's blue on blue, it's almost invisible. It doesn't catch your eye. Even the interest checking account is muted. Everything is dark and gloomy, like Gotham City."

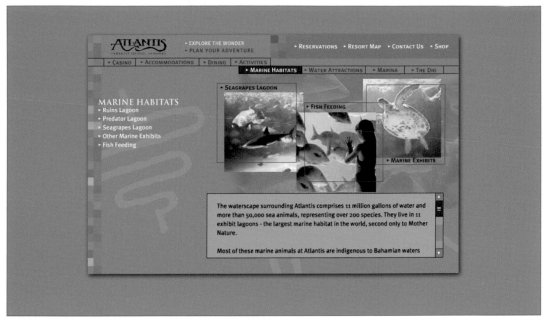

www.atlantis.com

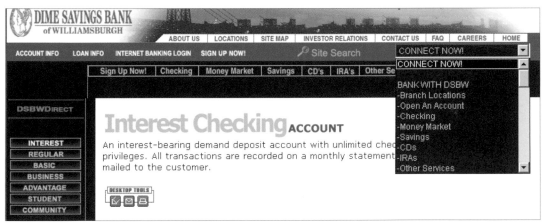

www.dimewill.com

Gary Daugherty

philosophy   projects   profile   contact

iborhood retail/office

Gary Daugherty - Architect   ? ©   site by: **Roadside Multimedia**

www.gdarchitect.com

Here's an extreme example of poor contrast. If you happen to have a low-resolution monitor or your screen settings aren't properly optimized, you might not be able to see this page at all.

(Facing page)   The small writing coupled with the light-colored text on the Nestlé site made reading difficult for some of our test viewers:

"The writing doesn't seem to stand out. A light blue on white background doesn't stand out. You have to peer into the screen to see what you're looking for."

www.nestle.com

Two Ways to Make Colors Pop

- When possible, use black and white color combinations, or use colors that vary significantly in intensity. A rough way to test whether or not your color choices are distinguishable is to view your screens in grayscale. The important elements on your page should still be discernable in grayscale.

- Provide a secondary cue when you use color to distinguish important information. This is especially necessary if red and green are among the colors used.

Common Color Blindness

Bear in mind that approximately 8 percent of men and .5 percent of women have some form of color blindness that prevents them from differentiating certain colors. Red/green color blindness is the most common. People with red/green defective color vision cannot distinguish colors that fall within the middle and long wavelength range.

You want colors to be perceived as they are presented, especially when color is used to convey meaning. Choosing the wrong color combination, such as red text on green background, can make it impossible for some people to read because the text and background color is perceived to be the same.

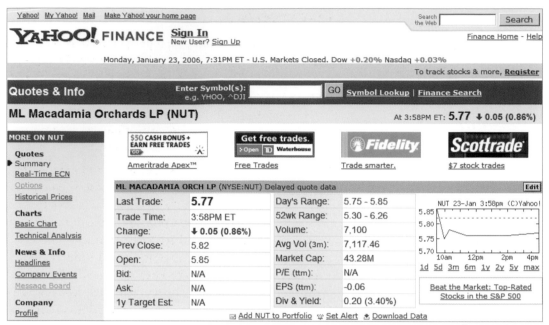

finance.yahoo.com

Yahoo! uses color-coding to give users a quick view of whether stocks are up or down. At the top of the page, green helps indicate that the general stock market was up the day this screen shot was taken. If you are color blind and can't discern green, you can still intepret this by the secondary clue of the plus sign. The main stock was down that day, as signaled by the color red. Again, a secondary cue—the arrow pointing down—helps color-blind users. In principle we would prefer consistent notation: either arrows or plus and minus signs. But in practice both notations are clear, and this minor inconsistency in the user interface is not likely to cause any usability problems.

Text Images

Text images are sometimes appropriate for snippets of text such as buttons, but not for large blocks of text. Designers who want to use fancy, nonstandard fonts sometimes attempt to circumvent the issue of browser compatibility by making the text an image. While a few judiciously chosen areas of text images are fine in most cases, a Web site based on graphics is problematic for several reasons:

- Graphics cause file bloat. Remember, half of the world is still using dial-up connections and has low patience for sites that load slowly. It's common for people to leave a site before it even finishes loading. Even if you're planning to use graphical buttons and headers, think about how many you'll have on your site and multiply that by the file size of each element. It could add up to be very a large amount. When it comes to reducing file size, don't underestimate the power of plain HTML. It's also easier to make changes to HTML text.

- Graphics-based text is not searchable, and we repeatedly hear people complain when they can't search for words on Web sites. PDF documents and sites that have graphics-based content are flat, making it nearly impossible for people to use the Search feature on their browsers.

- Graphical text is not selectable. When doing research, people like to select an area of content and paste it in a program such as Word for future reference or printing. Also, it's common for people to copy an address and paste it into mapping programs to get driving directions.

- Graphical text doesn't scale. Even if the text on your Web site is resizable, the graphics remain the same size.

- Screen readers can't readily read graphical text. Alternate text must be specified for the text to be read by the screen reader.

Graphics cause file bloat. Remember, half of the world is still using dial-up connections. It's common for people to leave a site before it even finishes loading.

www.bacararesort.com

Make sure the areas that people may want to copy and paste, such as addresses, are selectable. The Flash-based version of this site neglects to make the content on this page selectable. There is an icon for a printer-friendly version of the page, but it will be missed because its design is too obscure and it is far away from the main area of the page. Even worse, the site overtakes the browser window, robbing people of their browser controls.

Moving Text

People are annoyed by blinking or moving text on Web sites because it distracts them from what they are trying to do. They also associate dynamic text with advertising and are likely to ignore it. Ironically, moving text is one of the tactics intended to grab people's attention that actually ends up driving them away because they think it is promotional and untrustworthy.

As we saw in our studies in Japan, moving text is particularly problematic for international users, who sometimes have to look up foreign words in a dictionary as they read. But it is really not good for anyone. People want to control their own reading pace, and dynamic text takes that control away. Text that moves too slowly is also irksome. People typically can read static text much faster than dynamic text, and they hate having to wait for missed text to reappear. People with impaired vision or conditions that cause lack of head control, such as cerebral palsy, may not be able to focus on and maintain continuous eye contact with displays that constantly move or change.

www.socialsecurity.gov

More Information

For details on our test of 24 Web sites with teenagers, visit *www. nngroup.com/reports,* and see "Teenagers."

Very few people in our study even noticed the moving text at the top of the U.S. Social Security homepage. Those that did could see only a little text at a time in the miniscule content area, and if they couldn't read it fast enough, they had to wait for it to recirculate. Scrolling text may be effective on specialized venues such as news sites to create a feeling of excitement and breaking news. But it is inappropriate for the Social Security Administration's target audience, who wants direct content and isn't looking to be entertained.

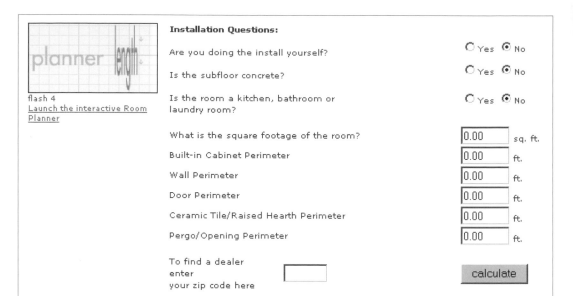

www.pergo.com

We asked people to use Pergo.com to figure out what supplies they would need to install a new kitchen floor. The site included a big animated graphic with flying phrases such as "room planner," "set up room size," "length," and "width" that were supposed to draw users' attention to a feature to help them calculate their room size. But no one saw it. One poor user was cursing as he tried to calculate his kitchen floor size by hand. To test the usability of the Room Planner application, we actually had to direct people to it

8 Writing for the Web

With a few exceptions, people visit the Web for its utility, not its beauty. Having a visually appealing site is good, of course, but content is golden. After all, when people enter queries into search engines, they don't type in aesthetic attributes—they're looking for information.

Good writing makes a huge difference in page views, time spent on a site, and sales. The essential rule of site usability holds for written content as much as it does for design: Customers choose clarity over confusion.

Don't underestimate the role of effective writing in creating a successful Web site. As goal-oriented people, Web users want to get to their destination, find the interesting or useful information they're looking for, and move on. They don't have the time or the inclination to wade through a sea of text that never gets to the point. Having clear, solid content is one way to attract and retain viewers, and efficient, intuitive access to that information is a major factor in their satisfaction levels.

How Poor Writing Makes Web Sites Fail

Disorganized, poorly written content commonly makes users unable to complete basic Web tasks such as choosing a product. In our study, we saw people purposefully navigate to the correct area of a site and still be defeated by convoluted content. They'd stare blankly at screens, baffled by the verbiage. And even after reading the information several times, often they still didn't get it.

When users find sites that make it easy to find their answers, they tend to trust and revisit them. Good design gets out of people's way yet helps them satisfy their desire to know. Visual flair can help incite curiosity and interest in the content, but designs with little or no information value don't retain customers. In fact, eye-tracking studies conducted by the Poynter Institute (www.poynter.org/eyetrack2000) found that for online news content, headlines and text are noticed first, even before images. Content should be the focal point on your Web site.

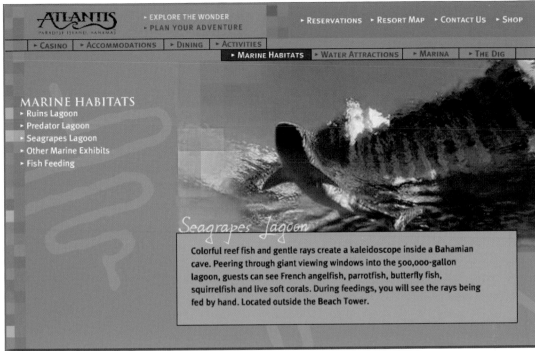

www.atlantis.com

People thought the layout and language used to describe this topic was easy to comprehend. Extraneous text is carved out, leaving only the essentials.

"This is nice and clear. It's got a picture. The text is nice and bold with lots of bullet points... [The page uses] simple words: 'You're hooked up to equipment to monitor your heart.' It's everyday language."

What is a Stress Test?

Why do I need a stress test?

A stress test, sometimes called a treadmill test or exercise test, helps your doctor find out how well your heart handles work. As your body works harder during the test, it requires more fuel and your heart has to pump more blood. The test can show if there's a lack of blood supply through the arteries that go to the heart.

Taking a stress test also helps your doctor know the kind and level of exercise that's right for you.

The results of your stress test may help your doctor decide if you have heart disease, and if so, how severe it is.

What happens during the test?

- You're hooked up to equipment to monitor your heart.
- You walk slowly in place on the treadmill.
- It tilts so you feel like you're going up a small hill.
- It changes speeds to make you walk faster.

- You may be asked to breathe into a tube for a couple of minutes.
- You can stop the test at any time if you need to.
- After slowing down for a few minutes, you'll sit or lie down and your heart and blood pressure will be checked.

www.americanheart.org

| American Stroke Association |
| Diseases & Conditions |
| Children's Health |
| CPR & ECC |
| En español |
| Healthy Lifestyle |
| Advocacy: You're the Cure |
| Fund Raising |
| Publications & Resources |
| Heart & Stroke Encyclopedia |
| News |
| About Us |

Stem Cell Research

AHA Policy

The American Heart Association funds meritorious research involving human adult stem cells as part of our scientific research grant program. We do not fund any research involving stem cells derived from human embryos or fetal tissue.

The American Heart Association recognizes the value of all types of stem cell research and supports federal funding of this research. We are committed to supporting medical and scientific research to help us pursue our mission to reduce death and disability from cardiovascular diseases and stroke.

What are stem cells, and how can they be used?

Stem cells are cells within the body that have the potential to develop into one or many kinds of cells. Stem cells potentially could treat or cure many diseases and conditions. These include Parkinson's disease, Alzheimer's disease, diabetes, heart disease, stroke, arthritis, birth defects, osteoporosis, spinal cord injury and burns.

There are many types of stem cells. Two broad classifications of stem cells are human "**pluripotent**" stem cells and **adult** stem cells. Pluripotent stem cells potentially can develop into any kind of cell in the body and come from two sources:

- fetal tissue from miscarriages and abortions
- embryos created for in vitro fertility treatments but not selected for implantation

The American Heart Association does not fund any research involving stem cells derived from human embryonic or fetal tissue.

DID YOU KNOW?

The exact cause of 90-95% of all high blood pressure cases is unknown.

read more...

www.americanheart.org

Unfortunately, not all pages on the American Heart Association site are written clearly. For example, the organization's information regarding stem cell research is repetitious. Rather than get to the main point, it repeats secondary information such as the organization's policy and funding practices.

The over-emphasis on auxiliary details causes people to question the association's motive. Rather than provide information on the potential of stem cell therapies, the site focuses on political obstacles to the expansion of stem cell research, which users view as self-serving.

In addition, bolding words such as "adult" and "pluripotent" doesn't help because it is given no context and so seems arbitrary. Few people know what *pluripotent* means, but the site provides no definition.

"What's sticking out is that the American Heart Association does not fund any research involving embryonic tissue. It already told me that up front. Also, it says the American Heart funds meritorious research. I don't know why it's telling me that. I find that it's self-congratulatory."

"Having spent a couple of minutes on this site, I don't find that I am any wiser than when I started. I would go somewhere else to find out any more details in a simpler format. I am taking a disliking to the American Heart Association as a result."

Content writers commonly assume that users understand the distinctions among the products and services touted on their Web sites, but that's a mistake. For example, many people who visit investment sites are baffled by industry-specific terms such as "brokerage," "annuities," and "mutual funds," all of which are familiar if you work in the financial world. If potential investors come to your site to learn more but feel bombarded by unfamiliar jargon with no clear way to find the information, they may well go elsewhere.

⤏ Investments

Brokerage
Manage your investments online with Chase Investment Services Corp. – and receive real-time quotes, free news, and online trading of mutual funds, stocks and options.

College Planning
It is never too early to begin planning for your child's or grandchild's college education. Chase Investment Services Corp. offers many ways to start saving today.

JPMorgan Funds
Access JPMorgan Funds. Get fund information, investor tools and online account access.

Annuities
Annuities offer a combination of features and benefits that you may not find with other investment products.

Retirement Planning
The tax-deferred earnings potential of an IRA makes it a wise choice for many investors at all income levels - and making your retirement investment decisions online makes it even easier.

Rollover IRAs
Try our useful investment tools and articles to find out what you might do today to help make your financial dreams come true.

Forms and Disclosures
Investment forms are available as downloadable PDF files.

Mutual Fund Investing
Learn more about mutual fund investing and how your investments are affected by breakpoints and revenue sharing.

www.bankone.com

Many people had difficulty deciphering the difference between the various investment options on this site. Financial jargon compounded with superfluous writing makes it impossible for people to make confident product decisions. For example, the description for Rollover IRAs rambles on about trying out investment tools and articles but doesn't directly say what this option actually is.

"I'm not familiar with all this stuff. I would read more about it and maybe talk to somebody. The language here is too difficult for people to understand."

"This [site] gives me a lot of information. Understanding it —not!"

Write for the way people read on the Web. Design your content to match human behavior and tailor it for optimum scannability and comprehension

Understanding How Web Users Read

The Web is a user-directed medium, where people adopt information-seeking strategies to save time. They tend not to seek information in a linear fashion. Instead, they rely on the visual cues that give off the strongest signal that their answer is nearby. People direct their attention to these areas and ignore everything else.

We aren't suggesting that people *never* read information on the Web. How much people actually read depends on their goals and the level of information they need. In general, people scan first to sniff out the main points and then, if necessary, comb the page for more details. People who need in-depth information (such as for research projects) still scan, but reading is more deliberate on content-targeted pages.

If people are able to quickly recognize cues that point them to the targeted information, they'll happily follow the trail. However, if they don't immediately see anything of significance or feel overwhelmed, they'll abandon that path (or page) and try something else. Sometimes this means going back and selecting something else from a previous page.

Burn your users too many times, however, and they leave the site altogether and may never return. Regardless of how inherently interesting or important *you* think your content is, if your site doesn't make it easy for visitors to quickly grasp your purpose, their excitement vaporizes right at the point where the payoff should be.

What does this mean for your Web site? Write for the way people read on the Web. In order to capture and hold their attention, design your content to match human behavior and tailor it for optimum scannability and comprehension.

Life would be great if only users would read your content carefully. Don't they know that it's good?

No, they don't. Even if your content is in fact good and valuable, users most likely won't know that during their initial visit to your site. Scanning is an efficient method to home in on useful content. It takes less cognitive effort, so users can focus attention on fruitful areas.

Basic information-foraging theory (discussed in more detail in Chapter 2) states that users maximize their rate of gain across their entire time on the Internet. For any one topic a reader might need to research, there are likely to be hundreds of Web sites that contain seemingly endless amounts of related text. When faced with this much information, users absolutely must be able to scan and prioritize. Within a very few well-spent seconds, they decide whether to stay and read more, or move on to the next site.

Writing for Your Reader

You must be in touch with the interests, culture, needs, and limitations of your users in order to write for them. Information must be filtered and translated into a form your target reader can digest. For example, doctors need to understand the physiological and psychological effects that cigarette smoking has on their patients so that they can treat them. But they must also be able to explain the effects of smoking to their patients in lay terms. So must a medical-advice site intended for patients. Whatever your subject matter, if you're writing for a lay audience, avoid technical or industry jargon.

Who is your intended audience—IT professionals, teenagers, parents of school-age kids? Identifying your target audience helps you effectively communicate ideas and keeps you focused on the right subject and tone. Your readers want content that addresses their concerns and speaks to them at their level, in a voice they can relate to.

On the other hand, don't make the mistake of talking down to your audience. For example, in our study of teenagers, they often complained that adults are out of touch and don't understand their situations. They resented sites that came across as judgmental and particularly detested insincerity. When adults try to be "cool" or talk down to them, young people can detect it in a heartbeat. In our tests, we found that teens appreciated anecdotes that they could relate to. Supporting text with relevant illustrations or photographs was also key in facilitating learning and retaining their interest. Their enthusiasm quickly plummeted, however, when confronted with large blocks of text and ineffective examples.

www.theinsite.org

TheInsite.org had a section on how to resolve conflicts with siblings. While this topic initially piqued a lot of interest in a test with teenage users, many participants were skeptical of the advice given on the site because the language sounded too clinical. It was written in an adult tone that teens couldn't relate to. Several users chuckled at the phrase, "Use 'I feel' statements." They responded better to terms such as "cool off" and "listen." Users also expected to get concrete examples, which this site lacked.

"I'm thinking that this is a bunch of lies. Nobody does this. Make it more realistic and keep it real."

"This Web site was not satisfying because it didn't show examples of how to get along with each other."

President ∗ News ∗ Vice President ∗ History & Tours ∗ First Lady ∗ Mrs. Cheney

YOUR GOVERNMENT   KIDS   ESPAÑOL   CONTACT   PRIVACY POLICY   SITE MAP   SEARCH

The White House
PRESIDENT GEORGE W. BUSH
HOME

EMAIL UPDATES [   ] SEARCH

Issues
- Homeland Security
- Hurricane Recovery
- Immigration
- Jobs & Economy
- Judicial Nominations
- National Security
- Pandemic Flu
- Patriot Act
- Renewal in Iraq
- Social Security
- **More Issues »**

News
- Current News
- Press Briefings
- Proclamations
- Executive Orders
- Radio

RSS RSS Feeds

Major Speeches
- Progress in Iraq
- National Security
- Jobs & Economy

Interact
- Ask the White House
- White House Interactive

Your Government
- President's Cabinet
- USA Freedom Corps
- Faith-Based & Community
- OMB
- NSC
- **More Offices »**

Appointments
- Nominations
- Application

January 23, 2006 | Last Updated 10:59 p.m. (EST)

President Discusses Global War on Terror at Kansas State University

President Bush on Monday said, "Part of the job of a President is to be able to plan for the worst and hope for the best; and if the worst comes, be able to react to it. On September the 11th, the worst came. We got attacked. We didn't ask for the attack, but it came. I resolved on that day to do everything I can to protect the American people." **full story**

- In Focus: National Security
- In Focus: Renewal in Iraq

President Calls "March for Life" Participants

President Bush on Monday said, "You believe, as I do, that every human life has value, that the strong have a duty to protect the weak, and that the self-evident truths of the Declaration of Independence apply to everyone, not just to those considered healthy or wanted or convenient. These principles call us to defend the sick and the dying, persons with disabilities and birth defects, all who are weak and vulnerable, especially unborn children." **full story**

President's Radio Address

In his weekly radio address President Bush said, "America's economy is strong and growing stronger. Small businesses have been a driving force behind the tremendous growth and job creation of recent years. By adopting sound policies that help our small businesses continue to grow and expand, we

More Photos | White House photo by Kimberlee Hewitt

President George W. Bush meets with members of the U.S. Walker Cup Team in the Oval Office at the White House, Monday evening, Jan. 23, 2006. White House photo by Kimberlee Hewitt

PHOTO ESSAY: Mrs. Bush's Visit to West Africa

NATIONAL SECURITY

Fighting a Global War on Terror

On Monday, President Bush discussed the missions in Afghanistan and Iraq, and spoke about the importance of tools like the Patriot Act and the National Security Agency terrorist surveillance program, that are being used to prevent attacks and save lives. Click here to learn more.

SETTING THE RECORD STRAIGHT

- Democrats Continue to Attack Terrorist Surveillance Program
- Critics Launch Attacks Against Program to Detect and Prevent Terrorist Attacks

MORE »

www.whitehouse.gov

Teenage students avoid governmental sites, assuming they won't be able to relate to the content. Users suggested that their interest would be bolstered if sites used simpler language and had topics with which they could identify.

"We like to be treated equal to adults. Just use less complicated language. Teens process information differently from adults. Instead of using complicated words, take it slow. Most people go to a Web site to look up something. They want to understand it. Adults might understand topics differently and have different views. They have more experience and think differently."

Use Simple Language

Out of respect for your users' time and reading skills, keep your writing simple and concise. Using sophisticated words won't make you appear smarter or earn points with your users. Most people prefer a conversational tone to a formal tone because it's more personal and direct. Match your writing to their reading level to ensure maximum readability.

Don't overwrite. Superfluous verbiage makes people work unnecessarily hard to find the information they need, and convoluted language and fancy words alienate users; choose short words over long ones. For example, rather than use the term "carcinogenic," you might choose a simpler yet descriptive phrase such as "causes cancer."

Three Guidelines for Better Web Writing

- Skip the jargon. The terminology your organizational or industry uses is not usually part of your customer's vernacular. Simple terms might not seem artful or original, but they're understandable.
- Avoid acronyms. Government Web sites are especially notorious for sprinkling acronyms throughout their pages, assuming that audiences know what they mean.
- Bar sarcasm, subtle word play, and clichés such as "happy as a clam" or "caught with your pants down," which don't translate well on the Web and distract readers. Your audience is coming to your site for direct content, not for cleverness. Remember that the Web is truly a worldwide medium, and idioms don't easily cross borders.

(Facing page, top) This site attempts to insert humor into its product description. Unfortunately, some people didn't get the joke. The reference about "taco sauce" being a road-trip essential wasn't considered humorous.

"It says the removable flip-up rear seats let you configure the Element to fit most road-trip essentials, including your favorite taco sauce—I don't get that."

(Facing page, bottom) Our test users on the Social Security Administration Web site had difficulty finding answers to basic questions such as retirement age and benefit amounts. Even when staring at the page that contained the answers, people felt helpless because they couldn't interpret esoteric terms such as "Total Reduction" and "Total % Reduction." This is an example of using internal jargon instead of straightforward language to explain concepts.

"I thought it was over my head. They didn't talk in layman's terms. This is like speaking Greek to the average person."

Suggested Starting Price $16,100
BUILD & PRICE YOUR ELEMENT

Big on function and versatility, the Element gets you (and your stuff) where you need to go.
The removable flip-up rear seats let you configure the Element to fit most road-trip essentials, including your favorite taco sauce. And you can expect quick, simple loading of bikes, boards and more with the clamshell tailgate and side cargo doors. So grab your friends, stow your gear and get gone. Playtime just got easier.

automobiles.honda.com

Social Security Online
www.socialsecurity.gov

Full Retirement Age is Increasing

Home   Questions?   How to Contact Us   Search

Find Your Retirement Age

No matter what your full retirement age is, you may start receiving benefits as early as age 62.

Full Retirement age goes from 65 to...66...67

Note: *If you were born on January 1st of any year you should refer to the previous year in the chart below.*

Year of Birth	Full Retirement Age	Age 62 Reduction Months	Monthly % Reduction[1]	Total % Reduction[1]	Monthly % Reduction (spouse[2])	Total % Reduction (spouse[2])
1937 or earlier	65	36	.555	20.00	.694	62.50
1938	65 and 2 months	38	.548	20.83	.679	62.92
1939	65 and 4 months	40	.541	21.67	.667	63.34
1940	65 and 6 months	42	.535	22.50	.655	63.75
1941	65 and 8 months	44	.530	23.33	.644	64.17
1942	65 and 10 months	46	.525	24.17	.634	64.58
1943--1954	66	48	.520	25.00	.625	65.00
1955	66 and 2 months	50	.516	25.84	.617	65.42

www.socialsecurity.gov

www.san-diego-vision.com

This is an example of how using the wrong words can cause people to misinterpret the information. The tab labeled "Practice Information" is meant to lead visitors to information about the organization. People in the medical field commonly use the word "practice" in this way, but average people don't expect to find corporate information under "practice." They were looking for a more widely accepted term such as "About Us."

The International Adult Literacy Survey (IALS), a collaborative study by seven governments and three intergovernmental organizations, discovered that even in industrialized countries, a large percentage of adults have low literacy or poor reading comprehension.

In Sweden, where overall literacy is the highest, 28 percent of the participants scored in the lower literacy ranges—at about an eighth-grade reading level or below. A 2003 study conducted in the United States by the National Center for Education Statistics found that 43 percent of Americans aged 16 and older fall in the same category.

While most users *prefer* clear, simple language, site visitors with poor reading skills *need* it. Though people with low literacy tend to use the Web less, they still need and deserve accessible sites. In the United States and the United Kingdom, where literacy levels lag behind those of other developed nations, the number of Web users with low literacy may be as high as 30 percent. As Web usage continues to grow, this proportion will rise.

Make low-literacy needs a priority, especially if your site targets a broad general audience. We advise writing text that's aimed at the sixth-grade reading level, especially on high-exposure pages such as the homepage, category pages, and product pages. Pages deeper inside the site can be written at an eighth-grade reading level. Have a good Web content editor review the text for simplicity or use one of the many readability tools available. If the reading level is too high, reduce it by using simpler words with fewer syllables, and shorter sentences and paragraphs.

Tone Down Marketing Hype

Don't go for the hard sell. Give people the facts and let them come to their own conclusions. Good content sells itself.

Don't go for the hard sell. People prefer factual language and are turned off by anything that sounds overly promotional or exaggerated. Credibility is important on the Web, and organizations need to work hard to earn and keep it. Highly self-congratulatory statements come across as self-serving, and people are repelled by them. Extraordinary claims cause people to pause, evaluate their accuracy, and try to separate the facts from hype. Give people the facts and let them come to their own conclusions. Good content sells itself.

www.accenture.com

If you've never heard of this company, its homepage wouldn't help you understand what it is that it actually does. "High performance. Delivered" is a tagline that might describe virtually any business. Similarly, the highlighted quote in the center of the page is another example of empty marketing blather, and it doesn't describe what services or products the organization provides either. Toning down the marketing spin and using more descriptive phrases would improve usability and enhance credibility.

Accenture's description of its services isn't much better. The marketing lingo dilutes the message and doesn't clearly describe the services. Again, this text could apply a myriad of businesses.

Global Home ▸ **Research & Insights** ▸ Services

Services

Committed to delivering innovation, Accenture collaborates with its clients to help them achieve high performance. Our professionals leverage leading-edge technologies and tools to identify new opportunities and drive business process improvements.

www. accenture.com

Sometimes a little self-congratulation is appropriate, such as when you're highlighting noteworthy accomplishments. The goal is to appear knowledgeable without coming on too strong. If you have received noteworthy awards, go ahead and mention a few that will be meaningful to your users, especially if your organization is relatively unknown. However, don't pad your list with outdated or unrelated accomplishments such as design awards if you're not a design agency.

Take care to keep advertising out of the corporate areas of your site and other sections where people expect straight talk, such as "About Us" and "Investor Relations" sections. People who access these areas are specifically looking for company facts. Strong marketing language detracts from the facts, casting doubt on the credibility of the organization.

Writing Samples: Before and After

Notice how each of these samples can be rewritten to be more concise and understandable. The revised passage on volcanoes is more suitable for a general audience including children and teens.

From www.health.gov:

Consume a variety of nutrient-dense foods and beverages within and among the basic food groups while choosing foods that limit the intake of saturated and *trans* fats, cholesterol, added sugars, salt, and alcohol.

Our shorter, simpler version:

Eat a variety of foods from each of the basic food groups. Limit saturated and trans fats, added sugars, salt, and alcohol in your diet.

Question: How do volcanoes form?

From www.space.com:

Volcanoes form when *chambers of magma,* or hot molten rock, boil to the surface. These magma chambers often remain sealed for hundreds of years between eruptions, until the pressure builds sufficiently to break through a *vent,* which is a crack or weak spot in the rock above.

Simpler version from www.encarta.msn.com:

Volcanoes form when the planet needs to let heat escape from its interior. Rocks that melt deep beneath the planet's surface become liquid magma. The magma rises from Earth's interior to spew forth from a volcano at the Earth's surface.

This article is good if you're looking for a high-level summary of treatment options for stroke patients. The content is admirably clear, with medical concepts described in common language. Even so, it is written at about a grade 12 reading level, which, sadly, is beyond the capability of many high school graduates in the U.S.

www.healthlink.mcw.edu

Ask yourself whether somebody reading the first two sentences on your page will take away the information you want to convey.

Keeping It Short and Sweet

We can't stress this enough: Long, rambling text frustrates audiences. In general, the word count for Web content should be about half of that used in conventional writing.

Cutting back is easier said than done. It takes courage and practice to carve your writing down to the essentials. But cutting back on word count doesn't mean leaving out important details. When done well, trimmed and scannable content conveys the same information and is more helpful to your readers.

Summarize Key Points and Pare Down

Start with the conclusion, then reveal supporting facts. This structural convention is known by journalists as the inverted pyramid. It gives readers the gist quickly and then lets them burrow into the details if they choose to read on. If the first part of the article is dull and unfocused, however, people will likely quit reading anyway.

People on the Web don't usually stay on the same page for an extended amount of time and feel more productive clicking hyperlinks and traversing from topic to topic. Rather than overwhelming site visitors with extensive content, layer the information on different pages. Start with the key points first and then make it easy for people to drill down. Layering your content satisfies the needs of both casual browsers and serious researchers without sacrificing scannability and completeness.

That said, don't dice your content so fine that it feels disjointed. Keep closely related information on the same page rather than make your users jump from one incomplete part to the next. As long as a page contains highly related information people don't mind a bit of scrolling.

When running long documents, it's not enough to simply break them into smaller parts with a generic *Continue* link at the bottom of each page. Instead create links such as "The Vice President's Response" or "Day Three of the Race," which tell people what information comes next when they click.

If you just want to know what you can bring back into the country from travel abroad, this page won't help. People in our study struggled with the convoluted content. The first few paragraphs should have answered the question, but instead they address specific situations and consequences that apply only to a limited number of users. While this level of detail is important, it doesn't belong at the beginning. The bold-face text "along with any vehicle used to transport them" might have some significance to the writer, but it doesn't to readers.

"It's smacking me with too much information first off. There's loads of information. Loads of text really."

Public & travel
Your customs allowances
Banned & restricted goods
VAT refunds for visitors
Shopping on the Internet
Travellers' charter
Notices for travellers

Your customs allowances - what can I bring back

Jump to other links in this section:

You do not have to pay any tax or duty in the UK on goods you have bought tax paid in other EU countries which are for your own use, and which have been transported by you.

'Own use' includes goods for your own consumption and gifts. But you cannot bring back goods for payment, even payment in kind, for re-sale, or for business purposes. These would then be regarded as held for a commercial purpose. You may be breaking the law if you sell goods that you have bought. If you are caught selling the goods, they will be taken off you and for serious offences you could get up to seven years in prison.

If you bring back large quantities of alcohol or tobacco, a Customs Officer may ask about the purposes for which you hold the goods. The Officer will take into account all the factors of the situation and your explanation. If you are unable or refuse to provide a satisfactory explanation the officer may well conclude that those goods are for a commercial purpose and not for your own use. If the Officer is satisfied the goods are being brought into the UK for a commercial purpose, and are not for own use, the goods, **along with any vehicle used to transport them**, will be liable to seizure and may not be returned.

When travelling to Spain, UK citizens need to be aware that the Spanish authorities have domestic legislation, which places documentary obligations upon anyone holding or moving large quantities of duty-paid cigarettes (above 800). One of the practical effects of this is that UK travellers, in the same way as everybody else who is holding or moving large quantities of duty-paid cigarettes in Spain (between 800 and 1200), must produce a receipt from a legitimate retailer and, for even larger quantities of cigarettes (over 1200), a form known as a 'Documento de Acompanamiento'.

Failure to provide the required document could result in the Spanish authorities taking the goods from you. The Spanish authorities do ensure, however, that people are free to purchase, hold and move as much tobacco as they like provided that they carry

www.hmce.gov.uk

Our users who visited this site had difficulty understanding what an IRA account was because the information was poorly organized and explained. The site elaborates specific details before establishing the main points, causing confusion. The first sentence attempts to describe the account, but the definition is so generic that it might almost apply to many other accounts. In addition, it's not clear what the differences are between "Traditional" and "Roth IRA" accounts. Convoluted banking jargon such as "Employer's Qualified Pension Plan" and "mandatory distribution" makes it arduous for people to pick the right product.

Traditional & Roth IRA ACCOUNTS

A Traditional Individual Retirement account is a tax advantage account designed to offer customers financial security after retirement. If an individual is covered by an Employer's Qualified Pension Plan, contributions may be fully or partially tax-deductible, or phased out completely depending on the customer's adjusted gross income. Withdrawals can be made at any time but are subject to taxes and penalty. After age 59½, distributions can be taken without IRS penalties. Mandatory distributions are required after age 70½. IRS regulations simplified the required distributions by providing a uniform distribution period for all individuals of the same age.

A Roth IRA has no maximum age restrictions, is not deductible, and is not subject to mandatory distribution. Eligibility to contribute to a Roth IRA is based on the customer's modified adjusted gross income. Ordering rules for tax and penalty free distributions apply for qualified and non-qualified withdrawals.

www.dimewill.com

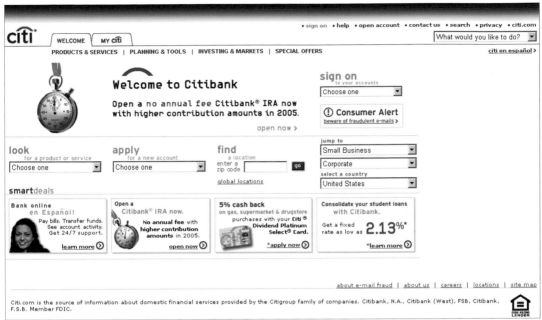

www.citibank.com

There's no need to literally welcome people to your site. While this might be considered a minor criticism, the point is to reduce unnecessary verbiage whenever possible. One word here and there slowly adds up, unnecessarily increasing the complexity of the site. Also, notice the use of buzzwords such as "look," "apply," and "find." These terms might leave people wondering: Look for what? Apply for what? Find what? Better to use more descriptive phrases.

Tip: Writing Descriptive Labels

We've selected a few label names from the Citibank Web site and renamed them to give you an idea of how using the right names can improve communication. The original labels are clever and snappy but not the best at conveying meaning. The revised version is better because it lets people know what they're going to get without any guesswork.

Original Labels	Suggested Labels
Look	Products and Services
Apply	Apply for an Account
Find	Locations

products   clients   about us   contact

Know What?

Can locators be used in wireless applications?
Absolutely! We perform our own wireless integration. This gives us the ability to work more closely with our clients and is both faster and more cost-effective than using third party integration.

How do you handle International locations?
Our World locator enables true proximity searching for locations all over the world!

Want to know more?

The Know-Where Solution

Your customers found your web site. We'll send them to your nearest stores.

Electronic commerce makes up less than 2% of all retail sales. In most cases, making a sale means getting your customer to a real world store. That's where Know-Where Systems excels. We can get your clients to your nearest location where they can buy your product. No matter if your business has a few dozen locations in one town or tens of thousands of distributors all over world, Know-Where has a store locator solution for you.

With years of experience in web-based locators and a world class engineering team, we have automated process of building, customizing and maintaining store locators. This lets us offer a locator that is better, faster and cheaper than any other available. There is simply no locator service more flexible and powerful than Know-Where.

We believe your customers should have best experience possible. With many compelling advantages, both for client and their customers, our experience and technology combine to produce a superior locator service.

Find out more about our products!

What Now?

Once you've learned more about the powerful solution that is Know-Where Systems, how can you take advantage of our services for your project? In just a few quick steps, we can get you well on your way towards becoming another one of our over 300 satisfied clients...

These are just three of the hundreds of Know-Where enhanced clients. Take a look at more.

www.know-where.com

Avoid meaningless headers. "Know What?" and "What Now?" might be cute in concept, but they don't really communicate anything useful.

(Facing page, top) The repetition of words such as "Click here to" and "Click here for" clutters the page, making it difficult to quickly scan the links and hone in on the important ones. Most people now know how to recognize links, so you can eliminate the instruction to click and identify links with information-carrying words.

(Facing page, bottom) Overuse of the words "Palm Beach County" diverts attention from the key terms on this site, making scanning difficult. Visitors already know they're in a section on Palm Beach County, so repeating it adds no value.

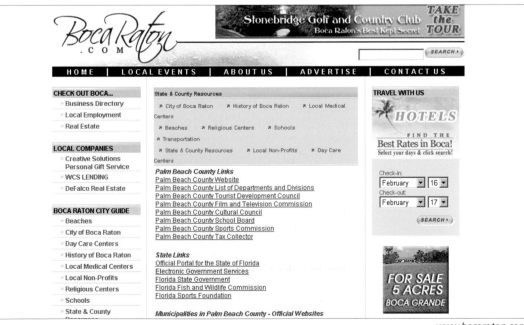

www.bocaraton.com

What's the key term here? In this design, the links appear to be the most prominent, but they convey the least amount of information. Better to simplify this screen by eliminating the links and instead making the most important information, such as times and dates, clickable. The title of the page already tells us that all listings are for 'O' by Cirque Du Soleil, no reason to repeat it.

Show	Time	Date
SOLD OUT 'O' BY CIRQUE DU SOLEIL-WED	7:30 PM	Wednesday August 10, 2005
SOLD OUT 'O' BY CIRQUE DU SOLEIL-WED	10:30 PM	Wednesday August 10, 2005
'O' BY CIRQUE DU SOLEIL-THURS	7:30 PM	Thursday August 11, 2005
'O' BY CIRQUE DU SOLEIL-THURS	10:30 PM	Thursday August 11, 2005
'O' BY CIRQUE DU SOLEIL-FRI	7:30 PM	Friday August 12, 2005
'O' BY CIRQUE DU SOLEIL-FRI	10:30 PM	Friday August 12, 2005
'O' BY CIRQUE DU SOLEIL-SAT	7:30 PM	Saturday August 13, 2005
'O' BY CIRQUE DU SOLEIL-SAT	10:30 PM	Saturday August 13, 2005
'O' BY CIRQUE DU SOLEIL-SUN	7:30 PM	Sunday August 14, 2005
'O' BY CIRQUE DU SOLEIL-SUN	10:30 PM	Sunday August 14, 2005
'O' BY CIRQUE DU SOLEIL-WED	7:30 PM	Wednesday August 17, 2005
'O' BY CIRQUE DU SOLEIL-WED	10:30 PM	Wednesday August 17, 2005
'O' BY CIRQUE DU SOLEIL-THURS	7:30 PM	Thursday August 18, 2005
'O' BY CIRQUE DU SOLEIL-THURS	10:30 PM	Thursday August 18, 2005
'O' BY CIRQUE DU SOLEIL-FRI	7:30 PM	Friday August 19, 2005
'O' BY CIRQUE DU SOLEIL-FRI	10:30 PM	Friday August 19, 2005
'O' BY CIRQUE DU SOLEIL-SAT	7:30 PM	Saturday August 20, 2005
'O' BY CIRQUE DU SOLEIL-SAT	10:30 PM	Saturday August 20, 2005
'O' BY CIRQUE DU SOLEIL-SUN	7:30 PM	Sunday August 21, 2005
'O' BY CIRQUE DU SOLEIL-SUN	10:30 PM	Sunday August 21, 2005

www.bellagio.com

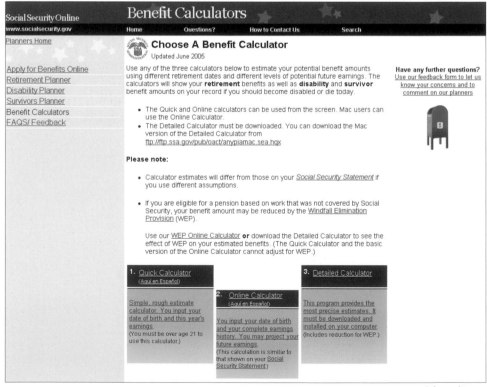

www.socialsecurity.gov

In 1998 John Morkes and Jakob Nielsen conducted a study demonstrating how formatting very technical information according to Web guidelines can significantly improve usability. They compared two versions of a white paper posted on a B2B (business to business) Web site—one in its original form, and the other using more Web-ready, concise writing. The results were astounding. The revised version scored significantly higher on all usability parameters.

Compared to the original, the version presented in a Web-optimized format enabled readers to:

- Complete the task 80 percent faster
- Make 80 percent fewer errors
- Recall 100 percent more facts
- Score their satisfaction with the Web site 37 percent higher

(Facing page, bottom) The title says to choose a calculator, but the main page doesn't show the choices clearly, and the names of the calculators don't help. Extraneous notes and tips clutter the page, while the tools people want are mostly hidden below the viewable browser window. Bolded words such as *retirement* and *disability* call attention to random terms that don't communicate anything useful.

"Oh, my God! Way too much text!"

Formatting Text for Readability

Well-established Web-formatting techniques can create visual cues that significantly improve the readability of your site's text, helping people scan pages quickly and access the areas that pertain to them. The most common and effective conventions are:

- Highlighted keywords
- Concise and descriptive titles and headings
- Bulleted lists and numbered steps
- Short paragraphs
- Making sure that the most important point on a Web page is stated within the first two lines

Highlight Keywords

Highlighting carefully chosen keywords can attract readers' attention to specific areas of the page. Using design treatments such as such as boldface or colored text adds emphasis and draws the eye to important elements, as we discussed in more detail in Chapter 7.

Highlighting entire sentences or long phrases slows readers down, so single out just those words and phrases that communicate key points. Emphasizing too many items with color highlight or bold text causes diminishing returns; nothing stands out, and the page just looks busy.

Design treatments commonly associated with hyperlinks (such as blue, underlined, and bold text) automatically make them stand out. In fact, in some cases, these are enough, and you don't need any additional highlighting.

The judiciously bolded words attract the reader's attention to critical areas, making it easy to get the gist of the message by scanning quickly.

Statistics
Coronary heart disease is America's No. 1 killer. Stroke is No. 3 and a leading cause of serious disability. That's why it's so important to reduce your risk factors, know the warning signs, and know how to respond quickly and properly if warning signs occur.

Heart Attack Warning Signs
Some heart attacks are sudden and intense -- the "movie heart attack," where no one doubts what's happening. But most heart attacks start slowly, with mild pain or discomfort. Often people affected aren't sure what's wrong and wait too long before getting help. Here are signs that can mean a heart attack is happening:

- **Chest discomfort.** Most heart attacks involve discomfort in the center of the chest that lasts more than a few minutes, or that goes away and comes back. It can feel like uncomfortable pressure, squeezing, fullness or pain.
- **Discomfort in other areas of the upper body.** Symptoms can include pain or discomfort in one or both arms, the back, neck, jaw or stomach.
- **Shortness of breath.** This feeling often comes along with chest discomfort. But it can occur before the chest discomfort.
- **Other signs:** These may include breaking out in a cold sweat, nausea or lightheadedness

If you or someone you're with has chest discomfort, especially with one or more of the other signs, don't wait longer than a few minutes (no more than 5) before calling for help. Call 9-1-1... Get to a hospital right away.

Calling 9-1-1 is almost always the fastest way to get lifesaving treatment. Emergency medical services staff can begin treatment when they arrive -- up to an hour sooner than if someone gets to the hospital by car. The staff are also trained to revive someone whose heart has stopped. Patients with chest pain who arrive by ambulance usually receive faster treatment at the hospital, too.

www.americanheart.org

Use Concise and Descriptive Titles and Headings

Our eye-tracking studies show that users often read only the first words of search listings, so it's no good to save your information-carrying keywords for the end of the title.

The main page title is especially important because it serves as the link to the page in search engine listings. Users speed through those listings, so your page title must convey your purpose in just a few words. Our eye-tracking studies show that users often read only the first words of the search listings, so it's no good to save your information-carrying keywords for the end of the title.

Within a given page, effective headings and subheadings catch your reader's eye and announce the purpose of the content. They serve as signposts for the content's organization, breaking text into manageable chunks and making it easier to read and comprehend. Their main purpose is to point readers to the content they seek. That means they need to be short (60 characters maximum) and meaningful. Resist the temptation to write cute or clever headings.

Fancy titles such as "Go Red For Women," and "911" don't adequately describe the content. They are meaningful in context, but keep in mind that most people won't take the time to figure it out. Even when titles are bright, bold, and graphical, people ignore them if the meaning is obscure. Simply dressing up text won't make it any more appealing.

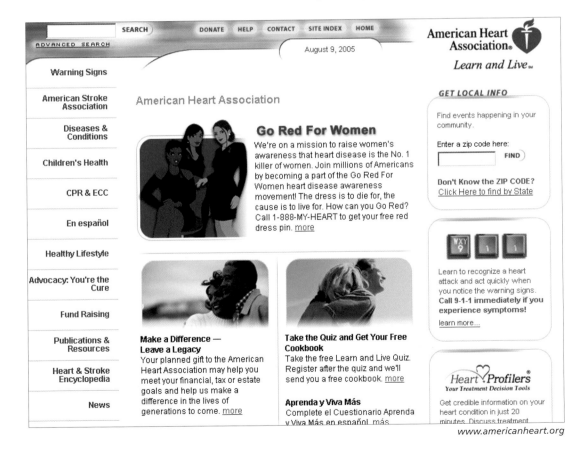

www.americanheart.org

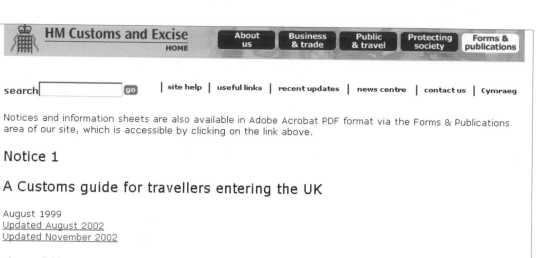

It's difficult to tell what information this page contains from the title "Notice 1: A Customs guide for travelers entering the UK." Many people don't know what "Notice 1" means or what "A Customs guide" includes. Users are overwhelmed by the wordy links and the use of obscure dates and terms.

"This is confusing—lots of things about date changes and guides and not much on relevant topics. There are lots of things about when things changed, but no lists of things you are looking for. Too much detail with regard to charters and dates and not enough details about the information you need."

"It's not user friendly. What I like now is a list of commonly asked questions. It's talking about documents and versions. The amount of text is quite confusing."

"It's all in government jargon. For a site intended for public access, there should be commonly used information, not government stuff. I'm tempted to phone somebody up."

Use Bulleted and Numbered Lists

When describing steps or items in a series, use bulleted or numbered lists. Use bulleted lists when items require no particular order and numbered lists for step-by-step instructions, sequenced items, and items referenced by number.

Vertical lists have more white space around each item, giving the eyes pause and making each piece stand out on its own. As a result, they are more effective than inline lists, making key points easier to reference and understand. Similarly, whether numbered or bulleted, vertical lists are more effective than run-in lists at conveying a sequence of events or ideas. Studies comparing the two show that vertical lists can improve usability by 47 percent.

Compare these two different formats and notice that the spa treatments listed in the second example are easier to read. Listing the offerings vertically makes it easier for users to scan choices than it would be on an inline list.

Spa Moulay Getaway   CHECK AVAILABILITY

6/20/05 - 1/29/06

Relax with our Spa Moulay Getaway which includes one night's deluxe accommodations, two Select* 50 minute Spa treatments and a Welcome Amenity. Valid thru 1/29/06.

*Select spa treatments include your choice of the following services: 50 minute Raindrop, Swedish, or Aromatherapy massage, 50 minute Holistic Facial, A haircut and style, 80 minute Spa Moulay Manicure & Pedicure.

Spa & Golf Package   CHECK AVAILABILITY

6/20/05 - 12/30/05

Enjoy the best of both worlds with our Spa & Golf Package. Includes one night's deluxe accommodations, one select* 50 minute spa treatment and one golf voucher for Reflection Bay or the Falls golf course.

*Select spa treatments include your choice of the following services.:
- 50 minute Raindrop
- Swedish or Aromatherapy massage
- 50 minute Holistic Facial
- A haircut and style
- 80 minute Spa Moulay Manicure & Pedicure.

www.hyatt.com

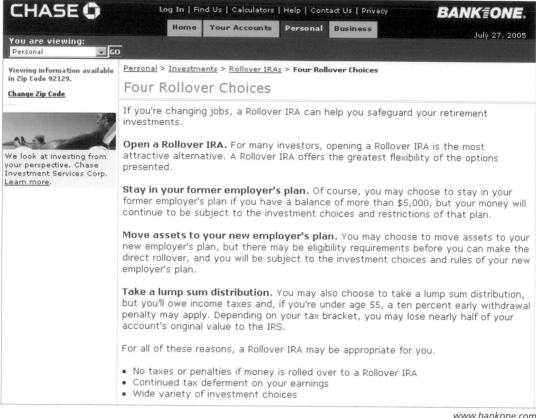

The writing here is an improvement over other examples we've shown you. Sentences are generally short and simple, and key terms are bolded, so the options stand out. It would be better to have a lead-in sentence and number each option so that people clearly know each one is a choice.

Top Seven Guidelines for Presenting Lists

- Use vertical lists when you have four or more items to emphasize. Shorter lists are generally overkill.
- Introduce a list with a clear, descriptive lead-in sentence or phrase. The lead-in doesn't have to be a complete sentence as long as each item in the list completes the sentence.
- Indent vertical lists and begin run-over lines under the text, not the bullet.
- Don't leave too much space between the bullet and the start of the text. Having wide gaps between the bullet and the text is difficult to read; the eye must travel farther to make the connection.
- When possible, omit articles such as "a," "an," or "the," and repetitive words from the beginning of list items.
- Use parallel phrasing for each list item.
- Don't overuse lists, as they can lose their effectiveness.

Goods you buy in the EU

You do not have to pay any tax or duty in the UK on goods you have bought tax paid in other EU countries for your own use and transported by you, but please remember the following:

- 'Own use' includes goods which are for your own consumption and gifts. You cannot bring back goods for payment, even payment in kind, or for re-sale. These would then be regarded as held for a commercial purpose.
- You may be breaking the law if you sell goods that you have bought. If you are caught selling the goods, they will be taken off you and for serious offences you could get up to seven years in prison.

If you bring back large quantities of alcohol or tobacco, a Customs Officer may ask you about the purposes for which you hold the goods. This particularly applies if you have with you more than the following amounts:

- 3200 cigarettes
- 200 cigars
- 110 litres of beer
- 90 litres of wine

- 400 cigarillos
- 3 kg of smoking tobacco
- 10 litres of spirits
- 20 litres of fortified wine (such as port or sherry)

These questions and checks could be about:

- The frequency of your travel
- The amount and type of goods purchased
- The reason for purchasing goods
- The method of payment used
- Levels of consumption
- Whether all your goods are openly displayed or concealed.
- Any other relevant circumstances.

The Officer will take into account all the factors of the situation and your explanation. If you are unable or you refuse to provide a satisfactory explanation the Officer may well conclude that those goods are for commercial purposes and not for your own use.

www.hmce.gov.uk

Bulleted lists can be helpful, but using them too often reduces their effectiveness.

Tip: Parallel Phrasing Is Important

Each item should have a consistent style of phrasing. Widely varied wording is ungrammatical and confusing to readers. Notice that in the non-parallel examples, the three phrases begin with different types of words and only the first completes the lead-in sentence. The revised list flows better because each phrase starts with a similar type of word (in this case, a verb) and completes the lead-in sentence.

Non-parallel

Students sign up for newsletters to:

- Find out what's new
- How other people in their age group are doing
- Contests

Parallel

Students sign up for newsletters to:

- Find out what's new
- See what other people in their age group are doing
- Enter contests

This is hardly an overview. The large wall of text intimidates readers. Chunking the information into smaller paragraphs would make the content feel more approachable.

Keep Paragraphs Short

Another way to improve readability is to break up content into small chunks. Short paragraphs surrounded by white space appear more approachable than a solid wall of text. Information shortened into digestible pieces facilitates scanning by allowing people to see natural breaks and absorb the information in manageable pieces.

There are no hard-and-fast rules about how long or short paragraphs should be, although it's helpful to keep them under five sentences. Each paragraph should have one topic sentence and one idea. Too many ideas in a single paragraph increase its complexity and make readers work to decipher the main idea. People should be able to read the topic sentence and decide whether they need to read the rest of the paragraph.

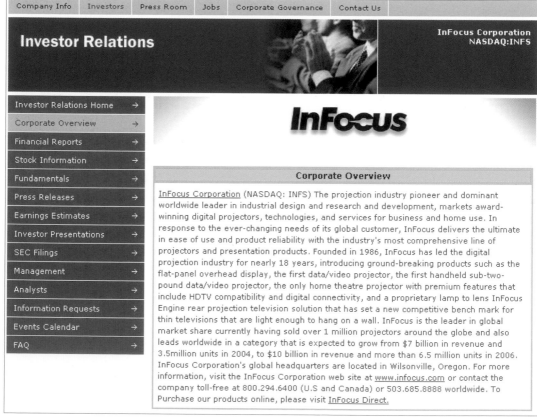

www.infocus.com

Behaviors

Interesting Facts:

- Sagebrush grows slowly. Dense stands of sagebrush -- which take 25 or perhaps even 100 years to recover from fires -- can be the most important to sage-grouse.
- Though more than 170 species of birds and mammals live in sage-steppe grasslands, sage-grouse are one of the only bird species that extensively eat sagebrush.

Voice: When flushed, a coarse "wut" or "kak, kak, kak" call. Males also coo and make popping vocalizations by expelling air through esophageal pouches during courtship.

Diet: Sagebrush almost exclusively during winter, and forbs (small flowering plants) in other seasons, while chicks eat insects and forbs. Unlike many other birds, sage-grouse are not adapted to digest seeds, and do not eat wheat, corn or other agricultural grains. They will, however, eat alfalfa, dandelion and other introduced forbs.

Habitat Type: Sage-grouse are found on prairies and mountain foothills, primarily in areas dominated by sagebrush, forbs and grasses, in habitats known as "sage-steppe." The best sage-grouse habitats are in mature sagebrush stands, often 30-100 years old, with a dense under story of native perennial grasses and flowering plants. These arid lands are characterized by a blanket of sagebrush and scant rainfall and snow. These birds require various types of sagebrush, ranging from tall, well developed sage for shelter and food during deep winter snows, to dense sage thickets with lush native grasses beneath for nesting. Sage-grouse chicks need healthy, wet meadows and creek areas rich in insects, forbs and other plants.

Range: Gunnison sage-grouse are found in Colorado and Utah, while the greater sage-grouse are found in parts of 11 western states and two Canadian provinces: California, Nevada, Oregon, Washington, Idaho, Montana, North Dakota, South Dakota, Wyoming, Colorado, Utah, Alberta and Saskatchewan.

Breeding: Each spring the males gather on a traditional display ground, called a lek, to court the females. They have ornate and competitive springtime mating rituals. Up to 100 males may be seen performing on a single lek, a true spectacle of nature. After mating, females nest and raise up to a

www.nwf.org

Nice writing style—clear writing, simple words, and appropriate use of Web formatting techniques facilitate scanning.

9 Providing Good Product Information

It would be difficult to overstate how many online sales are lost because of unclear product information. At its best, shopping on the Web should be more convenient than shopping in stores, but too often it is not, because merchandise information is insufficient, hard to locate, or simply not there. Makes you wonder if organizations have their sights set on making money or losing it.

To sell or promote products online, you must give people the information they need to make confident purchasing decisions. This chapter discusses the most common pitfalls in presenting product info and provides strategies for ensuring that your customers get the sales support they need.

There are many potential advantages to shopping online. People can research products and compare prices at their own pace and on their own schedule. There's no time wasted traveling from store to store. Even better, there's no sales pressure, no pushy salespeople to fend off. Yet all too often e-commerce is neither convenient nor easy. Looking for good product information often leads to dead ends and frustration.

We watched people in our studies get to the right product area but ultimately abandon it because they couldn't find answers to their most basic questions: How much does it cost? What does it look like? Does it have the features I need? Does it work with what I already have? Efficient navigation and a good purchase process help customers buy things online, but clear product information is essential to making them *want* to buy online.

For all its convenience, online shopping also poses challenges to retailers that brick-and-mortar stores do not face: There's no tangible product to hold, no product displays or boxes to inspect, no salesperson to turn to for help. Web sites must bridge this gap by making the research process as painless as possible, anticipating people's questions, and making sure the answers are easy to find.

Unlike store shoppers, online customers can go elsewhere with just a click. Rarely do they call retailers to get answers to their questions, especially if there are other online alternatives. Unless you have exclusive products and services to offer, frustrated shoppers will leave your site and go to your competitors' rather than search for a phone number, wait in a telephone queue, or struggle with cumbersome telephone menus.

We do not cover all aspects of e-commerce usability in this chapter—we have an entire report series devoted to those issues. Instead, we focus here on how to get useful product information to your customers, whether or not you sell your products directly on your site.

Show Me the Money

Customer surveys show that one of the first things people want to know about a product or service is the price. The product picture or description might pique one's interest, but pricing information is foremost in people's minds. Be candid: Make it easy for users to get pricing information.

A price can tell people a few things at once:

- The value of the item
- Whether the item falls within their budget
- Whether they are shopping in the right customer segment

When no price is shown, people assume—often wrongly—that the product must be expensive. Showing the price at the first mention of the product helps alleviate customer doubts about whether they are in the right price category.

Price is also a key component in product comparison. Once people identify potential candidates for purchase, pricing is critical in making trade-off decisions. Why are these two similar-looking products priced differently? Is this additional feature worth paying the extra cost?

Price can also guide buyers to the right place for their needs. For example, if a person is shopping for copiers for a company of 500 employees, he or she expects the price to be significantly different than the price for a machine designed for small businesses. Bigger companies need beefier machines, which means higher price tags. Conversely, if the user is buying for a small business with only a few users, the price category will be much lower. Knowing the price at the beginning helps buyers quickly hone in on the items that are relevant to their situation while weeding out the rest.

At a time when Internet scams are prevalent, customers need extra assurance that organizations are credible before they'll commit to a sale. Being straightforward and clear about price is essential in garnering business. People view companies that hide costs as evasive and untrustworthy. Imagine going into a flooring store and asking for the price of installing tile, but the sales associate says he can't tell you until after you hand over your credit card. Now imagine a

---

At a time when Internet scams are prevalent, customers need extra assurance that organizations are credible before they'll commit to a sale. Being straightforward and clear about price is essential to garnering business.

Tip: Where To Display Prices

Prices should be displayed clearly on product lists and product pages. Don't make people click on the product link or picture to get pricing information. Having to click back and forth between the product listings and the product page is inconvenient for users.

store where the sales associate not only tells you the final cost, but also breaks it down by materials and service. Which company are you more inclined to do business with?

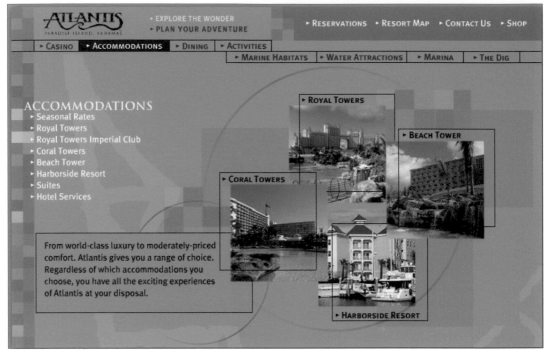

People in our study were initially drawn by the graphical presentation of this resort and immediately wanted to know about prices, but there was no obvious place to get them. The accommodation area had a small link called Seasonal Rates, but people didn't notice it because it was grouped together with links for the Towers.

"Looks pretty good to me, but how much is it going to cost me?"

"It doesn't say how much it costs. This is disappointing because I don't have a definitive answer. I don't know how much it costs and how to make a reservation."

(Facing page, top) Shopping on this site is unpleasant because customers must click on each item to see its price. Show prices at the category page level, not just on the deeper-level product pages.

"I don't like that they don't have prices, so you don't have a clue of what they are going to be."

(Facing page, bottom) This site leaves out prices altogether. Even if prices vary from store to store, showing estimated prices is better than nothing. Price can indicate product sophistication: For example, brand-name and designer apparel tends to be priced higher. People who are unfamiliar with this brand will wonder whether the price falls within their budget and their fashion sensibilities.

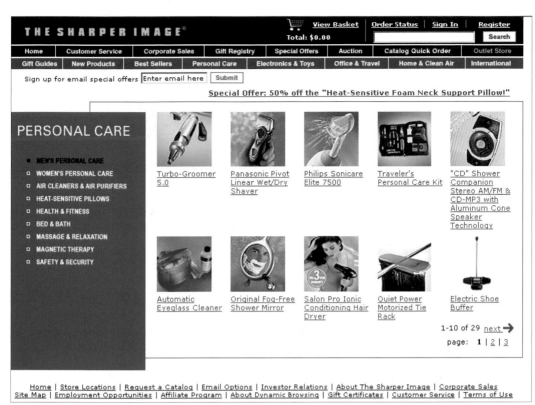

www.sharperimage.com

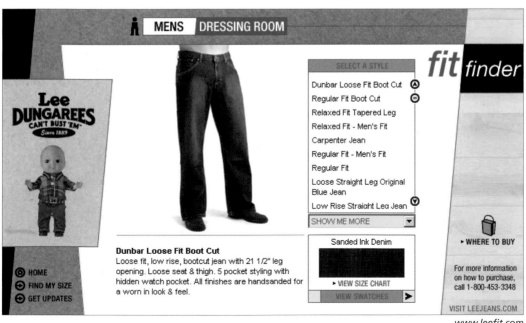

www.leefit.com

No Excuses

Companies make many excuses for why they don't reveal prices online: They don't want competitors to know their prices, prices vary for different customers, prices fluctuate, and so on. All of these excuses may be legitimate, but they don't help your customers. Not showing price works against their needs and creates a hostile shopping experience.

Don't play tricks on customers when it comes to cost. Repeat online transactions rely on consumer confidence, and companies that uphold their advertised claims win points with customers.

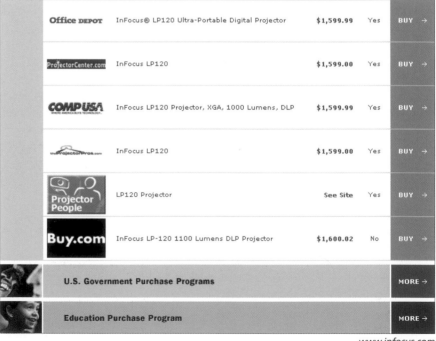

www.infocus.com

This site does a good job of revealing vendor prices for its products. Even though governmental organizations have their own purchase programs, seeing the cost gives them an idea of the price range.

People were initially attracted to the advertised price of the January White Out package on the Fairmont Chateau Whistler ski resort site. When they followed the link, however, the price changed from $1,049 (Canadian) for five nights to $529 per night. The seemingly inconsistent pricing information hurts an organization's credibility.

January White Out - Fairmont Chateau Whistler

A a member of the 'Leading Hotels of the World.

Nestled at the foot of both Blackcomb & Whistler Mountains, discover the Fairmont Chateau Whistlers majestic chateau-style hotel. Impeccable service, outstanding cuisine, and luxurious accommodation defines The Fairmont Chateau Whistler.

Starting From $1,049 CAD ($739 USD) Per Person

- 5 nights accommodations at the Fairmont Chateau Whistler
- 4 out of 5 day dual mountain lift ticket

Note: Rates are for 5 nights accommodation and a 4 out of 5 day lift ticket to both Whistler & Blackcomb Mountains. Based on 2 people sharing a Fairmont Room between January 5 - 31, 2004. Images may not represent actual room type included in this package. Rates are quoted in CAD (USD) funds, exclusive of taxes and fees. Advance purchase and other restrictions may apply. Rates are subject to availability at the time of booking and may change without notice. Policies and Conditions for travel products will be collected and presented for your perusal once you have created a travel plan.

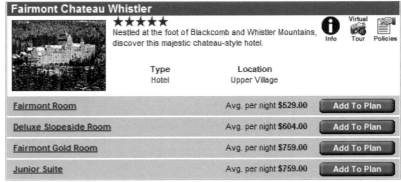

www.whistlerblackcomb.com

Tip: Approximate Prices Are Better Than None

If you can't give the actual price of a product online, give the approximate price or price range. There are many situations where users accept approximate prices, understanding that the final price will be different. For example, in the B2B (business to business) sector, big customers commonly negotiate special rates that are not available to the general public.

Purchasers for such companies know they won't have to pay list price but still need to get a ballpark figure. Pricing structures may also vary for a specific service. For example, a moving company typically can't provide fixed prices on its Web site. But it could quote typical fees for moving, say, a three-bedroom household within the same city or across the country.

Disclose Extra Fees

Disclose additional fees such as taxes and shipping as soon as possible, and certainly on the first page of the shopping cart. Don't expect people to wait until the end of the checkout process to get the bottom line. Most people won't waste their time filling out forms or giving personal information unless they know what they're spending, and an unexpected surcharge is an unwelcome surprise.

For example, a user in our study who was shopping for a vase on KitchenEtc.com was apprehensive about purchasing the item because the shipping and insurance costs weren't apparent. She was an experienced Internet shopper and didn't want to be fooled by hidden costs. Without the total cost, she didn't want to shop on this site.

"There wasn't any mention of shipping," she said. "Typically glassware requires insurance and is heavy; shipping can be expensive. I doubt that I would go back to this Web site.... It doesn't say how much the shipping is, so that is a concern."

Customers on this site don't get the final total until they've registered and entered complete shipping information. Placing such obstacles in customers' path turns them away.

By the same token, if you offer free or discounted shipping, say so. Let customers know whether taxes apply. Legitimately saving people money is not something to be shy about. Saving customers money on supplementary charges can swing them favorably in your direction.

www.target.com

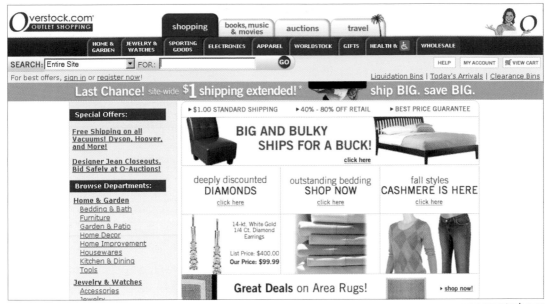

This site advertises its one-dollar shipping fee prominently on the homepage, so there's no ambiguity, leaving customers free to focus on shopping.

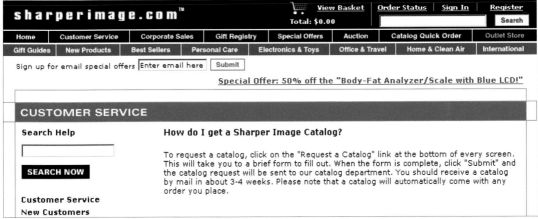

If you have complimentary items, make sure that's clear—even for items that are customarily free. Many companies give away catalogs on their Web site and neglect to indicate that they're complimentary. A participant in our study refused to sign up for a catalog because it didn't mention price, so she assumed there might be a cost.

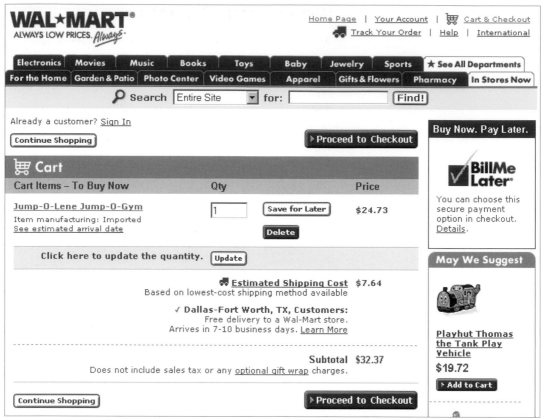

www.walmart.com

This site shows the estimated shipping price on the shopping cart page, before requiring any personal information. Saving people from unnecessary steps before they've made the commitment to buy is a smart strategy that facilitates a pleasant shopping experience. Of course, the exact final cost should be shown before people check out, preferably right after the shipping address is entered.

Win Customer Confidence

All too often, Web sites are drenched with marketing hype instead of accurate descriptions of the products and services they sell. Customers will trust a site that clearly explains a product or service and includes images, but too much detail up front can be overwhelming. When information is extensive, we suggest layering it. A few carefully placed accolades and positive reviews also help assure consumers that they are putting their trust (and money) in the right place.

Describe the Product

Shallow product descriptions are another culprit in the failure of online sales.

Common mistakes are:

- Not sufficiently explaining the offering
- Not having adequate images to show the details

Product descriptions need to be detailed enough to give people a good sense of the product or service and help them differentiate among the choices. Precise descriptions help people make confident purchase decisions.

The rules for writing for the Web that we discussed in Chapter 8 apply to presenting product information as well. Be concise. Be diligent in leaving out unnecessary words or fluffy language. For a broad audience, use common, everyday terms.

When reading online, users will skip over information that they don't understand, such as links or navigation items that use made-up words or jargon. Having your content overlooked is bad on any site. But it's worse if users overlook product descriptions: When people don't understand something, they sometimes assume the worst. For example, if a bank says in its description of checking accounts that it charges one dollar for something called "POS" and users don't know what POS means, they will fear that they'll have to pay a lot of these fees. (In the likely case that you don't know either, POS stands for "point of sale" and refers to potential fees imposed when you use a bankcard to pay at a supermarket or other store.)

Figuring out the differences between various checking accounts on this bank site is not an easy task. The description contains too many industry terms, making it virtually impossible for potential customers to understand the options. The wording might make perfect sense to someone who works in the banking industry but not to general audiences. For example, participants didn't know how to interpret ATM/MasterCard Check Card, Relationship balance, Telephone Banking accessible, or POS.

"I'm a little bit unsure. People are confused by ATM. Does it work as debit card, or is it a credit card? This is a little misleading. If you can clarify that line, that would help. What's a foreign ATM?"

Regular Checking ACCOUNT

A non-interest bearing demand deposit account with unlimited check writing privileges. All transactions are recorded on a monthly statement that is mailed to the customer.

DESKTOP TOOLS

Product Features	Product Benefits
• Unlimited check writing • Consolidated statement with checks • Personalized checks available • Free ATM/MasterCard® Check (Debit) Card • Telephone Banking accessible • Insured up to $100,000 (FDIC) • Relationship balance of $3,000 or more avoids foreign ATM charges of $1.00 for a withdrawal or POS, transfers and balance inquiries of $.50.	• Easy to open • Convenience • 24-hour access for information • Safety of funds • Saves money

Min $ to Open	Min. to Earn Interest	Min $ to Avoid Fee	Monthly Fee	Fees Waived
$1.00	N/A	$2,000 avg. daily balance in checking or $3,000 relationship	$12.00	First 3 months

www.dimewill.com

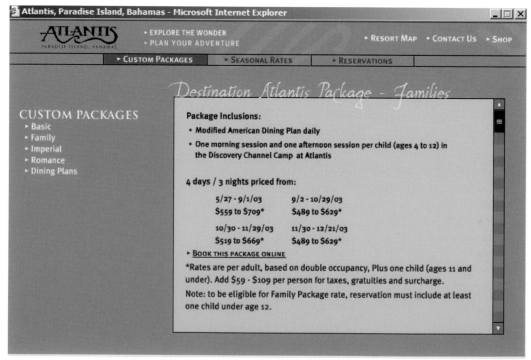

www.atlantis.com

prev (31 - 38)

Fri, 10/07/05 08:15 PM	**Juan Gabriel**	Gibson Amphitheatre at Universal CityWalk Universal City, CA	**Find Tickets** On Sale Now
Sat, 10/08/05 08:00 PM	**Charo**	Spotlight 29 Casino Coachella, CA	**Find Tickets** On Sale Now
Sat, 10/08/05 08:15 PM	**Juan Gabriel**	Gibson Amphitheatre at Universal CityWalk Universal City, CA	**Find Tickets** On Sale Now
Wed, 10/12/05 07:30 PM	**Juan Gabriel**	Save Mart Center Fresno, CA	**Find Tickets** On Sale Now
Sun, 10/16/05 08:15 PM	**Ana Gabriel**	Gibson Amphitheatre at Universal CityWalk Universal City, CA	**More Info** Presale Begins: Wed, 08/24/05 10:00 AM
Sat, 10/22/05 08:00 PM	**El Grupo Fantasma**	Roxy Theatre Hollywood, CA	**Find Tickets** On Sale Now

www.ticketmaster.com

It's aggravating not to be able to get a description of upcoming shows. If you're curious about Charo's show, for example, you can't click on the listing for it to get information. The blue text appears clickable, but it's not. Why assume that people already know what they want before they get here? It is a huge missed opportunity.

(Facing page, bottom) Incomplete information squelched people's enthusiasm for this product. While it's nice to offer discount packages, this site didn't have enough information for people to buy confidently. They couldn't figure out exactly what they would get for the price. For example, what's included in a "Modified American Dining Plan"? People's tendency not to purchase if they don't know what they're getting increases with high-ticket items.

"I would rather go someplace where I could talk to someone on the phone and get the specific questions answered rather than get a vague collection of information when I want something specific."

Test Driving an Auto Site

We asked people to use the Honda Automobiles site (http://automobiles.honda.com) to find a car that would suit a family with two small children. This task wasn't as straightforward as you might expect. Vague feature listings and product descriptions tripped people up.

User research would have helped Honda identify common questions that people want answered. Here are a few user comments:

"I wouldn't have thought that I would have to spend ten minutes to find that out that the car doesn't have air conditioning."

"It doesn't tell me what's in the trim package."

"The audio system—it doesn't say what brand it is."

"DX and EX—I don't know anything about Hondas."

"I don't know anything about front side airbags, but I don't see anywhere I can highlight that."

Provide Pictures and Product Illustrations

When presented properly, meaningful illustrations and images can complement text descriptions to show, rather then tell, what items look like. Space on Web pages is usually limited, so make your images count. Don't waste valuable real estate on images or graphics solely for decoration. Instead, support your customers' browsing behavior by choosing images that show the relevant details they care about. Keep your site efficient by setting image size and resolution as low as possible, but make sure you retain sufficient detail for customers to comfortably make out the important elements.

Make it possible for users to enlarge photos for a close-up view of products. Seeing a specific detail or assessing a texture helps increase shoppers' confidence in purchasing online. It's gratifying that most sites obey this guideline and offer zoom features, but sometimes sites implement this feature incorrectly.

The worst mistake is when a user clicks the "enlarge photo" button and the site displays the same photo. Such do-nothing links and buttons waste time and increase user confusion.

Almost as bad are sites that let users enlarge photos but only by a minute amount. When users ask for a big photo, show them a *big* photo. People are even willing to wait for it to download. It's often best to offer an enlargement that fills up the most common screen size used by your customers (1024 by 768 pixels at the time of this writing). Other times, it's better to offer a range of close-ups to give users the details they need without requiring them to scroll a very large photo.

Yes, initial pages should use small photos to avoid hogging bandwidth and real estate. Yes, you want to be aware of download times and watch your page weight quota. Even in this broadband age, slow response times are still common. Be sensitive to people with slow connections, as large files can take too long to load, or even worse, lock up their computers. People's willingness to wait for images to download has its limits; they especially don't like waiting very long if the payoff isn't worth the effort.

www.crutchfield.com

Crutchfield offers two levels of enlargements of the photos on its site. Notice how the larger picture includes sufficient detail to give you a very good idea of the style of the headphones and controls on this satellite radio. Of course, images this big can't be on the primary product page for two reasons: They download too slowly and would leave too little space for other product info. But it facilitates sales to make detailed photos available when users ask for them.

Amazon provides a clear close-up that shows the details of a ring. In addition, the site shows the product with other bands so that users can see its relative size. It would be better to include a side view to show the thickness of the ring. And for small objects, it's often a good idea to include a known item such as a coin in the photo to give users an easy way to gauge the size.

(Below) The photos are too small to show enough of the kind of detail that would help people quickly discern differences among the choices without clicking on each to get a larger picture. Photos on the initial page should be small, but they need to be large enough to show salient details for each product.

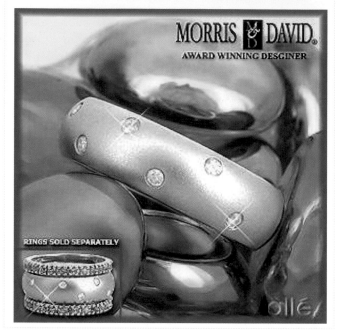

www.amazon.com

www.kitchenetc.com

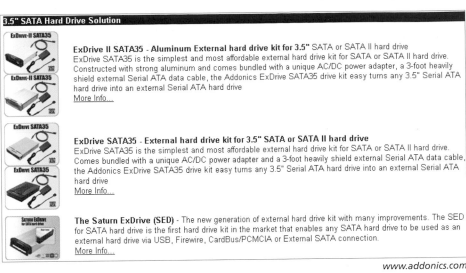

The use of thumbnails here is meaningless because viewers can't make out the differentiating details for each product. The text is illegible and the products look similar in these small-scale photos.

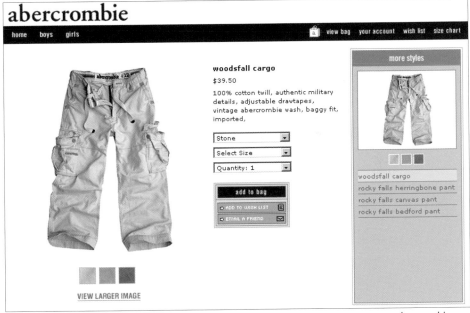

What, no back view? People want to know what the back of trousers look like.
Are there pockets, and do they have flaps? Are the pants in a wrinkly fabric?

This site does a good job of illustrating the item in views that people care about. Showing the beads against a ruler gives an idea of their size. It would have been ideal to include a picture of a person wearing them to give customers a sense of how they might look while being worn.

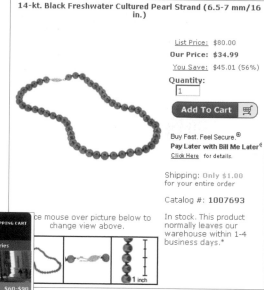

What is Cordura fabric, and what does the inside of the bag look like? It would be nice to get more close-ups of the fabric and an inside view of the bag. To the site's credit, it has a nice chart at the bottom of the page detailing the bag's dimensions, but it's too far down the page and away from the Select Size input area to be noticed.

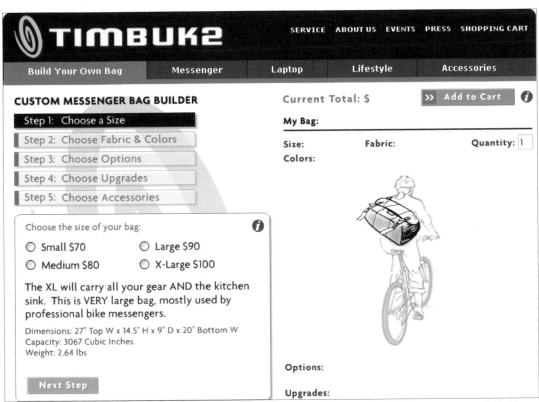

A simple sketch can help people choose a bag size. This simple low-resolution drawing of a bag on a person sufficiently illustrates its relative size.

> *Don't overwhelm your customers. Layer information by revealing the key points first, and make it easy for shoppers to get the specifics.*

Layer Product Pages

Presenting ample specifics and details about your products doesn't mean overwhelming your customers. You don't need to present all the details at once; layer the information by revealing the key points first, and make it easy for shoppers to get the specifics. Customers shouldn't be forced to find related information in separate parts of the Web site. Product pages should have links to all other product-related topics such as:

- Product details
- Photos, illustrations, and demos
- FAQs
- Customer and expert reviews
- Troubleshooting and maintenance
- Accessories and parts
- Manufacturer information
- Coupons/rebates

Manufacturers' sites should always provide detailed information on all their products. It's common for people to visit the manufacturer's site when product information is lacking elsewhere, so providing rich product information can save the sale for you if a retailer's site is lacking.

This is a good example of an effective product page. A bulleted list provides a high-level snapshot description of the product, while links guide interested customers to deeper information. Offering related accessories is also a nice way to boost sales while being helpful to customers. Showing prices for each accessory item is a plus.

www.sharperimage.com

Here's another good product page. Links to detailed product information are grouped together and prominently shown. This page gives just enough detail without being overwhelming. Including the delivery fees early in the shopping process also facilitates shopping.

www.potterybarn.com

(Facing page, bottom) This product page provides only superficial information and no access to details that customers care about. The brief summary doesn't give the specs that customers need to make purchase decisions. The page should support both new and returning customers, but related resources—maintenance manuals, warranties, replacement parts—are missing. People expect a product page to be the one place that has complete information about a specific item or service. When they don't see it, they assume that the site doesn't have it.

Crutchfield offers rich information about the fairly complicated electronics products it sells. But instead of overwhelming users with all the information on one screen, the site makes good use of hyperlinks to layer the information. The initial display (shown here) provides an overview that is probably too detailed. Additional information is available through the tabs in the description area or by following links like "request a copy of the manufacturer's warranty." Of course, this strategy only works if the links to the additional information are clear, and the links on this page are indeed pretty self-explanatory.

www.crutchfield.com

www.cummins.com

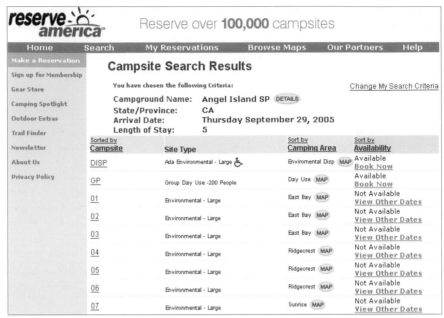

www.reserveamerica.com

www.reserveamerica.com

(Facing page, top) It's virtually impossible to confidently choose a campsite on this site. The generic description for each campsite makes it difficult for people to differentiate among the choices. The incremental detail that people get with each click isn't worth the effort and it's mostly unintelligible. The average camper isn't going to know what is meant by the codes or site descriptions such as Environmental–Large.

(Facing page, bottom) If you click for details on one of the campsites, the next page gives hardly any additional useful information. You're still baffled by what Environmental Sites or DISP mean, or what the campsite looks like. The information on vehicles doesn't make sense. Does it mean that they aren't allowed on the campsite? Without clear and complete information, people will abandon the online reservation process.

(Below) Even if you click the Campground Details link, the link names are meaningless. Who knows what the difference is between East Bay and Groups Platform? At this point, most people give up, leave the site, or telephone someone for assistance.

www.reserveamerica.com

Display Bona Fides

Acknowledging awards and recognition for the quality of products and services is one way to enhance your organization's credibility and build trust online. Instead of just listing them in a Press Releases section, consider mentioning recent awards directly on the appropriate product page. Major awards should also be shown in your About Us area. But don't feature old awards. They will just clutter your page and might undermine your credibility, suggesting that you haven't recently done anything noteworthy.

If your products have been favorably reviewed in the press or on respected Web sites, feature quotes from the reviews and link to them. Such links add enormous credibility because they show that you are not afraid to let users read the full review. Most users won't click the links, but having them there still works wonders.

http://automobiles.honda.com

Honda missed an opportunity to highlight important accomplishments that could sway customers in its favor. Telling customers about safety awards on other relevant pages, such as the product and safety pages, would have helped.

Support Comparison Shopping

Getting people to your site is half the battle. The challenge is keeping them engaged and interested. Some Web designers think that having as many product options as possible gives people the greatest flexibility, and thus, the best shopping experience. The opposite is true: Once again, less is more.

Having a few applicable choices is often better than loading up the site with a lot of similar-sounding ones that require extensive effort to differentiate. People don't like confronting a sea of choices. What is easier, comparing a few products, or comparing 10 or 20? Factor in each item's unique features, and the complexity of making an educated decision increases exponentially.

This image shows only a fraction of the available credit card offers. The screen scrolls on and on with many more similar offers. While providing choice is nice, having too much choice intimidates users and makes it impractical to make meaningful comparisons.

"I think they offer way too many cards."

"I started feeling overwhelmed by how many cards there are on the Web site."

www.bankone.com

Facilitate purchase decisions by making it easy for people to narrow down their options and make side-by-side comparisons. Notice here the operative phrase is "side by side." Remember, people don't want to wade through wordy content or jump back and forth between different product pages to compare items. Good comparison tables tend to be the most efficient method to communicate differences between similar items.

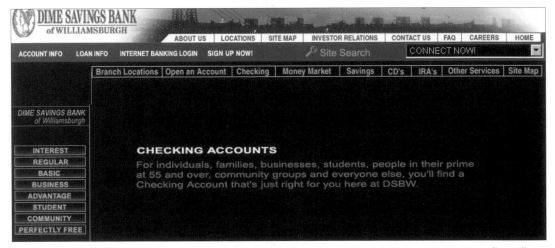

www.dimewill.com

People complained that comparing similar accounts was too cumbersome and required more effort than they wanted to make. The site didn't have a comparison table to help potential customers differentiate among the options. Instead, they had to select the account type shown in the list on the left and read the description for each one.

"It says to find the checking account that's right for me, but it doesn't guide me to which one. I have to go through each one of them. Maybe they can set up a page that can bring it all together. So it sets up the advantages and disadvantages of each kind. It's a lot to read if I'm only looking for a few specific things. It's better to have a chart. It's kind of losing my attention."

"Where do I find out what's right for me? It's too much work to see which one is right for me. Oh my goodness…yada yada yada."

"They should have a brief description of the accounts with bullets all in one place instead of making you have to go through each page individually. It would be nice to have a side-by-side comparison."

Let's look at the comparative tables from the Honda Automobiles Web site. Customers who were looking at the Accord might ask, "What are the differences between the various levels?" Different tables on the site provide slightly different angles on the answer, some better than others.

This bad example is taken from the Accord Sedan homepage. The main differentiating factor is cost, but what do DX, LX, and EX mean? This chart leaves people wondering what they get for the price. They won't find an easy answer here: They must click on each of the items, remember the features for each, and compile their own comparison data.

"I would want to have a picture showing what the differences are between EX and DX. Especially if I'm spending more money for an EX, I want to know what I'm getting for my money."

"As a consumer, I want to have it easier to compare them."

WHICH ACCORD SEDAN FITS?

There are many choices when it comes to the Accord Sedan. Click a trim level below, and decide which one is right for you.

Starting MSRP	Trim Level
$16,295	DX
$17,995	Value Package
$19,775	LX
$22,200	EX
$23,800	EX with Leather
$23,950	LX V-6
$25,800	EX with Leather and Honda Satellite-Linked Navigation System™
$26,850	EX V-6

http://automobiles.honda.com

This is better. This version gives more details about each car, but the formatting is atrocious. The text runs together, making it difficult for people to scan the information and quickly pick out the differences.

LX | Starting at $19,300.00
For the ultimate combination of performance and value, the Accord LX Sedan should be at the top of everyone's list. In addition to the DX features, there's a remote entry system with power window control, air conditioning, cruise control, power mirrors and door locks, and another 4 speakers for the AM/FM/CD audio system. Also available are side airbags.
Manual Transmission: $19,300.00
Manual Transmission with Front Side Airbags: $19,550.00
Automatic Transmission: $20,100.00
Automatic Transmission with Front Side Airbags: $20,350.00

EX | Starting at $21,700.00
The Accord EX Sedan provides an extra level of refinement and comfort. Inside, you'll find standard front side airbags, an AM/FM/6-disc in-dash changer and 6 speakers, steering-wheel-mounted audio controls, premium interior trim, ambient console lighting and a driver's seat with power height adjustment. Outside, there are 16" alloy wheels, 4-wheel disc brakes with electronic brake distribution and a power moonroof with tilt feature.
Manual Transmission: $21,700.00
Manual Transmission with Side Curtain Airbags: $22,000.00
Automatic Transmission: $22,500.00
Automatic Transmission with Side Curtain Airbags: $22,800.00

LX V-6 | Starting at $23,300.00
The Accord LX V-6 Sedan has a 240 hp, 24-valve VTEC® V-6 engine, one of the most powerful V-6 engines in its class. It offers all the standard features of the 4-cylinder LX Sedan, plus 4-wheel disc brakes with electronic brake distribution, front side airbags, 16" wheels with full covers, a Traction Control System (TCS), an AM/FM 6-disc in-dash changer and a driver's seat with 8-way power adjustment.
V-6 Automatic Transmission: $23,300.00

http://automobiles.honda.com

This one's best. It's a fine example of a well-designed comparison table: The clean and simple design makes scanning easy. The table could be improved, however, by making the descriptions hypertext. Terms such as "Drive-by-Wire Throttle System" are a mystery and need further explanation. For long tables that require extensive scrolling, make sure to repeat the top headers to preserve context. Remember to list features in priority order—based on your customer's perspective, not yours.

Specifications
2005 Accord Sedan

TRIM DESCRIPTIONS | FEATURES SUMMARY | FULL SPECS

🖶 Printer-Friendly Format

TRIM LEVEL Starting MSRP	DX $16,295	Value Package $17,995	LX $19,775	EX $22,200	LX V-6 $23,950	EX V-6 $26,850
Engine Type	In-Line 4-Cylinder				V6	
Valve Train	16-Valve DOHC i-VTEC®				24-Valve SOHC VTEC®	
Drive-by-Wire Throttle System™					Standard	
5-Speed Manual Transmission	Standard					
5-Speed Automatic Transmission (available)	Standard					
4-wheel double wishbone suspension	Standard					
Dual-Stage Front Airbags (SRS)	Standard					
Front Side Airbags with Passenger-Side Occupant Position Detection System	Standard					

http://automobiles.honda.com

Refine and Sort

If your Web site is bulging at the seams with all sorts of products and services, give people the ability to refine the selection to only show the relevant ones, so all items don't have be to considered. Separating the useful from non-useful items makes comparison–shopping less daunting.

(Facing page, top) Staples provides a variety of sorting parameters to narrow down its list of products so customers can focus their searches. The short bulleted descriptions highlight the top features so that the items are differentiable. However, it is better to include sorting options by other features people care about—such as lumens and resolution, in the case of projectors. Portability is important for travelers, so weight is another important criterion.

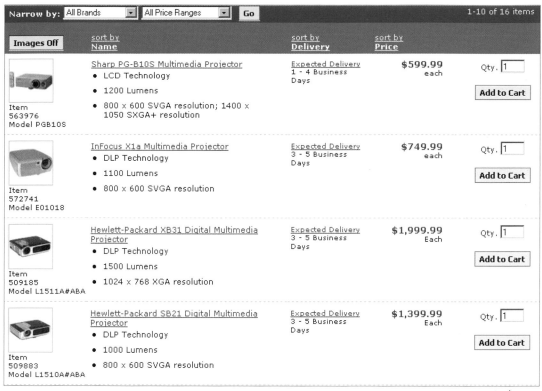

Narrow by: All Brands ▾ All Price Ranges ▾ **Go**

Images Off

	sort by Name	sort by Delivery	sort by Price	

Sharp PG-B10S Multimedia Projector
- LCD Technology
- 1200 Lumens
- 800 x 600 SVGA resolution; 1400 x 1050 SXGA+ resolution

Expected Delivery
1 - 4 Business Days

$599.99 each

Qty. 1   **Add to Cart**

Item 563976
Model PGB10S

InFocus X1a Multimedia Projector
- DLP Technology
- 1100 Lumens
- 800 x 600 SVGA resolution

Expected Delivery
3 - 5 Business Days

$749.99 each

Qty. 1   **Add to Cart**

Item 572741
Model E01018

Hewlett-Packard XB31 Digital Multimedia Projector
- DLP Technology
- 1500 Lumens
- 1024 x 768 XGA resolution

Expected Delivery
3 - 5 Business Days

$1,999.99 Each

Qty. 1   **Add to Cart**

Item 509185
Model L1511A#ABA

Hewlett-Packard SB21 Digital Multimedia Projector
- DLP Technology
- 1000 Lumens
- 800 x 600 SVGA resolution

Expected Delivery
3 - 5 Business Days

$1,399.99 Each

Qty. 1   **Add to Cart**

Item 509883
Model L1510A#ABA

www.staples.com

Comparison-shopping on this site is cumbersome because the sorting options are limited. Price is obviously an important criterion, but it's not the only one on which people base their purchase decisions. People would have to go through the products one at time to read the features and separate the useful from the useless ones. Imagine having to do this manually for more than 40 items!

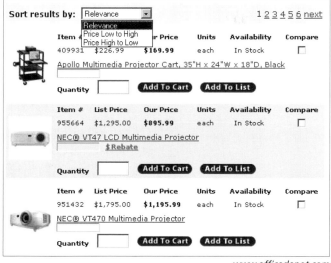

Sort results by: Relevance ▾   1 2 3 4 5 6 next

Relevance
Price Low to High
Price High to Low

Item #	List Price	Our Price	Units	Availability	Compare
409931	$226.99	**$169.99**	each	In Stock	☐

Apollo Multimedia Projector Cart, 35"H x 24"W x 18"D, Black

Quantity _____   **Add To Cart** **Add To List**

Item #	List Price	Our Price	Units	Availability	Compare
955664	$1,295.00	**$895.99**	each	In Stock	☐

NEC® VT47 LCD Multimedia Projector
$Rebate

Quantity _____   **Add To Cart** **Add To List**

Item #	List Price	Our Price	Units	Availability	Compare
951432	$1,795.00	**$1,195.99**	each	In Stock	☐

NEC® VT470 Multimedia Projector

Quantity _____   **Add To Cart** **Add To List**

www.officedepot.com

California State Parks

Discover the many states of California.

| Park List | Regions | County/City | Activity/Facility | Weather | **State Parks Home** |

(1 - 25) of 55 items that match your search   You are viewing page 1 of 3 pages

New Search | List | **Activities** | Facilities | Icon Key | Full Screen   << | < | **[1]** | [2] | [3] | > | >>

Multiple Region Search

Name																					
Admiral William Standley (SRA)											•										
Anderson Marsh (SHP)							•	•	•	•	•							•			
Annadel (SP)						•		•	•	•		•									
Armstrong Redwoods (SR)							•			•	•	•									
Austin Creek (SRA)			•		•					•		•									
Azalea (SR)										•	•										
Bale Grist Mill (SHP)							•			•											
Benbow Lake (SRA)	•		•		•			•	•	•							•				
Bothe-Napa Valley (SP)		•	•	•	•	•		•			•	•						•	•		
Caspar Headlands (SR)								•													
Caspar Headlands (SB)								•													
Clear Lake (SP)		•	•	•			•	•	•	•	•						•		•		•

www.parks.ca.gov

| Park List | Regions | County/City | Activity/Facility | Weather | **State Parks Home** |

Search | Help   ○ My CA ● This Site [_____] [search]

♿ **Click here for Parks with Accessible Features**

Click a single item name or **select multiple items across categories** and click any 'go' button

Find Parks that offers: **any** ● or **all** ○ of the requested activities.

Activities   go

☐ Beach Wheelchair	☐ Bike Trails	☐ En route Campsites	☐ Environmental Campsites
☐ Exhibits and Programs	☐ Family Campsites	☐ Fishing	☐ Group Campsites
☐ Guided Tours	☐ Hike or Bike Campsites	☐ Hiking Trails	☐ Horseback Trails
☐ Nature Trails	☐ Off-Highway Vehicles	☐ Primitive Camping	☐ Scuba Diving
☐ Surfing	☐ Swimming	☐ Wildlife Viewing	☐ Windsurfing

Facilities   go

☐ Boat Mooring	☐ Boat Ramps	☐ Boat Rentals	☐ Boat-in Camps
☐ Campers (Max. Length)	☐ Food Service	☐ Lodging	☐ Parking
☐ Picnic Areas	☐ Restrooms	☐ RV Dump Station	☐ RV Hookups
☐ Showers	☐ Supplies	☐ Trailers (Max. Length)	☐ Visitor Center
☐ Vista Point			

Other   go

☐ Historical	☐ Museums	☐ No Avail Drinking Water	☐ Reservations Recommended

www.parks.ca.gov

(Facing page, top) A comparison chart that spans over three long pages is too unwieldy. Matching up the dots with the correct columns and rows is a tedious process. The icon headings on the top row are too small and nondescript. People can hover the cursor over each one and get descriptions, but that's too much effort for more than 50 items. In this case, having a way to winnow the list based on important features would be more useful.

(Facing page, bottom) This site offers a method to choose camp-sites based on desired features. Unfortunately, it is so hidden that many people in our study didn't know it was available. Note: The default should be set to all of the requested activities rather than to any one requested activity. The three Go buttons are confusing because it's not clear if people must click the associated button for each category.

Support Sales with Quality Content

Companies are slowly getting the message that marketing hype and pushy sales tactics turn Web customers off. Some organizations understand that customers value good content and are posting informational articles to their sites in support of this. Obviously articles and other content support the sales of their products as well. But customers will find them truly useful if they are concise and informative, in a factual manner that suits the Web—not the pushy style of late-night TV commercials. Keep the marketing language to a minimum; let the content speak for itself.

One of the best places to fill people in on your products or services is on relevant informational pages. Ads or links to buy products that are well integrated within the content are seen as helpful because they're available when people most need them. Regrettably, some sites we studied did a great job of providing informative articles but missed opportunities to sell their products—or even let people know they sell them.

Remember, people don't always get to your site's home-page. Search engines often take them through deep links directly to specific pages inside the site, which means that they may never see your offerings. Placing product mentions or links to product pages in an article ensures that people will know you carry products relating to their interests. People won't need to browse your site any further if your articles answer their questions.

Four Reasons for Informational Articles

- They enhance credibility by showing your expertise and genuine motivation to help
- They help customers differentiate between alternative products
- They provide information to support customers' purchase decisions
- They contain keywords that enhance search engine visibility and increase traffic to your site

---

In one of our studies, people searched pg.com (the Procter & Gamble site) for food products that might be appropriate for a new kitten. Most were unable to accomplish this simple task. After exploring the site for an extended period, they didn't think that the site recommended kitten food.

There was a link labeled "May we recommend a product for your cat?" But it was far off in the left-hand margin, which people often associate with unimportant information. It would have been advantageous to embed this link in the body of the article so that it was noticeable.

To its credit, the site made it easy for people to get to the right place. The upper levels of the site had a prominent and clear link to "Pet Nutrition & Care," and the articles in this section were interesting and informative. Even the site's search engine brought up relevant articles for "kitten food." But the product links were overshadowed by the other elements on the page and people left without realizing that it actually sold the product it was promoting.

The P&G site has well-written articles that kept the interest of people in our study, but many who were researching what to feed their kittens left it thinking that the company didn't sell anything. The link to "All Pet Nutrition & Care Products" was at the bottom of the page, so it went unnoticed. The Feature Products header didn't clue people in to the fact that the company made products because titles underneath such as Does Your Cat Have a Sensitive Stomach? appeared to relate to article content.

www.pg.com

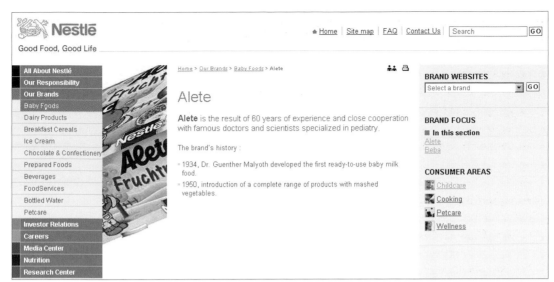

People were disappointed with the Nestlé Web site because it doesn't offer product recommendations. The Baby Foods section provides only superficial information about different brands. Nestlé misses the mark by ignoring consumer-related questions and focusing primarily on branding instead. For example, selecting the Alete brand baby food only provided branding history. People expected to find the products, information about which babies they're intended for, and the benefits.

"It talks about breastfeeding, but not about the product. I would like to have categories for formula according to the child's age, milk products, etc."

"They don't actually give me much information."

"I just read a little bit about their baby foods, but I can't find anything [more in-depth]. There's nothing that you can click on."

"I didn't like that bit of information; it didn't explain much to me."

More Information

For 207 design guidelines on e-commerce usability, as cited in this chapter, go to www.nngroup.com/reports, and see "ecommerce." For guidelines on presenting the complex products found on business-to-business sites, see "b2b."

10 Presenting Page Elements

A company has only a browser-size canvas on which to present its message on the Web. People garner their impressions of a Web site based on what they see at a glance, and there's no guarantee that that will be everything on the first screen—even items that are bold and flashing. Web users have learned through experience to expect certain items in certain areas and to ignore others. Understanding users' behavior and expectations can help you create layouts that satisfy them and make it more likely that they'll get your message.

Web designers must convey abundant information about a company or organization in a very limited space. Emphasizing the information that is of the highest priority to users is critical to attracting their interest. Conducting user testing will help you understand your audience so that you can match your site's design to its needs.

Common page layout mistakes include:

- Page not structured in prioritized order
- Interactions overly complex and don't offer guidance
- Related areas not grouped in close proximity
- Elements not properly aligned to create order
- Elements not placed where people expect
- Too many elements on page

Following usability guidelines for presenting page elements can help you avoid these mistakes.

Should You Design for Scrolling?

As we discussed in our dissection of user scrolling habits in Chapter 2, most users don't scroll most of the time. That's partly because most pages are not worth scrolling. And you can bet that users definitely won't scroll unless the first screen makes it clear that they're in the right place and it's worthwhile to read on.

Users tend to look smack in the middle of the page. If need be, they will also look to the left or the top to check out the navigation. They will rarely look all the way out in the right margin to check the scroll bar, especially if they don't think they will be using it. (This also explains why users rarely discover that a new window has been opened, even though in systems such as Microsoft Windows, this is clearly indicated by another tab in the taskbar.) People also tend not to look at the very bottom of the screen unless they think they have a reason to do so. They assume that items at the bottom of long pages are unimportant, so they don't scroll down very far.

You might argue that people should notice the browser scroll bar—it's right there! But remember, to effectively process information, people cannot pay attention to everything on the screen. They adopt strategies to help them separate useful from useless information, and home in on areas that give the strongest information scent, ignoring the rest. The less you put on the page, the more likely they are to see it.

www.grand-canyon.edu

Though the browser scroll bar says otherwise, the exaggerated white space at the bottom of the screen creates an "illusion of completeness"—a term coined by our colleague Bruce "Tog" Tognazzini to refer to page designs that appear to be complete even though there is more invisible information available. Most people won't even notice that there are three more screens of information on this page.

In general, it's safe to design for limited scrolling as long as you show the most important information first. But some Web sites have taken cautionary advice about scrolling to the opposite extreme and made their pages non-scrollable. This can be damaging, leading to pages with only navigation and no content. Better to provide the right visual cues and context to make users see the value of scrolling. The placement of critical elements on the page can dictate whether people scroll or not.

Four Rules of Scrolling

- If people expect something to be in a particular place, they will not look for that item elsewhere or scroll to find it
- If there's white space at the bottom of the viewable area of the screen, people usually assume that's the end of the page and don't scroll any farther, even when their browser scroll bar indicates otherwise
- People interpret ad-like elements that appear immediately above the fold as the end of a page because ads are commonly placed in peripheral areas of the page
- Placing indicators such as headers or content that can be seen just above the bottom of the screen strongly suggests that there's more content below

(Facing page, top) The white space and the graphics that are lined up horizontally across the screen make it appear as if it's the bottom of the page even though there's more important information below. People looking for the Corporate Info link might miss it because it's hidden underneath the viewable area, creating the illusion of completeness.

(Facing page, bottom) Where would you go to find the calendar of events? There are multiple links to buy tickets but nothing about a full list of upcoming shows. The information does exist, but it takes four screens of scrolling to get there. Here the problem is not the illusion of completeness, because there's clearly more on this page. The problem is that the information below the fold doesn't seem relevant. If you're interested in taking your visiting aunt to a Mozart concert next week, you aren't looking to learn about the five-star subscription plan, which appears to be the type of information that will be found farther down the page.

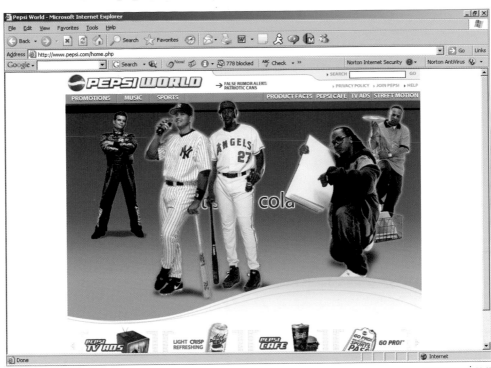

www.pepsi.com

www.artcenter.org

Corporate Overview on this site is not really an overview. The extremely long page doesn't optimize the use of hyperlinks. Don't give your audience a wall of text. Partitioning content into hierarchical pages is a more effective way of presenting detailed information.

After we took the screen shot in the previous figure, Pixar redesigned its Corporate Overview page. The new design is an improvement, but the copy could still use some editing, and the lack of formatting makes scanning difficult. To the site's credit, however, major sections have been truncated by navigational links, making the information appear more manageable.

Prioritizing Web Usability

There are situations when longer pages are better than short, fragmented ones; it's advantageous then to have highly related information together. Having a continuous article appear on one page makes the information feel more cohesive and mitigates unnecessary work. Scrolling requires less effort than clicking Next, Next, Next. Of course, you want to layer extremely long detailed content to utilize hyperlinks. This is what the Web is good for.

Home > Solutions > Getting Your Color Right

Getting Your Color Right

07.13.05

ENLARGE ↗

⊙ Discuss Total posts: 1

ADVERTISEMENT

Partner Services:
▶ Dell Business Systems
▶ Dell Home Systems
▶ MPC (MicronPC)

By M. David Stone

Printing photos has changed dramatically since the days when getting acceptable color took a great deal of knowledge or even more luck. Today, you can pick almost any printer, camera, and scanner at random and use them together without a problem. If you have a well-trained eye, you might quibble with the color, but most people are usually satisfied with it.

For those who aren't, the fixes run the gamut, from simple steps that anyone who prints photos should know about to complex tools of interest only to professionals and the most demanding photo enthusiasts. We'll focus on the simple fixes here and take a look at the advanced tools in the sidebar "Color Calibration Tools."

next >

 Print ⊠ Email Save ▽ Reprints

www.pcmag.com

The Next link at the bottom of the bottom of the screen doesn't tell people what you'll get by selecting it. Does the article continue or does the page move on to the next article? The table of contents at the top right hand corner of the screen can help people navigate to specific sections of this article, but it's placed in the peripheral area of the page, away from where people look.

Avoid cramming content into small scrolling areas. Requiring people to scroll in a tiny space is like forcing them to read through a peephole. Maximize the size of the scrollable area to reduce eye fatigue and make reading more enjoyable, especially if there's a lot of content. Another danger of having small scroll areas is that the scroll bar has the tendency to zip through too quickly, causing people to miss important information.

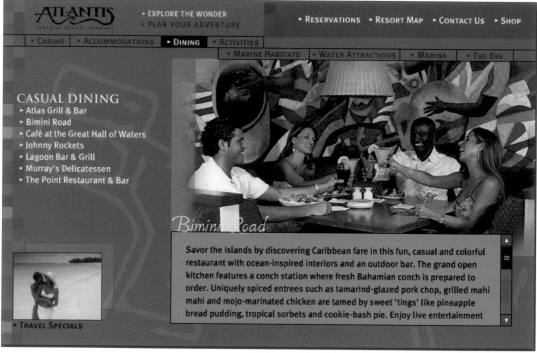

www.atlantis.com

A small scrolling area like the one shown here makes reading uncomfortable. People in our test even tried to increase the size of the site to see more content.

Guiding Users, Step by Step

When an interaction requires multiple steps, gently guide users through an expected linear process, but don't overwhelm them with options. Your goal is to create an experience that they find satisfying; people don't mind clicking through multiple pages as long as each click brings them closer to the desired result, at a reasonable pace. Interactions that are consistent with people's expectations feel pleasant. In fact, people who have a good experience on Web sites think their task takes less time (or clicks) than it actually does.

Don't make people solve complex problems to proceed to the next page. Having a structured process helps them avoid making mistakes such as skipping steps. If a feature requires multiple steps, it's helpful to lay out a linear process so people know what to anticipate.

Users will expend the effort to learn software that they've purchased or are required to use for work, but not to use Web sites. If the site doesn't serve their needs immediately, there are thousands of others vying for their attention. It's easier to find answers on a competitor's Web site than try to figure out a complex interface. Remember this: If it looks too cumbersome to use, people will bolt.

Tip: Beware of Magic Numbers

Our clients sometimes ask whether there is an acceptable number of a navigational items or clicks to get people from point A to point B. There is no magic number. But sometimes people misuse cognitive psychologist George Miller's 1956 research on human memory to insist that there is. Miller suggested that humans could retain up to seven, plus or minus two, bits of information at once with little processing. This rule simply doesn't apply to Web design. Miller's study was intended to research the limitations of short-term memory; Web site navigation is generally concerned with recognition and interpretation, not memorization.

Once our users arrived at this page, they couldn't figure out what to do next. The complex interaction model on this site prevented them from successfully making an online reservation. The instructions say, "Set your options, then click 'Search,'" but people didn't know what that meant. The most salient clickable element was the green Search button, which gives an unintelligible error message when nothing is selected. People didn't know that they had to select participants one at a time and customize each package. Having a more structured linear workflow could have made this interaction doable.

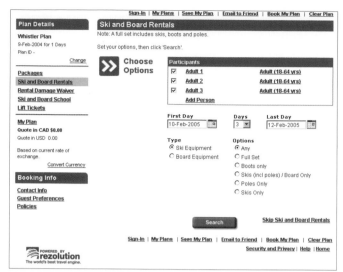

www.whistlerblackcomb.com

The City of San Diego Web site lets people submit street repair requests online. Unfortunately the process is so clumsy that our users eventually gave up. They couldn't figure out how to work the map controls and the process asked for the same information twice. People were required to enter the street name manually, as well as to identify it on a map. This redundancy caused much confusion because they couldn't figure out how the map related to the form.

Interestingly, most people chose the text method over the map method, saying that fancy maps have the tendency to be troublesome. They felt that typing in text was more efficient and less error-prone.

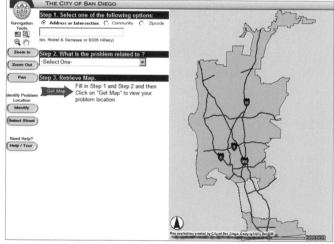

www.sandiego.gov

Sometimes Web sites include instructions to explain the interface. Often, a slight nudge in the right direction helps. However, adding layer upon layer of instructions to explain your interface is a sure sign that something's awry with your design. Good interaction design rarely needs instructions; the presentation is self-explanatory.

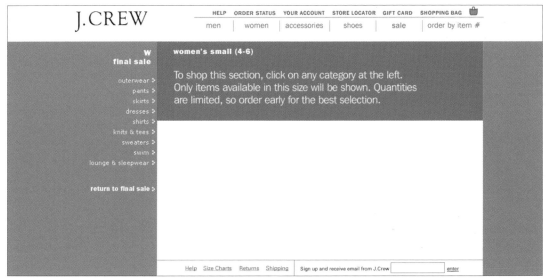

www.jcrew.com

This interface is complicated by unnecessary instructions. When customers encounter this page, they have to stop, read the text in the blue area, and figure out what it means. In this situation, there's no need to tell people what they already know: (1) to click on a category, and (2) only their size will be shown. They already expect that. Why slow them down with useless instructions?

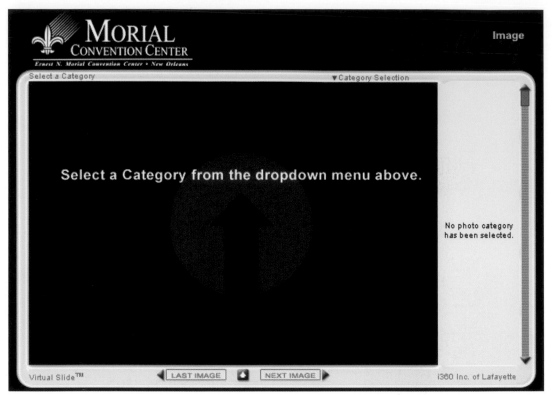

On the Web site for the Morial Convention Center, the navigational menus are completely hidden. The site's interaction model is so obscure that it requires instructions. It would only take a bit more screen space to make users' choices visible. It would also be better to reconsider the use of buttons with non-predictive labels such as Next Image, which don't tell users what they'll see. People don't have time to click things in the vague hope that they will be rewarded.

Keep Like with Like

Grouping associated items together ensures that they are noticed. It's common behavior to look for related objects in the same area. If they're not there, people often assume that they don't exist or that something is amiss. For example, if people were looking for product specifications, they'd probably look somewhere near the product description. If it's located elsewhere on the page, they most likely won't notice it.

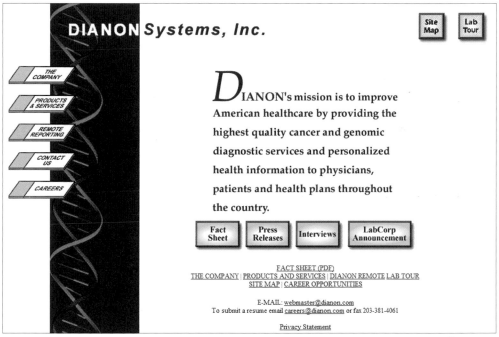

www.dianon.com

The navigational areas are sprinkled throughout this page with no apparent hierarchical order. For example, corporate information is placed on the left, bottom and top of the page. Having like items in different places causes people to aimlessly hunt around.

"I'm thinking this is a horrible site because nothing makes sense to me. On the homepage, they have options on left, bottom, and upper corner. And nothing seems clear about what it's going to lead you to."

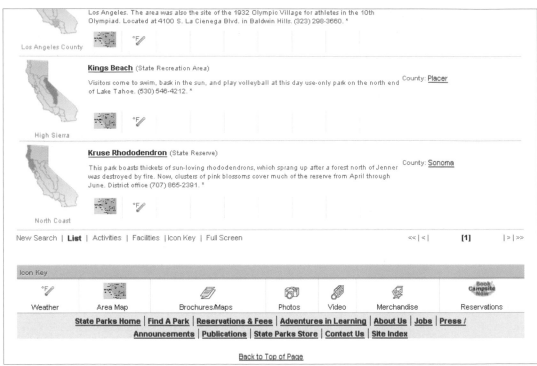

Los Angeles. The area was also the site of the 1932 Olympic Village for athletes in the 10th
Olympiad. Located at 4100 S. La Cienega Blvd. in Baldwin Hills. (323) 298-3660. *

Los Angeles County

Kings Beach (State Recreation Area)

Visitors come to swim, bask in the sun, and play volleyball at this day use-only park on the north end   County: Placer
of Lake Tahoe. (530) 546-4212. *

High Sierra

Kruse Rhododendron (State Reserve)

This park boasts thickets of sun-loving rhododendrons, which sprang up after a forest north of Jenner   County: Sonoma
was destroyed by fire. Now, clusters of pink blossoms cover much of the reserve from April through
June. District office (707) 865-2391. *

North Coast

New Search | **List** | Activities | Facilities | Icon Key | Full Screen   << | < | [1] | > | >>

Icon Key

| °F Weather | Area Map | Brochures/Maps | Photos | Video | Merchandise | Book Campsite Now Reservations |

State Parks Home | Find A Park | Reservations & Fees | Adventures in Learning | About Us | Jobs | Press /
Announcements | Publications | State Parks Store | Contact Us | Site Index

Back to Top of Page

www.parks.ca.gov

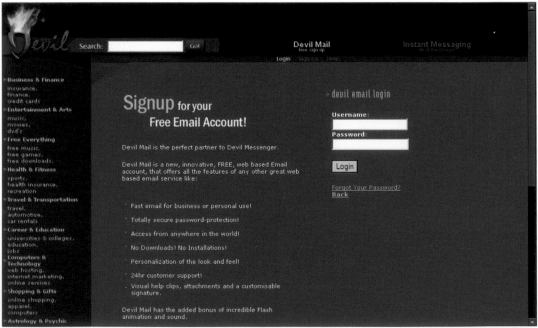

www.devil.com

(Facing page, top) The icon key on the California State Parks Web site appears too far down a long page, so many people didn't know it existed. Presenting the icon legend at both the top and bottom of pages might provide better visual cues. However, since the meaning of the icons is not evident, text links would work better.

(Facing page, bottom) Almost every user in our tests had difficulty signing up for Devil Mail because the sign-up button was hidden below the viewable area of the page. The login area appeared to be the only actionable area of the page, so users tried to sign up there. The illusion of completeness strikes again.

For Web applications, place the input area in close proximity to the output/results area. People can easily miss visual feedback when the two areas are spaced too far apart or not within the same viewable or work area.

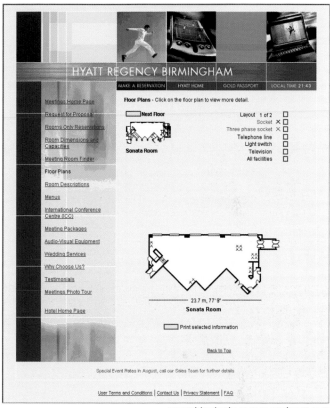

www.birmingham.regency.hyatt.com

This small online application is intended to help meeting planners select meeting rooms that are appropriate for their event needs. When users interact with the list of room features (say, Light switch), the diagram updates to show the location of the chosen features. However, the floor plan diagram is so far below the input area that people didn't even notice when it was updated. Even worse, people who viewed the screen at 800 by 600 pixels didn't see the floor plan at all because it's pushed below the viewable area. The illusion of completeness made small-screen users think that the small room diagram was all that was available on the page. (Try covering up the bottom half of this screen shot to see why.)

Users with low vision who use screen magnifiers don't have the full visual context of the screen and have to move their magnified view around to various areas to get context. So any changes or feedback that appear outside the magnified area can easily be overlooked. Putting the active areas close to each other helps all users, but especially those with low vision, who can see only one part of the screen at a time.

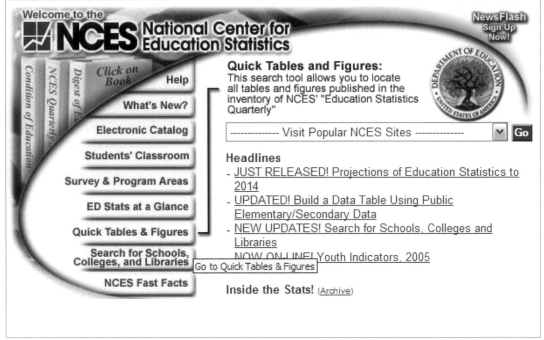

www.nces.ed.gov

Notice that the description for the left-hand navigational items appears at the top of the page instead of by the items. When related items are placed too far apart, people don't notice the change. This is even more problematic for audiences who use screen magnifiers and won't know if changes occur outside their viewable area.

www.nick.com

The area above the dotted line is what users see without scrolling on a 1024-by-768-pixel screen. Clicking the characters in the green area, which is above the fold, reveals the shows—but the visual feedback occurs below the fold. Kids can easily miss shows because they can't see changes without scrolling the page. Place visual feedback and input areas in close proximity and in the same viewable area so that information isn't lost.

Sloppy Formatting of Forms

Careless formatting of forms is another area that trips people up. When fields appear scattered and disorganized, it's difficult to tell which label goes with what widget. Properly aligned widgets and spacious layouts help people recognize groupings and understand the relationship between them.

The lack of structure on this form creates visual cacophony. Highly associated entries such as street number and street name are awkwardly separated. The text boxes are spaced so far apart that people in our study misunderstood their association. It's better not to split fields for street addresses.

The crammed layout makes it difficult to tell which text boxes the labels and examples refer to. The lack of indentation and proper spacing caused people to overlook the radio buttons and assume that they were required to enter the location in both ways.

Note: ▦ information is mandatory.

Location Information:

▦ Please complete the following information to initiate your service request.

⦿ **Address**

Address / Number: &   **Street Name:**

Ex: (1135)   Ex: (Broadway Ave, Camino del Rio S, etc.)

○ **Intersection or closest Cross Street**

Street Name: &   **Cross Street:**

Ex: (Broadway Ave, Camino del Rio S, etc.)

▦   **Location Description:**

Ex: (By the west curb, in front of stop sign, etc.)

Problem Information:

▦   **Problem Category:**   -Select One-   ▼

▦   **Describe Problem:**

(Limit your description to a maximum of 255 characters)

Continue   Reset

www.sandiego.gov

People can easily miss the radio buttons and checkbox on the right because they're too far removed from the main input area.

Registration Steps:
▶ 1. Accept Waiver ▶ **2. Complete Form** ▶ 3. Submit Payment ▶ 4. Print Receipt

31st Annual Midnight Madness Fun Bicycle Ride
Adult

PARTICIPANT INFORMATION

(indicates required information)

You must have a bib number, helmet and bike light to participate in Midnight Madness.

First Name: *

Middle Name:

Last Name: *

Gender: *   ○ Male ○ Female

Birthdate: *   MM ▼ / DD ▼ / YYYY ▼

Email: * ⊘

Enter Email Again: *

Yes! Send me health and fitness news, information about local events and special offers.   ○ Yes ○ No

Day Phone: *   xxx-xxx-xxxx   ext.

Evening Phone: ext.

Address Line 1: *

T-Shirt Size * *(The 30th Annual Midnight Madness t-shirt features nine-color art, including a reflective moon and San Diego skyline, screened on a navy blue 100% cotton tee. One shirt is included with paid registration; add $2 for XXL.)*

○ Small
○ Medium
○ Large
○ X-Large
○ XX-Large - $2.00

Additional Shirts *(Extra shirts may not be available after the event, so place your order now!)*

☐ S   Qty.   @ $10.00 ea.
☐ M   Qty.   @ $10.00 ea.
☐ L   Qty.   @ $10.00 ea.
☐ XL Qty.   @ $10.00 ea.

www.active.com

The two-column layout on this page doesn't match the registration workflow that users are accustomed to. People are used to completing similar information in the same place, working from top to bottom. Having to go all the way to the bottom of the form and scroll all the way up again—with questions midway diverting their attention—is jarring and leads people to overlook or forget about the choices in the panel on the right.

Registering in the wrong place is a common mistake among users. Most registration screens have an area reserved for new customers, but more often than not they use the other side because it has input areas while the new user side does not. People are highly attracted to text boxes because they appear actionable. Users would rather do something than read something. That's why they gravitate toward open boxes and ignore everything else on the registration page.

New users tried to register using the Member Login area of this site. The text boxes are much more prominent than the Register button for new registrants on the opposite side of the page—too far away for users to notice it. New members tried creating usernames and passwords in the member area and wondered why the system rejected their entries.

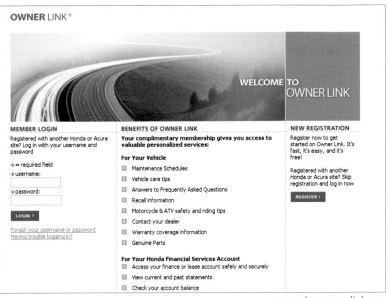

www.ahm-ownerlink.com

www.reserveamerica.com

Similarly, people ignored the Not Registered Yet? area on this site and went directly to the Member Sign In side. Formatting both sides more evenly would have attracted more new users. Better yet, let new users enter information in the member side and have the back-end handle the rest.

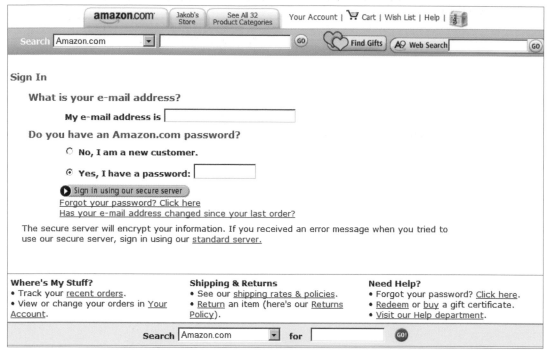

This is the preferred solution for having a login screen that is accessible to people who are not registered users. The first question is the same for everybody, and the second question clearly presents two radio buttons, with the Yes button chosen by default if the computer has a cookie indicating that the user is likely to be a returning customer. This screen has a bit too many design elements—for example, even though Search should usually be ubiquitous, there's no need to present three Search boxes to compete for the user's attention on a login screen. Among the page's other positive elements are clear links to resolve two common problems: forgotten passwords and changed e-mail addresses. Just-in-time help is usually better than requiring users to find the answer to a problem in a comprehensive online documentation system where they are just as likely to get lost.

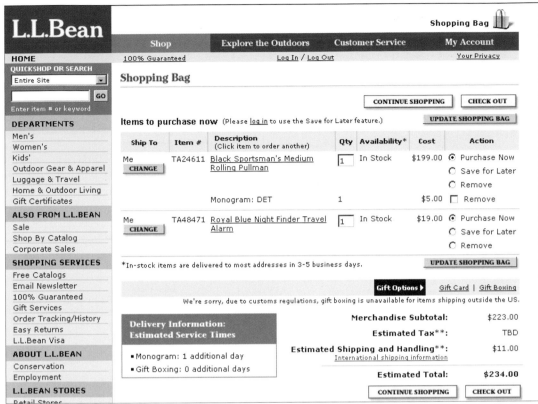

Offering Save for Later and Remove buttons is nice, but edit tools should not be given such prominence in the order summary area. Also, the Purchase Now option is redundant because it's understood that shopping carts are meant for purchases. Removing unnecessary options and placing things in the right areas unclutters the interface and improves scannabilty.

Satisfy Your Users' Expectations

As the Web matures, commonalities emerge across Web sites that shape people's expectations of yours. For example, links to corporate information are commonly found at the top and bottom of the homepages. Placing them anywhere else can cause unnecessary confusion. The advantage in understanding people's expectations is that you can give them what they need exactly the way they want it. There's no need to over-design for fear of it not being noticed. Simply placing items where people expect them ensures that they will see them.

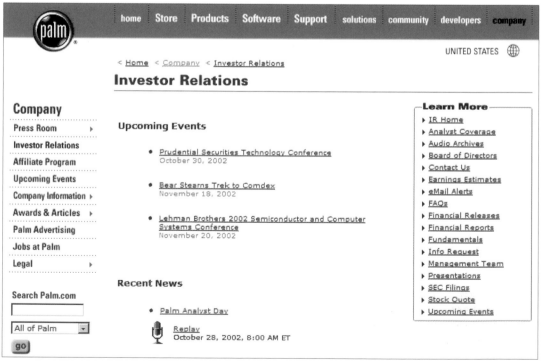

www.palm.com

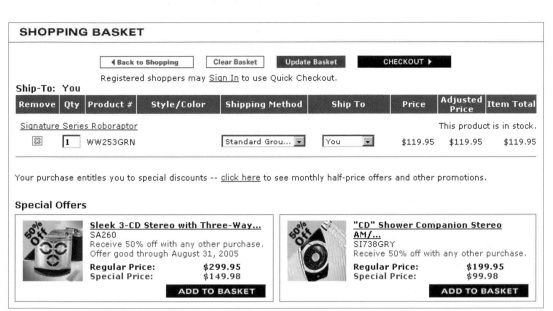

SHOPPING BASKET

◀ Back to Shopping | Clear Basket | Update Basket | CHECKOUT ▶

Registered shoppers may Sign In to use Quick Checkout.

Ship-To: You

Remove	Qty	Product #	Style/Color	Shipping Method	Ship To	Price	Adjusted Price	Item Total
Signature Series Roboraptor							This product is in stock.	
⊠	1	WW253GRN		Standard Grou... ▾	You ▾	$119.95	$119.95	$119.95

Your purchase entitles you to special discounts -- click here to see monthly half-price offers and other promotions.

Special Offers

Sleek 3-CD Stereo with Three-Way...
SA260
Receive 50% off with any other purchase.
Offer good through August 31, 2005
Regular Price: $299.95
Special Price: $149.98
ADD TO BASKET

"CD" Shower Companion Stereo AM/...
SI738GRY
Receive 50% off with any other purchase.
Regular Price: $199.95
Special Price: $99.98
ADD TO BASKET

www.sharperimage.com

The checkout button is in a peculiar place. Checkout buttons are typically found at the bottom of the shopping cart, not at the top. It's natural for people to review their order from top to bottom, then see the checkout button at the end of the list. Disrupting a user's mental model creates a jarring experience, requiring people to look harder than they should.

(Facing page) Even though the Learn More area on this site is emphasized with boldface and a highlighted box, people bypassed it because it was placed in the wrong area. They didn't think these links were important because main navigational elements are commonly on the left side of the screen, not the right. Also, having a box around the links made them appear secondary. Boxed areas are commonly associated with advertising, especially when they're placed in the periphery.

Placing the Add to Wish List button where people expect to see the Add to Shopping Bag button makes this layout error-prone. Also, the blue Shopping Bag button blends in with the other blue text on the page, making the gray Wish List button stand out even more. So although it is slightly smaller and lighter in color than the Add to Shopping Bag button, it has more prominence.

The placement of the Add to Shopping Bag button is better here. The Add button, which is the highest-priority action button here, is placed immediately after the last selection, followed by the less-important Add to Wish List and E-Mail a Friend buttons. The order and stacked layout of the buttons make it less likely that people will accidentally click on the wrong one.

Using White Space

What's not present on your site is as important as what is. A page's "white space"—the parts that don't have any text or illustrations—is important in content and visual design because it helps people process information into manageable units. Having adequate white space around groupings draws users' attention to key points without causing eyestrain.

Visually crowded sites are overwhelming—making it difficult for users to quickly identify what's important and create order. Providing enough space around different groups relieves spatial tension. The idea is to maximize the perceptual distance between groups while minimizing the distance between items within a group.

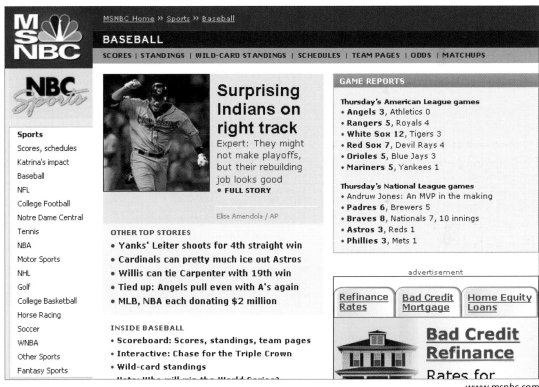

www.msnbc.com

The generous use of white space around each major grouping visually pulls related topics together. The sparse compartmentalized presentation creates order so that information isn't competing for attention.

We know screen real estate is limited, and attempting to cram too much information on a page often does more harm than good. Screens that are packed with choices, text, links, and bright colors cause eyestrain, especially if users stay for any extended period of time. Increasing white space on your site means making trade-offs. Some elements might need to be removed or made less prominent. In most instances, it's worth it. Less is more.

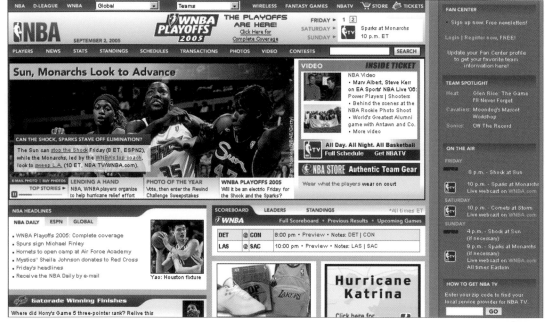

www.nba.com

The extraneous use of graphical treatments and lack of white space creates a busy-looking homepage. It's difficult to separate the headlines and the content because everything blends together. With so much visual activity, how do users know where to go first?

11 Balancing Technology with People's Needs

As technology continues to improve and more users have high-speed access, multimedia Web sites are becoming more prevalent. Done well, video, animation, and sound can enrich the user experience and delight audiences. Implemented inappropriately, multimedia is repellant and reduces your site's value. In this chapter, we'll discuss strategies to help you avoid common pitfalls and use multimedia to your advantage.

In the ten or so years since the Web became a widely used tool, it has turned into a multimedia environment. Many non-technical users have become familiar with following hyperlinks, scrolling to read text, clicking on images to enlarge them, seeing text and images animate, and even using VCR-like onscreen controls to play audio and video. As the technologies that enable people to produce multimedia improve, Web designers and developers are increasingly interested in supplementing their sites' text and images with audio, video, and animation.

But multimedia can be a blessing or a curse. Integrated thoughtfully—in proper context and skillfully implemented—motion and sound can aid usability, making content not only more entertaining and "immersive," but also more accessible. Unconstrained use of multimedia numbs the sensory experience, creating disruptive interactions and confusing site visitors with a cacophony of sights and sounds. In their enthusiasm for cool new tools, Web designers can lose sight of their primary responsibility: solving communication problems by making information easily available to their audience.

Flashback to 2000: A Note from Jakob Nielsen

Back in 2000 I published a controversial article in my Alertbox column called "Flash: 99% Bad." In it I claimed that while multimedia has its role on the Web, interactive animation technology tends to degrade usability rather than enhance it. This, I argued, was for three reasons: First, it made bad design more likely by encouraging gratuitous animation and idiosyncratic interface design, and designer-controlled action rather than true user interactivity. Second, it deviated from the Web's fundamental convention of interactivity. Third, and perhaps most serious, it consumed resources—specifically time, thought, and effort—that would be better spent enhancing a site's core value of providing information.

Of course I was overstating the case to provoke thought. Flash was not then and is not now inherently bad, and in fact can often be put to use very effectively. The ability to create a highly engaging Web site that has other dimensions of user interaction is very appealing. But when Macromedia first released Flash, Web creators and designers were so wowed by its capabilities that they applied it prolifically.

In the intervening years, Flash has matured as a product and to a large degree, designers have matured in their use of it. But the basic problem still remains: The overuse of bleeding-edge technology often has the opposite effect of what designers intend. Rather than assisting users on a Web site, it can prevent them from being fully engaged. The result is bloated, buggy designs that take too long to load, tie up people's systems, don't make sense, and ultimately drive people away.

Use Multimedia When It Benefits Your Audience

The most shameful phrase that emerged from the era of superfluous design was "Skip Intro." Garish, overproduced intro pages are inconvenient and arrogant. Making users wait for some pointless animation to download and play is basically saying to them, "We're pushing something we know you don't want, but we're going to do it anyway." Customers resent the lack of control and disregard for their time.

On the bright side, the use of splash pages has dwindled in recent years. Maybe it's just that the novelty has worn off, but more likely the companies have listened to usability experts (and to their users) and are putting multimedia to better use. That said, our previous assertion about multimedia still holds true today. Knowing how much interactivity is appropriate and which tools to use in different situations is essential to creating a successful Web site. Our recent studies show that most multimedia found on the Web these days still trips people up and causes antagonistic reactions. The fancier the design, the buggier it can be and the more problems it's likely to cause. And to make sure it works properly requires more time and effort in quality assurance.

(Facing page, top) Gateway provides an interactive feature that makes it easy to get close-ups of its products. Move the orange box to areas you want to zoom in on. Click on the green text to go directly to a particular component. No instructions are necessary because this is a simple, one-feature user interface and the interaction model works the way people expect.

www.atlantis.com

Atlantis.com does a good job of integrating multimedia into its Web site to create a tantalizing experience. While the site is visual, it loads quickly and the navigational elements are relatively consistent. The video gallery is effective because the interaction is simple. Select a picture on the left and the video plays on the right. A main downside, however, is that the site has an annoying splash page that plays every time a user accidentally clicks back too many times or reenters the Web site. There are also some hidden features on the site. For example, you can turn the page by clicking the upper corner of the book. Some people might not discover this, but it's not a big deal because the most important information is readily accessible.

▸ PS/2 Mouse and Keyboard Ports
▸ Serial Port RJ-45
▸ Dual 10/100/1000 Ethernet
▸ Low Profile PCI-X Slot
▸ VGA Port (1 of 2)
▸ USB Ports (2 of 3)
▸ Full-Height PCI Slot
▸ SCSI Connector
▸ Power Connectors
▸ Redundant Power Supply

PS/2 Mouse and Keyboard Ports
Connects a PS/2 mouse and keyboard to the server.

www.gateway.com

The 3D view of the car is both fun and informative. The designers have accommodated a broad audience by offering multiple ways to control the car, either by clicking the large buttons (easy for everybody) or dragging the mouse across the image (more immersive, but also requiring better mousemanship). The Photos tab gives people the option to see the car without having to manipulate the 3D model. Overall, this is a good implementation of multimedia. It could even be better if people were able to zoom in farther and see more details, such as the dials on the dashboard.

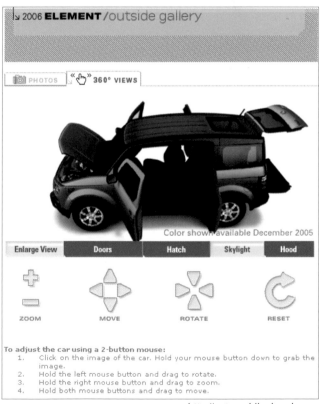

http://automobiles.honda.com

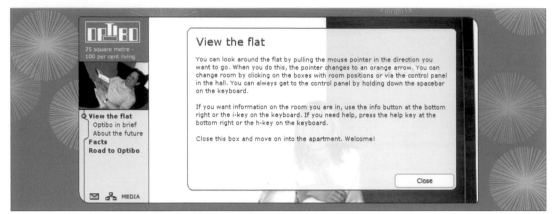

Lengthy instructions such as these indicate that the interaction design is too complex. People won't read them. If they can't figure out how the application works within a few seconds, they're gone. Better to simplify the interaction than to add more instructions.

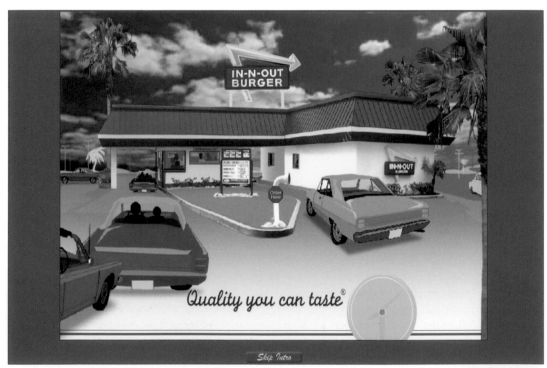

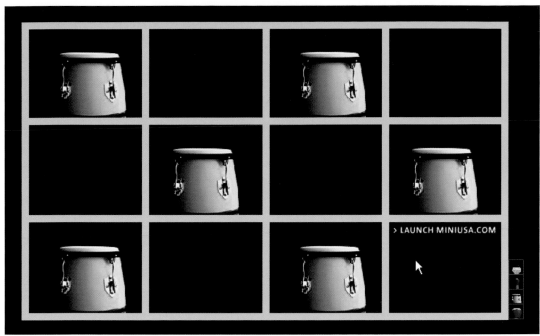

www.miniusa.com

The splash page on the Mini USA site was interactive. Moving the cursor over each graphical element prompted movement and sound. People could switch between the pictures by clicking on the icons on the lower right side of the screen.

Cool, right? Wrong. People in our study didn't know how to get past this screen. They clicked on the pictures, but nothing happened. You might think that Launch MiniUSA.com is so obvious, how can anyone not see it? The answer: Because "launch" is a technical term that some people don't recognize. One user complained:

"Are we talking about a car here? I'm trying to get on the Web site to see the actual car. But I can't get in it. It won't let me in.... I don't know what the matches and drums are all about. If it has anything to do with cars...it's weird. Bees, matches, and drums have nothing to do with cars."

(Facing page, bottom)   Originally the In-N-Out site launched with the company's theme song repeated several times while cars moved through the drive-thru line. As we were finishing this chapter, the company changed the design: Now the theme song only plays once, which is more than enough. Maybe it had received too many complaints about the previous design. In any case, this splash page remains useless because it serves no purpose to the user. There's a Skip Intro button, but why waste people's time with this gratuitous screen in the first place? People are better served with Web sites that start on the homepage. (In-N-Out's homepage is, in fact, pretty good, and it would have been much better if it offered the theme song via a button there instead of forcing users through a splash page.)

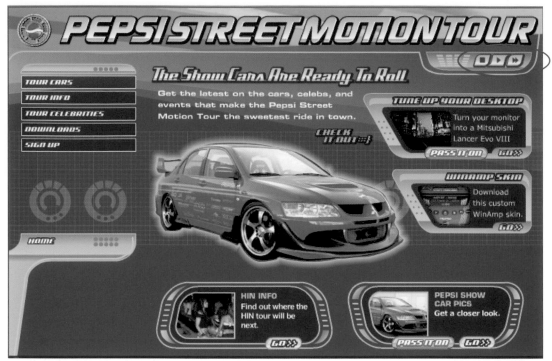

www.pepsiworld.com

www.pepsistreetmotion.com

(Facing page, top) Designers shouldn't assume that users would know what the audio control buttons in the upper right corner are meant for. People in our study accidentally selected arrow icons and were startled when audio turned on. Better to include text labels that say On, Off, and Pause. If your design uses resemblance icons to leverage a metaphor, it's best to maximize the resemblance by ensuring that the graphics look like the referenced system. In this case, they should look like the control buttons on a VCR or other consumer electronics. Such buttons are almost always square or rectangular.

(Facing page, bottom) The redesign of the Pepsi Street Motion Tour put text labels on the button controls, making it less likely to cause user errors.

Overcoming Barriers to Multimedia

Multimedia—or to use the more current term, rich media—can be instructive and engaging in ways static HTML pages cannot. Audiences appreciate audio on music sites, configurators on automotive sites, videos on entertainment sites, and virtual tours on hotel and real estate sites. Music and movie sites benefit particularly, because users can sample their products online. To use them wisely, you must take into account your users' equipment and needs.

Accommodate Low-Tech Users

In field studies where we visited people's homes, workplaces, and school environments, we discovered that many people work on old hand-me-downs or donated equipment that runs slowly and doesn't have the required plug-ins and applications to take advantage of advanced features. For example, many sites designed for children and teens offer multimedia and interactive features, but because young people often use old or borrowed computers, they don't benefit from these features. For this reason, make sure to provide alternative content for your users who lack access to the multimedia.

Also, use sound to complement your site, not as a primary way to deliver content. In almost all teen homes that we visited, teens didn't have speakers attached to the computer or they had them turned off so they could listen to the radio. If you're going to have a demonstration that uses sound, make sure it has a text version as well, so students can follow along without having to depend on the audio.

Tip: Providing Alternative Accessibility

Equipment incompatibilities are not the only causes of frustration when it comes to multimedia. Don't forget that some of your site's users may have disabilities that you should accommodate. Accessibility is always desirable because it expands your market, and for many government and educational sites, accessible Web design is a requirement.

For users with hearing disabilities, offer a textual alternative to audio, and optional subtitles for video. Visually impaired users can still use your site if you provide a text-to-voice option that will read content aloud for them.

Enemies of usability sometimes claim that we are old fogies who don't understand that young people like overblown and fancy Web design. Admittedly, we are in our 40s and 30s, respectively, and our personal taste doesn't run to the latest rap artist. But that's irrelevant. Personal taste has no role in judging usability. We conduct user research with the target audience and empirically ascertain what works for them. That's how we derive our usability guidelines: by observing real users visiting real Web sites.

We have tested plenty of sites with young users, including children from 6 to 12 years of age who do indeed like their sites flashier than traditional grown-up sites. The problem comes when a B2B site that sells, say, wood pallets uses a design that's more appropriate for kids than for seasoned warehouse managers.

In our testing with teenagers, we found that they like cool graphics and pay more attention to a Web site's visuals than adult users do. Still, the sites that our teen users rated the highest for subjective satisfaction were those with relatively modest, clean designs. They typically marked down overly glitzy sites as too difficult to use. Teenagers like to *do* stuff on the Web, and sites that are too slow or fancy inhibit that.

It's also a mistake to think that teens are so tech-savvy they can overcome any computer glitches. In contrast, we often found teens stumped by the same types of barriers to multimedia that get in the way of adult users.

Here are some quotes from users aged 14 to 17 from our teen study:

"You have to download it. I would go somewhere else because I don't have Acrobat Reader on my computer."

"Why do I need Acrobat Reader to see this page? Any Acrobat program is hard to get and it's expensive. Most people who go on here will not have it."

"For some of these games, you have to have Shockwave. My dad doesn't let me download anything…. You have to download Shockwave, especially if you want to download music. You have to buy Shockwave to get it all."

"Sometimes I get impatient when things take too long to load. I hate the Shockwave player. It's annoying. It takes forever to load. Some [games] have Shockwave, some don't. You have to find the one that doesn't have it so it goes faster."

"I'm thinking this is a game and you have to download the Shockwave player…. I'm doing other stuff because I don't want to sit there and watch it download. That's really boring."

As this last quote shows, teens frequently complained about sites that they found boring. Being boring is the kiss of death if you want to attract teens. That's one stereotype our research confirmed: Teenagers have a short attention span and want to be stimulated. That's also why they leave sites that are difficult to figure out. Remember that multimedia can be boring if it doesn't engage with users.

Design for Your Audience's Connection Speed

Statistics show that almost half of Web users still have dial-up Internet access, especially at home. While this proportion is dropping as more and more users get broadband access, it's important to keep in mind that many of your site's users still have slow connection speeds.

Connections may be slow even in broadband situations, such as in wireless connections, or in educational institutions, where response times can be slow due to factors such as bandwidth sharing, servers, and filters. Many media files are big and take a long time to download. Even with broadband connections, participants in our studies complained about slow download times and often abandoned a site or video because it took too long to load.

Bottom line: Optimize file sizes and minimize loading time. Even if you have designed a useful and intuitive interface, long response times can doom your project.

Provide a Simple and Accurate Loading-Status Indicator

You can often minimize people's impatience during long downloads simply by having a status indicator to provide visual feedback. A well-designed indicator reduces the perceived loading time because people see the progress and know what to expect. Keep it simple. It's most helpful to show the actual percentage of data transferred (for example, "50% loaded") so that users can assess how much more time the download will take. Impatient users leave sites that don't provide adequate feedback, often assuming the site is down because the page appears frozen. If they can see that the site is working, they tend to wait longer.

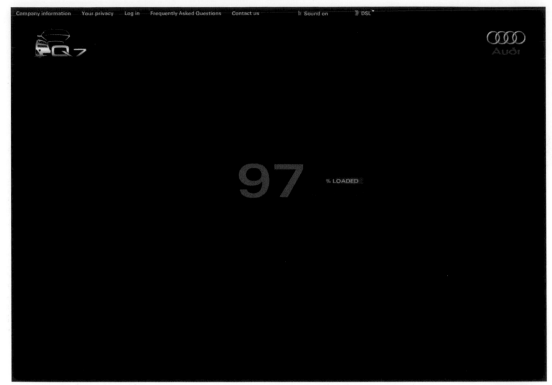

The Audi site has an appropriate counter that runs quickly and tells people the percentage of data loaded.

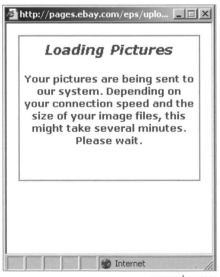

The information in this dialog box is vague and there's no animation or status indicator to let people know the system is working. It's impossible to tell how long the process will take or if the pictures are actually loading.

Travelocity doesn't have a status indicator. It's difficult to tell how long the process will take, but the twinkling stars give people some hope that the system is working. This is not a huge problem if the process is relatively quick. However, for long wait times, having an accurate indicator would minimize the perceived time, and people would be more likely to continue waiting.

Underestimate Your Users' Technical Knowledge

People are much more apprehensive about technology than you might think. Most people veer away from downloading plug-ins and clicking on unknown elements for fear of viruses, and because they dislike the long downloads.

Don't count on people to download new plug-ins. Adults fear viruses, spyware, and spam. Some schools actually block students from accessing multimedia content or downloading plug-ins. Parents warn their children against downloading anything on the family computer, for fear of contaminating it. Some users also automatically assume that there is a charge to download plug-ins, even when they're free.

If there's a compelling reason to require a specific plug-in or software, choose one that's common on most machines. It takes time for people to upgrade their system to the latest versions of software. Pick a version that's one iteration behind in order to capture a broad audience. The best solution is to provide non-multimedia content alternatives to people who don't have the proper plug-ins.

Deceptive dialog boxes such as these make it difficult for people to distinguish between a legitimate and unscrupulous security message. With virus scares proliferating, it's not surprising that people are fearful of downloading anything from the Web. (Did you notice the subtle word "advertisement" in the lower right? Most users don't.)

(Facing page, bottom)   People don't understand what messages like this mean. When people selected Play in the original window, they expected that the video would play automatically, not require them to commit to additional steps. To avoid messages like this getting in the way of your content, it's best to use file formats that are one or two versions behind the newest versions of the popular media players.

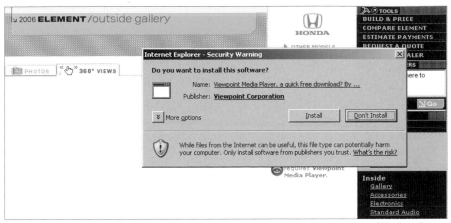

http://automobiles.honda.com

People are bewildered by security messages such as these. They're concerned about installing anything harmful but aren't sure whether the warning pertains to them. Some might install it in the hopes that nothing bad will happen; others might not take the chance and abandon the feature altogether.

www.mtv.com

Detect Users' Bandwidth

Don't require your users to select the bandwidth; many don't know what that means or how to find out, or they're using a borrowed computer and don't know the system's bandwidth. Asked to select the player or bandwidth speed appropriate for the media they want to play, many participants simply guess.

Take the guesswork out of the equation by measuring the user's connection speed in the back end and setting a cookie value accordingly. Give people with slow connections functionality geared toward low-bandwidth users. People who have faster load times can better handle the more robust version. Unfortunately, automatic bandwidth detection is still difficult with current technology, so in most cases, you're still best off aiming for a lower common denominator. But in two instances—when download delays would pose a major problem for narrowband users, or when you'd gain substantial additional benefits from a "fat" version of the application for broadband users—it's worth the additional effort.

www.bellagio.com

Most users don't know the difference between QuickTime and Windows Media Player. Even worse, this site abbreviates these terms, making them more obscure. It's better to remove the guesswork from the interface and let people see videos without having to select mysterious settings.

The video options on this page are overwhelming and too technical for average users, who don't know what 480p, 720p, and 1080p mean or how those numbers pertain to them. The "p" stands for progressive scan video, but this is too technical for people to know. The file size indicators might give people a clue, but they still don't tell people which format works best on their system.

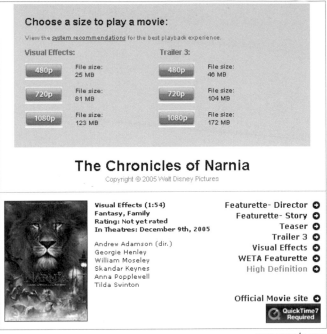

www.apple.com

People expect videos to play without them having to choose between options that are meaningless to them. If you offer different video sizes, it's best to identify them with simple words such as "big" and "small" because they refer to a concrete and observable aspect of making the choice. It also helps to tell users that the small version downloads the quickest.

www.miniusa.com

This splash page reminds viewers that they must have a specific screen resolution setting and have pop-up blockers disabled in order to access the site. This implementation is problematic for several reasons. First, most users won't even notice the message (as the instructions are in tiny letters and difficult to read). If they do notice it, they probably won't understand what it means. Then, too, many people don't know how to change their settings. Finally, a majority of people have pop-up blockers installed and won't even be able to access this site. Better to have a flexible design that works on most reasonable settings.

Stick to Familiar Interface Conventions

As we've said, people's mental model of how the Web works is predicated on their previous Web experiences. When they come up against elements that don't work as expected, they have to guess why this is so. For example, if users select a Play button to begin a video and nothing happens, they may conclude that the site is broken or that Play buttons on other sites won't work either. The site designer, on the other hand, may have a different explanation for why the video didn't work on the users' systems—their Internet connections were too slow, their players incompatible, users just need to be more patient. In the end, the reason doesn't really matter. Don't defend your interface. Fix it.

This real estate Web site uses a "virtual tour" to show the details of its properties. Unfortunately, many users don't know to click on the small symbol at the door, and so they will never "enter" the house and see the many pictures of its interior. Yes, you can pan the photos and see more of the rooms, but it's painfully slow to do so, and users quickly get lost in the house—if they ever do enter.

www.coldwellbanker.com

Don't let technology get in the way of your users' experience. Technically savvy designers are often tempted to create more sophisticated and interactive Web sites by experimenting with unusual designs and interactions. But ironically, sites that use cutting-edge technology intended to capture audiences run a high risk of alienating them when the technology doesn't work seamlessly.

If you have the urge to demonstrate your talent by creating something revolutionary, ask yourself, "If customers prefer simple tools, why not use them to the fullest instead of imposing new tools?"

People resist learning new interactions because, understandably, they don't like working harder than they have to. Stick to what people already know and are comfortable with. The more cutting-edge the technology, the more unfamiliar the interaction conventions will be to the average user, and the more you have to simplify the design.

This property listing shows a simpler way of exposing users to photos of a house: Show thumbnails and allow people to click on the photos they want to have enlarged. It would be better to show bigger photos that would allow users to see more details, but at least this user interface follows conventions for how to interact with photos on the Web. Underlining the labels for each thumbnail further enhances the perceived affordance of clickability. (See Chapter 6 for more on clickability.)

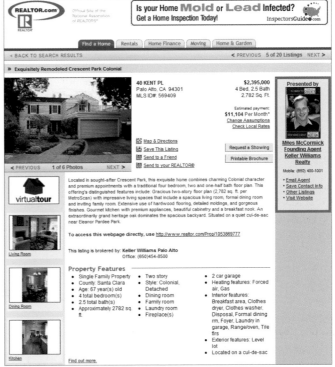

www.realtor.com

Atlantis.com homepage: The global navigational panel isn't apparent. It's hidden under the vague term Atlantis Navigator and tucked away in the upper left side of the screen. Once people click it, the navigational menu literally scrolls out, which is clever and matches the theme of the site. However, for something as important as global navigation, it's best to stick with a standard paradigm that people are accustomed to. Otherwise, they might not notice it.

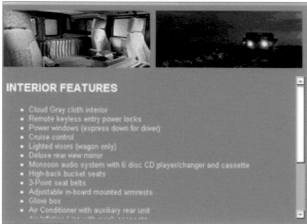

These are examples of good scrollbar designs. They look like scroll bars, so users easily recognize them.

Users of Haribon's map of the Philippines didn't notice the scrollbar because it looked like a North/South indicator for the map. There were several nonstandard elements in the design: The scrollbar was outside the area it controls, the top and bottom arrows looked as if they were part of the map as compass pointers, and there was no slider indicator.

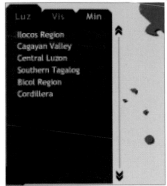

www.haribon.org.ph

A user couldn't create her virtual character because she didn't realize that the triangular arrows on the side of each boxed picture were scroll arrows.

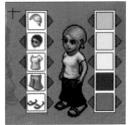

www.cokemusic.com

Tip: Scroll Bars Should Be Standard

People often overlook fancy scrollbar designs that depart too far from the norm. Make sure users recognize and understand how to use your scrollbar. Scroll bars should have both top and bottom arrows, and a scroll indicator. Provide scroll bars that are big enough to be controlled easily. Tiny scroll bars make it difficult for users to find and target the click zones. Traditional-looking scroll bars are most functional because they are most familiar.

Whenever you modify a standard GUI component, consider the usability implications of that modification because users may have difficulties interacting with nonstandard designs unless they are truly easy and intuitive. Being the first to showoff a slick design concept runs a high risk that people won't know how to interpret your design. The further you veer away from the norm, the higher chance you have of confusing or, even worse, losing your audience. If your design slows people down, causes them to make mistakes, and undermines their assumptions, it's the kiss of death. If you must do something unconventional, make sure you have a good reason for it, and user-test your system to make sure people understand it.

www.bk.com

Excessive use of multimedia is more damaging than beneficial. The Burger King site uses animation to present menu items. Users must catch moving targets that fade in and out to get detailed information. Such interaction frustrates people because it requires precision and excessive effort. One user commented:

"Something that is lame…they're flying around and you can't catch them with the cursor, or if you can, they move. That's just a pain. Just have it all up there so I can click on it."

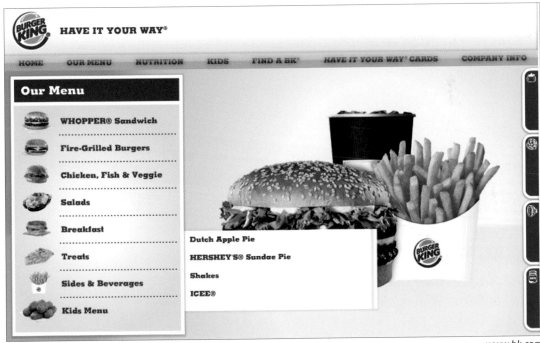

www.bk.com

Since the screen shot in the previous figure was tested, Burger King's site has been modified to be in line with people's expectations. The site now lists menu items in a more traditional navigational style. From a user standpoint, this is an improvement; static items are easier to click on than moving ones.

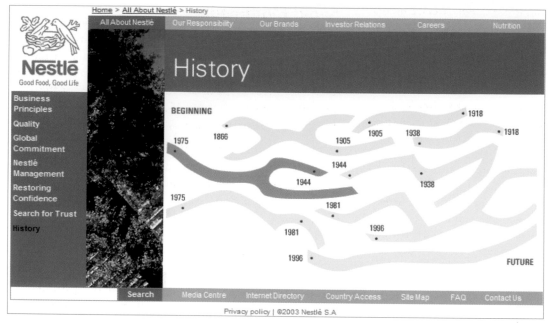

www.nestle.com

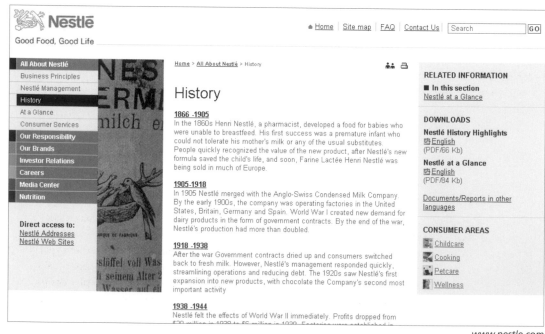

www.nestle.com

(Facing page, top) This is a historical timeline of the Nestlé Company. This esoteric representation of the timeline confused people. They didn't know what the graphical representation meant or how to interact with the interface. While fancy and slick timelines might seem initially appealing, they're often cumbersome and get in the way of people accomplishing their tasks. People can get the same information quicker from a simple HTML page than with this interactive timeline. Scanning a single page is easier than having to move the cursor over each part of the picture.

(Facing page, bottom) After our study, the Nestlé site replaced the interactive timeline with this one. This version is much easier to use. Nestlé did the right thing by choosing function over cleverness.

Avoid Multimedia Excesses

Use multimedia thoughtfully, and only when it adds substantial value to your site. Creating multimedia is far more costly and time-consuming than creating static illustrations, so when you're choosing between the two, opt for the most time- and cost-efficient format that will effectively illustrate the point you want to make.

In studies we conducted with teenagers, they were particularly impressed with Web sites that had videos to give them a better perspective on complex concepts. ChannelOne.com had demonstration videos, which teens appreciated because the videos made it easier to visualize the steps and helped them avoid having to read the instructions. For example, the clothing site Wetseal.com promoted its "Stylizer" program by explaining it with a video. Teenage girls felt that having a real person give a testimonial gave the program a personal touch. "[The video] is pretty cool," said one 15-year-old. "I like how it has 'What is a Stylizer?' and it gives you information about it."

Virtual tours on the White House site piqued other people's interest. The videos allowed users to see the White House as if they were walking through it, giving them a more realistic perspective of the layout than still photos could. We could go on and on with good examples, but you get the idea.

Tip: Rich vs. Poor Media

Levels of interaction run along a continuum. Choosing between a technology-rich and a plain-HTML design is not always a clear-cut decision. The best solution depends on your target audience and the communication problem you're solving. Sticking close to your audience's knowledge base, needs, and likely technology will guide your design decisions in the right direction. Rich media enhances the user experience in some cases, but mostly it's poor media that will make *you* rich because simpler designs make users focus on doing business with you.

A video tour of the White House appealed to many users. Note that in contrast to the virtual house tour on the real estate site on page 369, this tour doesn't require users to figure out how to move between rooms or pan the viewpoint. Instead, you can sit back and let the tour guide point out the items of interest as the camera automatically zooms. (Note: If you have a less famous tour guide, you probably can't get away with a seven-minute video on your site.)

Turn Down the Volume

> *Reserve features that chirp and chime for children. Audiences may enjoy a few whimsical effects, but once the novelty has worn off, they won't tolerate being hindered by them.*

Sound and animation can be very effective for providing user feedback and illustrating complex concepts. For example, sounds can be used effectively to confirm people's selections or to alert them when they've made an incorrect choice. Animation can help users visualize objects in three dimensions.

Sound and animation are often used simply to attract attention, and occasionally that's appropriate, such as when you want to point out breaking news headlines or something that needs the user's immediate response. However, a site that's peppered with too many blinking and moving elements quickly fatigues its viewers, making it difficult for them to focus on their tasks. Too many sound effects—especially if they're repetitive and play unexpectedly—are similarly distracting and irritating. Things that chirp and chime appealed to many young children when we tested Web sites with them, but teens and adults found them annoying. People lose patience with intrusive or persistent effects. Audiences may enjoy a few whimsical effects, but once the novelty has worn off, they won't tolerate being hindered by them.

Avoid audio rollovers. It's best to give users control over sound and video playback. Sound is disruptive in work environments (especially if people want to be stealthy about surfing the Web), and teens complain that sound on Web sites compete with other music and media that they're listening to. Sudden loud sounds and music are jarring and disruptive to coworkers in nearby cubicles. If your site has sound, make sure it starts softly and gradually gets louder, and give your users a way to adjust the sound. We've seen people jump out of their seats and cover their ears.

How Do You Turn This Thing Off?

Most people don't want to hear music playing continuously in the background, so give them an easy and obvious way to turn it off. Don't rely on the volume controls built in to their operating systems; most teens and many adults don't know where they are. Instead of having fancy controls, consider labeled buttons to turn the music on or off and standard slider controls for volume.

Make Videos for the Web

Pundits make much of the "convergence" of media, and the fact that people are increasingly using their computers as media centers. There are still significant differences between broadcast media and the Web—most significantly that the Web is interactive, and people want to be in control and move around it.

Make sure to produce and edit videos so they're tailored for online use. Since users dislike sitting through long video clips on the Web, break them up into small, compelling segments. Videos made for broadcast tend to be too long and can contain too many distracting visuals for small computer screens.

People don't sit passively in front of their computers, as they would in front of a television set; they want to click on things and drive their experiences. Most audio and video clips should be less than a minute long; very rarely should they last more than five minutes. The data from our eye-tracking study shows that even after a short 24 seconds, people's attention is diverted to other elements, especially if the subject is boring. For example, on a news site, people's eyes rested on the news anchor for a short time, but then wandered to mundane objects in the background, such as the trashcan or stop sign. Even more interesting, people's attention focused outside the video window on elements such as alternative headlines and options.

Tip: When to Take a Commercial Break

If your videos have commercials, it's better to play them after the primary clip than before. When commercials play before the main clip, people wonder if they've selected the wrong thing, or if the Web site is buggy. If you must play a commercial first, make sure to indicate this clearly, or users may close down your video before seeing the real content.

Eye-tracking diagram of a user watching a video clip on CNN. Red indicates the parts of the screen that were viewed the most; yellow and blue indicate areas that were viewed less. Even though the user only watched this video clip for 24 seconds, his attention soon drifted from the person being interviewed to other things.

The Practice of Simplicity

Throughout this book, we've been evangelizing simplicity, but ironically, the practice of simplicity is not at all simple. It's easy to build a bulky design by adding layer upon layer of navigation and features; it's much more difficult to create simple, graceful designs. Paring designs to essential elements while maintaining elegance and functionality requires courage and discipline.

Take interior decorating, for example. Why are some rooms more inviting than others? An amateur decorator might pack a living room with a jumble of furniture styles, patterns, and textures in a misguided attempt to dazzle. In contrast, skilled designers carefully select items that support their clients' needs, ruthlessly eliminating those elements that do not serve a real purpose. If an element doesn't complement the fundamental plan, it dilutes the impact of the room's decor.

www.nestle.com

The animation on this site interferes with its content. The tumbling man in the upper left distracts people from the content they came to the site to get. One user commented:

"I like these icons but they can be a bit too much … you get fed up seeing them come up all the time. The images and graphics are fine for a while, but then you want to get on with it, without the interference of the chap tumbling over."

It's the same with Web sites. Good designers get the maximum use out of limited space (both screen space and bandwidth) by paring down the interaction to the essentials. Gratuitous effects, graphics, and pictures take away from the important elements you want to display on your site. When everything is flashing and screaming for attention, nothing gets it.

Take a good, critical look at your site. See if you find any extraneous design elements that are cluttering it up. Make every effort to simplify the interactions on your site. Is there a slick or fancy feature that's more difficult to use than a simple static one? Every icon, picture, graphic, and animation should serve a purpose and communicate something meaningful. Before adding design elements to your site, ask yourself:

- Does this element simplify the user's task?

- Does this element add value to the user?

If the answer is "no," eliminate it.

www.bms.com

What does this picture of a sunflower have to do with corporate responsibility (not to mention its size and download time)? This useless photograph takes up prime screen real estate. People don't mind waiting a little longer for useful information, but they resent waiting for something meaningless. Use photographs to augment content, not to decorate the page.

Look at the two versions of the navigational menu on the Tiffany & Co. Web site. In the first design, the translucent menu opens on top of the image, making the menu extremely difficult to read. The second design is an improvement because the text is darker and doesn't compete with the background. While the first design appears elegant, it's too difficult to read and alienates customers. The second design balances aesthetics with usability. The menu is more legible yet maintains the site's elegance.

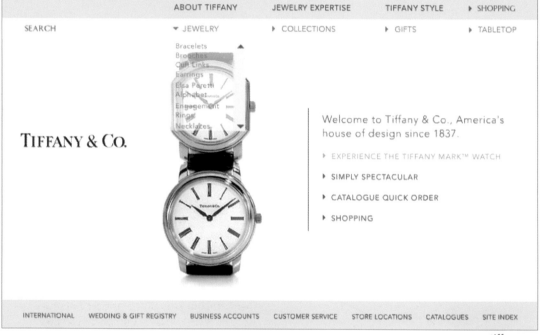

www.tiffany.com

An earlier version of the Tiffany & Co. Web site used transparent menus, which looked interesting but were difficult to read.

Since our study, Tiffany.com improved the navigational menu design without compromising aesthetics.

Improving Your Site: Sooner or Later?

This book contains many examples of designs that failed our user testing and have since been replaced by better designs. Hopefully, by the time you read the book, many more sites will have been updated to take advantage of our free consulting advice.

Sometimes, when you see the revised, improved design, you may say, "That's obviously the way to go" and discount the usability insight behind it. However, the better design was not obvious from the get-go, as proven by the fact that even rich companies with fat Web budgets may feature bad sites that hurt their business for years.

To a large extent, usability equals simplicity, which again implies that usability improvements are obvious. One of the big points we hope to drive home is that easy-to-use sites don't happen by themselves. You must employ usability methodology and test with your target users. We discovered all these usability problems through quick, cheap studies. Each company could have done so on its own instead of waiting until it had suffered lost traffic and floods of customer complaints.

Usability defects will surface sooner or later: The main issue is whether you discover them early in your project, before you have wasted untold time and money implementing a bad design. Sooner is better—and cheaper too.

Include only the features that will help people simplify their tasks. When interactions are too complex, people often can't find the information they need and can't benefit from the site. Complex interactions increase both learning time and the likelihood that people will be bewildered. It's better to have a few helpful features rather than many unhelpful ones.

Now let's look at two approaches to map design, the first interactive and the second one not. The interactive map shows the locations of restaurants in the city. Moving the cursor over each orange ball reveals the restaurant name, and clicking it shows the restaurant details. Simple, right? Actually, no. If you were not familiar with the restaurants in this city, you would have to click on each ball to find out about them. Click on a ball, back out, click on another ball, back out—whew!

The second map is easier to use. It reveals information about each establishment without forcing people to work harder than they have to. The map gives people the most relevant information at a glance without requiring any clicks. While the first map might seem slicker, it's not as functional as the simpler one.

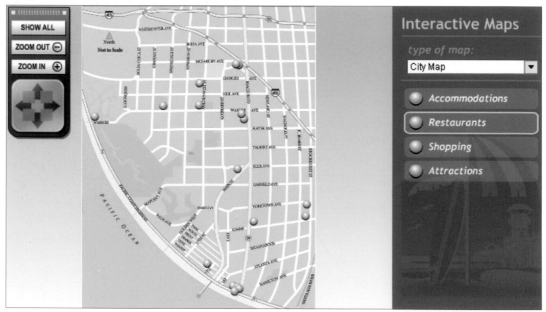

http://surfcityusa.com

This interactive map probably required more time and resources to create than a static map would, but it is less useable.

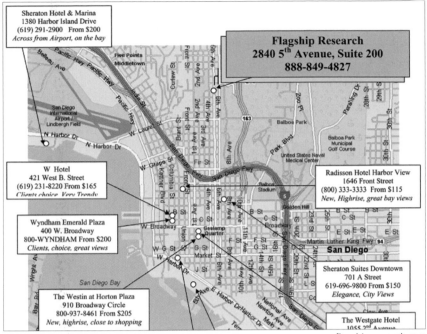

Sheraton Hotel & Marina
1380 Harbor Island Drive
(619) 291-2900 From $200
Across from Airport, on the bay

Flagship Research
2840 5th Avenue, Suite 200
888-849-4827

W Hotel
421 West B. Street
(619) 231-8220 From $165
Clients choice. Very Trendy

Radisson Hotel Harbor View
1646 Front Street
(800) 333-3333 From $115
New, Highrise, great bay views

Wyndham Emerald Plaza
400 W. Broadway
800-WYNDHAM From $200
Clients, choice, great views

Sheraton Suites Downtown
701 A Street
619-696-9800 From $150
Elegance, City Views

The Westin at Horton Plaza
910 Broadway Circle
800-937-8461 From $205
New, highrise, close to shopping

The Westgate Hotel
1055 2nd Avenue

www.flagshipresearch.com

This low-tech design serves its purpose, giving people relevant information quickly and easily.

Developing fewer features allows you to conserve development resources and spend more time refining those features that users really need. Fewer features mean fewer things to confuse users, less risk of user errors, less description and documentation, and therefore simpler Help content. Removing any one feature automatically increases the usability of the remaining ones.

In one study, we asked participants to use the Sydney Opera House Web site to locate a particular restaurant. Most people tried finding the answer using the Virtual Tour because it was the most prominent element on the site.

The robust feature allowed people to do advanced things such as:

- Move arrows around to view the building from various vantage points
- Watch balls shoot up and reveal the names of the locations
- Reveal more icons and photographs of the building
- Listen to sound effects resonate as different things are clicked

This Virtual Tour contained a lot of useful information. Most people couldn't figure out how it worked, however, and so they never saw much of the content. In addition, it was slow to load, had progressive disclosure, and the sound effects impeded people's progress. Users want direct answers when seeking information; feature-rich applications often hamper users because the interactions tend to be circuitous.

Here are some of the comments from our test users about this instance of fancy design:

"This ball shooting up is annoying. … I'm trying to figure out if any one of these balls indicates the Playhouse. … It took me a while to find the Playhouse."

"I didn't notice the little arrow. What am I supposed to do with that? I don't get what that is."

"I don't really want to do this grand tour. It takes a lot of time. You get all of this stuff coming up: music, intro— something I would rather not go through."

"Constructing maps and loading panoramas—this is more information than I would want to have. I don't need the architectural drawings. I just want to see where the restaurant is relative to the Opera House. I wish I had a list on here that showed the entities within the Sydney Opera House, like where I can find a restaurant, but I don't see it. I like the panorama view but I don't need that right now. I wish they had Search, so I could type in 'playhouse' and it would show me the Playhouse rather than bouncing around the entire multilevel Opera House."

"It's rather distracting, this 3D thing. It's a little overkill. This is like the USS Enterprise. If you've never been on it, you wouldn't know where to begin. It's pretty and dynamic, but how helpful is it?"

When you find users comparing your user interface to that of the Star Trek spaceship, it's usually not a good sign.

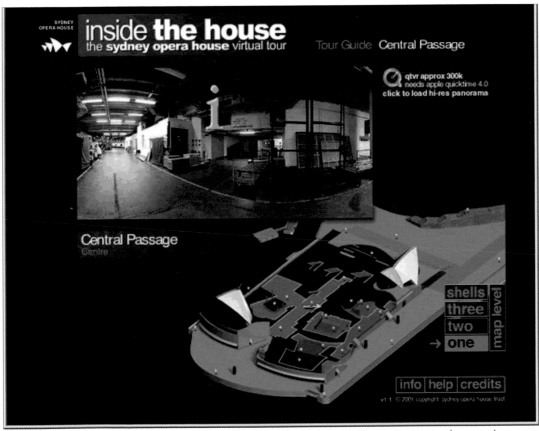

www.sydneyoperahouse.com

This virtual tour might be enjoyable for a few people who have a lot of spare time and curiosity, and want a challenge. However, for most visitors who need general information about the Sydney Opera House, this application is excessive. People didn't like having to hover their mouse over yellow balls in order to get basic information such as location names. Many people didn't notice or understand the myriad of icons such as the yellow arrow (shown here in the central corridor on the lower map) and the "i" (here superimposed on the upper photo).

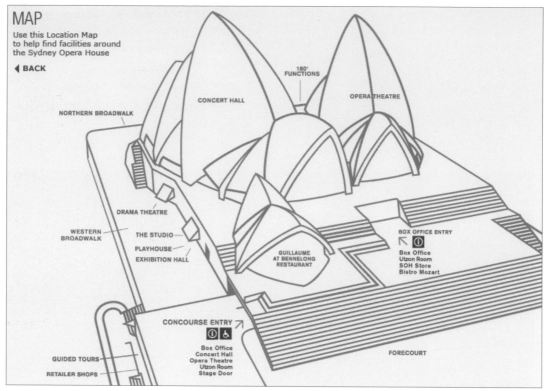

www.sydneyoperahouse.com

People were more successful at finding locations on a well-labeled static map than on a complex interactive one. The simple sketch has enough detail to give people context and orientation. Having the main areas labeled helps them make associations and understand the layout of the facility.

(Facing page, top)   This is the first of two splash pages on the Wynn Las Vegas Web site. Not only is this two-step entry process time consuming, the options on this page are based on the company's priorities, and not on the end users'. The first things people want is to find information about this hotel, not Buy Tickets or Book Now. Asking people to Buy Tickets and Book Now is premature. In addition, these terms are vague and have overlapping meanings in this context. At this stage, viewers might wonder what they are booking and buying tickets are for.

(Facing page, bottom)   This is the first of two splash pages for the Wynn Las Vegas Web site. Not only is this two-step entry process time-consuming, the options on this page are based on the company's priorities, and not the end users'. The homepage slowly loads with audio of Steve Wynn saying, "Unlike other Web sites, we filled it with surprises. Have fun, go find the surprises, and enjoy." People trying to compare hotels and book reservations don't want to find surprises, the want information quickly.

Prioritizing Web Usability

www.wynnlasvegas.com

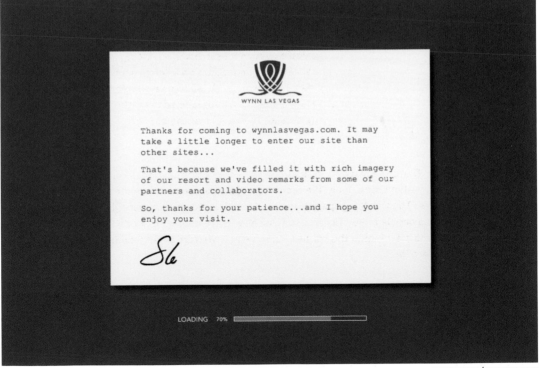

www.wynnlasvegas.com

There will always be new technology, but early adopters are a minority. It takes time for mainstream audiences to accept and learn new interactions.

Toward a More Elegant Design

There will always be new technology, but setting your sights too high backfires. Early adopters are a minority. It takes time for mainstream audiences to accept and learn new interactions. Effective interaction designers understand and support people's cognitive and physical abilities, and remain true to their objectives. Technology may change, but people's innate capabilities remain constant.

Careless, ineffective designs are overly adorned. Sophisticated designs are planned, organized, and unpretentious. Truly elegant Web designs are visually pleasing as well as functional. Moreover, function always comes before beauty. What good is a beautiful Web site if people don't have use for it, or it's not navigable? Before you rush out to build the most cutting-edge Web site, you should consider its purpose. What do your users want to achieve? Coming back to the user will help you decide what's best for your site.

More Information

For more details on our study of users with disabilities, go to www.nngroup.com/reports and see Users with Disabilites; for other studies cited in this chapter, see Children, Teenagers, and B2B Website Usability.

12 Final Thoughts: Design That Works

Design for users. That sounds so obvious, but it's not. Almost always, when we see bad Web sites, they were designed for the designers themselves or for their clients. The point is not what you like or what your manager or even the CEO likes. It's difficult to reject your own preferences, but the key to creating a good experience for users is to design with them in mind.

Remember, you are not your average user. Your boss is not your average user. Presumably, both you and your boss are smart, and you probably know much more about computers and the Internet than your average user does. But even if you are targeting an audience of highly educated geeks, you *still* are different from them in one key area: You know more and care more about your company and your products. To you, they are special, different, and probably better than the competition's.

Not so for prospective customers, who are evaluating all offers equally and may have no knowledge of your product line or your special internal terminology. Since their perspective is different from yours, they will judge your site differently. In the end, the only thing that matters is whether they like it and use it. Creating elaborate and unconventional interfaces because they seem more interesting isn't enough. Being interested in your users is what earns you their business and loyalty.

Know your target users. They have expectations for your site based on their experiences with others. A unique site that is incongruous with what's familiar disrupts their workflow and causes confusion. It's more difficult to learn something new than to repeat the familiar, and people are not on your site to work extra hard to get answers. Any additional cognitive burden on them translates directly into lost business for you.

Choose function before form. Creative designs are delightful, but don't assume that people want to be constantly stimulated or engaged. Using Web sites is not usually the key to happiness; for most people, it's something they want to get over with so that they can get back to playing with their kids. Because they don't care about technology, computers, or Web sites for their own sake, most people prefer sites that balance design with simplicity. They appreciate sites that are aesthetically pleasing, but they balk if the design gets in the way. Combine creativity and usability to achieve a harmonious and effective design.

Test Your Assumptions

The only way you can know what users like is to listen to them. Make sure to test your system on real target users. Give them tasks to do, observe their behavior, and listen to their feedback. Don't be afraid to modify your design and test again. No one can create the perfect usable design, especially on the first try. User testing is the simplest of all the usability engineering methods, so fast and inexpensive that there is no excuse for launching a site without testing it.

We encourage you to follow the usability guidelines that we've outlined in this book, as they apply to most situations. Our recommendations are based on years of experience and research with thousands of users. Our hope is that this book prevents you from making the mistakes other companies have made and gives you a better understanding of how people interact with Web sites.

Keep your users at the center of your design project. Be humble. Listen to them. They'll make you successful.

Index

3-click rule, 322
3D images, 109–110, 355
10-point rule, 221

A

Abercrombie site, 301
"About Us" sections, 115, 127,
    264, 267, 310
above-the-fold information, 39
absolute text size, 227
Accenture site, 266
accessibility, 226, 359, 390
accessories, product, 305
Acrobat Reader, 70, 360
acronyms, 262, 295
Active.com site, 340
ad avoidance techniques, 76–77,
    344
ad banners, 76–77
Add to Cart button, 76
Add to Shopping Bag button, 346
Add to Wish List button, 346
Addonics site, 301
Adobe
    PDF files, 70, 220, 247
    Reader, 70, 360
ads. See advertising
Advanced Search feature, 140, 150,
    153, 154, 159
advertising
    blockers, 77
    deceptive, 364–365
    most hated techniques, 75
    rich-media, 164
    search, 36, 39, 41, 43, 164–165
    techniques for avoiding, 76–77,
        344
    text-only, 164
AE.com site, 346
affordances, 206
Air Force user interface guidelines,
    85
all-cap text, 236, 238, 239
All Musicals site, 28
Amazon site, 86, 300, 342

America Online, 26, 138
American Eagle site, 346
American Heart Association site
    fly-out menus, 202–203
    "Learn more" links, 197
    page titles, 277
    Search box, 149
    search engine results page, 152
    text formatting, 276
    writing, 255–256
American Medical Association
    study, 128
Anderson Floors site, 201
animation. See also Flash
    effective use of, 377
    gratuitous use of, 88, 113, 380
    reduced use of, 131
    user familiarity with, 352
answer engines, 36
anti-aliasing, 222
AOL, 26, 138
Apple, 94, 95
architectural applications, 109
architectural SEO, 163, 167–168
architecture, information, 130, 133,
    172–174
archives
    homepage feature story, 15–16
    older information, 116
    usability study, xviii, 121
Arial Black font, 232
Arial font, 232, 233
Art Center site, 325
articles, informational, 317
artistic elements, 213
assumptions, testing, 395
Atlantis site
    hidden features, 354
    homepage, 101
    multimedia features, 354
    navigational panel, 188, 189,
        370
    pricing information, 288,
        296–297
    scrolling problems, 100, 101,
        328

text/background contrast,
    242–243
writing, 254, 255
Audi site, 362
audience
    designing site for target, 394
    font considerations, 221
    identifying, 259
    talking down to, 259
    writing for specific, 259–261
audio clips, 378–379
audio control buttons, 359
audio rollovers, 377
auto-buying sites, 298, 313–
    314, 359. See also specific
    manufacturers
awards, 310

B

B2B sites, 275, 291, 319, 360
Bacara Resort site, 248
Back button, 63–67, 88
background contrast, text and, 216,
    217, 219, 240–245
backtracking, 63, 64
Bag You! site, 339
bandwidth
    detecting user, 366–367
    and large photos, 299
    and usability problems, 84, 85,
        91–92
Bank One site, 207, 257, 280, 311
banner blindness, 76–77
bare-bones designs, 86
BASF site, 153
Bath & Body Works site, 182,
    186–187, 193–194
BBC site, 15–16
BBW site, 182, 186–187, 193–194
Bellagio site, 274, 366
below-the-fold information,
    45–46, 100
"best bets" functionality, 154–156
Bic Sport Surfboards site, 98
birthdate, 118

Advance praise for *Prioritizing Web Usability*

"There is a reason why Jakob Nielsen's advice is sought by so many organizations that are serious about the Web: He is the gold standard of advice. He translates between empirical studies, practical designs, and business concepts, untangling the morass of inconsistent Web lore. **This book by Jakob and Hoa Loranger is the best yet—concise, highly readable, and authoritative—a digest of all their experience.** It's the next best thing to having Jakob and his talented associates at work for you—and much more affordable.

This will be the definitive book on Web usability. I'm going to apply it to our own site."

—*Stuart Card, Senior Research Fellow, Palo Alto Research Center (PARC),*
  co-author, Readings in Information Visualization, Using Vision to Think

"Once again Jakob Nielsen, this time in collaboration with Hoa Loranger, provides Web designers everywhere with powerful design guidelines derived from actual observation of hundreds of Internet users.

In many ways this book **is an important update to Jakob Nielsen's book** *Designing Web Usability,* from 2000. Nielsen and Loranger show that technology improvements, better design skills, and behavioral adaptations among users of the Internet have resulted in a significant improvement of Web usability. The biggest change, however, is a renewed focus on the Web as a single, integrated resource, with search engines as the most important interface between user and information. These observed changes in search and navigation behaviors pose new challenges for Web designers as they seek to attract, retain, and satisfy a new generation of hurried and critical Internet users. Usability continues to be a defining factor in the success or failure of a Web site—this book **can help you prioritize existing problems and identify the solutions that will help make your site a success.**"

—*Klaus Kaasgaard, Ph.D, Senior Director, User Experience Research, Yahoo!*

"Jakob's first book had an incredible impact on designers make the Web a more usable tool for people to accomplish their goals. With the benefit of extensive research, this book **shows which insights are the most important to build an engaging user experience.**"

—*Kaaren Hanson, Director, Customer Centered Development, Intuit*